COMMODITY PRICES

COMMODITY PRICES

A Source Book and Index
Providing References to Wholesale
and Retail Quotations for More Than 5,000
Agricultural, Commercial, Industrial,
and Consumer Products

Compiled by
Paul Wasserman
Diane Kemmerling

Gale Research Company • Book Tower • Detroit, Michigan 48226

Copyright © 1974 by Paul Wasserman

**Library of Congress
Cataloging in Publication Data**

Wasserman, Paul.
   Commodity prices.

   "Updating and thorough revision of Sources of commodity prices, published in 1959 as a project of the Business and Finance Division of the Special Libraries Association."
     1. Prices–United States–Sources. I. Kemmerling, Diane, joint author. II. Special Libraries Association. Business and Finance Division. Committee on Sources of Commodity Prices. Sources of commodity prices. III. Title.
Z7164.P94W33   338.5'2'0973   73-19898
ISBN 0-8103-0369-8

CONTENTS

PREFACE. v

GENERAL ABBREVIATIONS. vii

ABBREVIATIONS OF PERIODICALS INDEXED. ix

COMMODITY PRICES. 1

LIST OF PUBLISHERS OF PERIODICALS INDEXED. 191

PREFACE

Commodity Prices: A Source Book and Index is an updating and thorough revision of Sources of Commodity Prices, published in 1959 as a project of the Business and Finance Division of the Special Libraries Association under the editorial supervision of the principal compiler of the present volume. The content of this new edition is based upon an exhaustive effort of examining at first hand as many current U.S. and Canadian publications as possible which provide regular or seasonal price information.

Commodity Prices offers a guide to current sources of detailed information on market prices for approximately 5,000 different products as quoted in 158 different sources. Because of its wide scope and coverage, the volume is particularly applicable to the requirements of librarians; trade association and chamber of commerce officers; business, financial, and economic researchers; government officials; and others who in the course of their work require access to current prices.

The basic body of the work is a dictionary arrangement of commodities. For each commodity listed, the following information is provided: name of the commodity, title of periodical publishing the price, frequency with which prices appear in the periodical, and market or markets in which price is effective. This basic section contains cross references and 'see also' references. The index at the back of the book gives an alphabetical list of periodicals covered in the main part of the volume. For each periodical the publisher, address of publisher and frequency are provided.

The terminology employed in listing commodities is normally based upon usage in the publications cited. Therefore, where trade terminology varies, a particular commodity may occasionally be listed under two or more headings if the various names used for the product do not suggest to the uninitiated that they all refer to the same commodity.

If a periodical reports prices in a large number of cities, this fact has been indicated by selecting and listing a few representative cities. If no indication of the scope of the reporting is given, it may be assumed that the market covered is nationwide. Prices covered may be wholesale, retail, future, or spot.

The earlier volume issued by the Special Libraries Association, and its predecessor, Price Sources (Department of Commerce, 1931), have both enjoyed wide usage as essential sources of information. The intent of the present volume is to contribute the same kind of information support to those who require current and viable present-day price information. Naturally, its compilers are indebted very much to the efforts of all those whose earlier work led to the rationale and general formulae which have been followed in the present compilation.

The compilers were assisted by Fred Leise who assumed responsibility for typing the manuscript. In spite of the exhaustive attempt to identify publications providing price details, there still may be gaps in the coverage of a book so ambitious in its comprehensiveness. If errors or omissions are noted, it will be appreciated if they are called to the attention of the compilers.

GENERAL ABBREVIATIONS

A   -   annually
Ala   -   Alabama
Alta   -   Alberta
Ariz   -   Arizona
Ark   -   Arkansas

BC   -   British Columbia
BM   -   bimonthly
BW   -   biweekly

Calif   -   California
Can   -   Canada
Colo   -   Colorado
Conn   -   Connecticut

D   -   daily
DC   -   District of Columbia
Del   -   Delaware

Fla   -   Florida

Ga   -   Georgia

Ida   -   Idaho
Ill   -   Illinois
Ind   -   Indiana
IR   -   irregularly

Kan   -   Kansas
Ky   -   Kentucky

La   -   Louisiana

M   -   monthly
Man   -   Manitoba
Mass   -   Massachusetts
Md   -   Maryland
Me   -   Maine
Mich   -   Michigan
Minn   -   Minnesota
Miss   -   Mississippi
Mo   -   Missouri
Mont   -   Montana

NB   -   New Brunswick
NC   -   North Carolina
ND   -   North Dakota
Neb   -   Nebraska
Nev   -   Nevada
Newf   -   Newfoundland
NH   -   New Hampshire
NJ   -   New Jersey
NM   -   New Mexico
NS   -   Nova Scotia
NY   -   New York

Okla   -   Oklahoma
Ont   -   Ontario
Ore   -   Oregon

Pa   -   Pennsylvania
PEI   -   Prince Edward Island

Q   -   quarterly
Que   -   Quebec

RI   -   Rhode Island

S   -   semimonthly
SA   -   semiannually
Sask   -   Saskatchewan
SC   -   South Carolina
SD   -   South Dakota

Tenn   -   Tennessee
Tex   -   Texas

US   -   United States

Va   -   Virginia
Vt   -   Vermont

W   -   weekly
Wash   -   Washington
Wis   -   Wisconsin
W Va   -   West Virginia
Wyo   -   Wyoming

yr   -   year

ABBREVIATIONS OF PERIODICALS INDEXED

ABER-ANGUS J - Aberdeen-Angus Journal
AGRI LET - Agricultural Letter
ALASKA BEV ANALYST - Alaska Beverage Analyst
AM MET MKT/MET NEWS - American Metal Market/Metalworking News
AM PAINT J - American Paint Journal
AM SHOE - American Shoemaking
AM TEXTILE RPTR/BUL - America's Textile Reporter/Bulletin
ARIZ BEV J - Arizona Beverage Journal
AUTO MKT RPT - Automotive Market Report
AUTO NEWS - Automotive News

BARRON'S - Barron's National Business and Financial Weekly
BEV MEDIA - Beverage Media
BEV NEWS - Beverage News
BUCK BEV J - Buckeye Beverage Journal

CALIF FARM - California Farmer
CALIF WINE - California Wineletter
CAN CHEM PROCESSING - Canadian Chemical Processing
CAN MIN J - Canadian Mining Journal
CAN TOBACCO - Canadian Tobacco Grower
CHEM MKTG RPTR - Chemical Marketing Reporter
CHEM PUR - Chemical Purchasing
CHICAGO HIDE - Chicago Daily Hide and Tallow Bulletin
COMM BUL - Commercial Bulletin
COMM REV - Commercial Review
COTTON DIG - Cotton Digest
COTTON-M REV - Cotton-Monthly Review of the World Situation

DAIRYMAN - Dairyman
DAIRYNEWS - Dairynews
DAIRY REC - Dairy Record
DAKOTA FARM - Dakota Farmer
DLY MKT REC - Daily Market Record

DLY NEWS REC - Daily News Record

EARNSHAW'S - Earnshaw's Infants, Girls and Boyswear Review
ENG MIN J - E/MJ Engineering and Mining Journal

FARM & DAIRY - Farm and Dairy
FATS & OILS - Fats and Oils Bulletin
FEED BUL - The Feed Bulletin
FEEDSTUFFS - Feedstuffs
FINISHERS' MGT - Finishers' Management
FIN POST - Financial Post
FIN TIMES CAN - Financial Times of Canada
FLA FIELD RPT - Florida Field Report
FOUNDRY - Foundry
FREE PRESS FARM - Free Press Weekly Report on Farming
FUELOIL & OIL - Fueloil and Oil Heat

HANDBAGS - Handbags and Accessories
HIDE & LEATHER BUL - Hide & Leather Bulletin
HIGH PLAINS J - High Plains Journal
HOG FARM MGT - Hog Farm Management

IDA FARM - Idaho Farmer-Stockman
ILL BEV J - Illinois Beverage Journal
IMPLEMENT & TRACTOR - Implement and Tractor
INDUS WK - Industry Week
IRON AGE - Iron Age

J OF COMMERCE - Journal of Commerce

KAN FARM - Kansas Farmer

ABBREVIATIONS OF PERIODICALS INDEXED

KY BEV J - The Kentucky Beverage Journal

LANCASTER FARM - Lancaster Farming
LEATHER & SHOES - Leather and Shoes
LIVESTOCK BREED J - Livestock Breeder Journal

MAN CO-OP - Manitoba Co-operator
MD-WASH-DEL BEV J - Maryland-Washington-Delaware Beverage Journal
MET WK - Metals Week
MICH BEV NEWS - Michigan Beverage News
MICH FARM - Michigan Farmer
MIN REC - Mining Record
MOD PCKG-ENCYCLO & PLAN GUIDE - Modern Packaging-Encyclopedia and Planning Guide
MOD TEXTILES MAG - Modern Textiles Magazine
MONT FARM - Montana Farmer-Stockman
MO RURAL - Missouri Ruralist

NATION'S RESTAURANT - Nation's Restaurant News
NATL LIVESTOCK - National Live Stock Producer
NATL PETRO NEWS - National Petroleum News
NATL PROVISION - National Provisioner
NATL WOOL - National Wool Grower
NEB FARM - Nebraska Farmer
NJ BEV J - New Jersey Beverage Journal
NORTH MINER - North Miner
NY TIMES - New York Times

OFFICIAL BD MKTS - Official Board Markets
OIL & GAS J - Oil and Gas Journal
OIL DLY - The Oil Daily

ONT MILK PROD - Ontario Milk Producer
ORE FARM - Oregon Farmer-Stockman

PACKER - The Packer
PA FARM - Pennsylvania Farmer
PAPERBD PCKG - Paperboard Packaging
PAPER TRADE J - Paper Trade Journal
PATTERSON'S - Patterson's California Beverage Gazetteer
PENNMARVA - Pennmarva
PLATT'S - Platt's Oilgram Price Service
POULTRY & EGG MKTG - Poultry and Egg Marketing
POULTRY TIMES - The Poultry Times
POULTRY TRIB - Poultry Tribune
PRODUCERS' GUIDE - Producers' Guide
PURCH WORLD - Purchasing World

RED POLL NEWS - Red Poll News
RI BEV J - Rhode Island Beverage Journal
RUBBER WORLD - Rubber World

SECOND RAW MATERIALS - Secondary Raw Materials
SEED WORLD - Seed World-Seed Trade Buyers' Guide and Directory
SHORTHORN WORLD - Shorthorn World
SOYBEAN DIG - Soybean Digest
STAT SUGAR TRADE J - Statistical Sugar Trade Journal
SUPER SER STATION - Super Service Station

TEA & COFFEE TRADE J - Tea and Coffee Trade Journal
TOBACCO/INTERNATL - Tobacco/International

ABBREVIATIONS OF PERIODICALS INDEXED

UN BUL STAT - United Nations - Monthly Bulletin of Statistics

UN LEAD & ZINC STAT - United Nations Lead and Zinc Study Group - Lead and Zinc Statistics

US AGRI MKTG SER - BEAN MARKET NEWS - US Agricultural Marketing Service - Bean Market News

US AGRI MKTG SER - BROILER MKTG GUIDE - US Agricultural Marketing Service - Broiler Marketing Guide

US AGRI MKTG SER - EGG MKTG GUIDE - US Agricultural Marketing Service - Egg Marketing Guide

US AGRI MKTG SER - FEED MKT NEWS - US Agricultural Marketing Service - Feed Market News

US AGRI MKTG SER - FRUIT & VEG PRICES - US Agricultural Marketing Service - Fresh Fruit and Vegetable Prices

US AGRI MKTG SER - GRAIN MKT NEWS - US Agricultural Marketing Service - Grain Market News

US AGRI MKTG SER - HONEY MKT NEWS - US Agricultural Marketing Service - Honey Market News

US AGRI MKTG SER - LIVESTOCK MKT NEWS - US Agricultural Marketing Service - Livestock Meat and Wool Market News

US AGRI MKTG SER - PEANUT MKT NEWS - US Agricultural Marketing Service - Peanut Market News

US AGRI MKTG SER - TOBACCO MKT REV - US Agricultural Marketing Service - Tobacco Market Reviews

US AGRI MKTG SER - TURKEY MKTG GUIDE - US Agricultural Marketing Service - Turkey Marketing Guide

US AGRI STABIL - SUGAR RPT - US Agricultural Stabilization and Conservation Service - Sugar Reports

US BUR DOM COMM - PULP Q - US Bureau of Domestic Commerce - Pulp, Paper and Board Quarterly Industry Report

US CONS & MKTG SER - COTTON PRICE STAT - US Consumer and Marketing Service - Cotton Price Statistics

US CONS & MKTG SER - DAIRY MKT STAT - US Consumer and Marketing Service - Dairy Market Statistics

US CONS & MKTG SER - POULTRY MKT STAT - US Consumer and Marketing Service - Poultry Market Statistics

US ECON SER - COTTON SIT - US Economic Research Service - Cotton Situation

US ECON SER - DAIRY SIT - US Economic Research Service - Dairy Situation

US ECON SER - DEMAND SIT - US Economic Research Service - Demand and Price Situation

US ECON SER - FATS & OILS SIT - US Economic Research Service - Fats and Oils Situation

US ECON SER - FEED SIT - US Economic Research Service - Feed Situation

US ECON SER - LIVESTOCK SIT - US Economic Research Service - Livestock and Meat Situation

US ECON SER - MKTG & TRANS SIT - US Economic Research Service - Marketing and Transportation Situation

US ECON SER - POULTRY & EGG SIT - US Economic Research Service - Poultry and Egg Situation

US ECON SER - STAT COTTON - US Economic Research Service - Statistics on Cotton and Related Data 1930-1967, Annual Supplement

US ECON SER - TOBACCO SIT - US Economic Research Service - Tobacco Situation

US ECON SER - VEG SIT - US Economic Research Service - Vegetable Situation

US ECON SER - WHEAT SIT - US Economic Research Service - Wheat Situation

US ECON SER - WOOL SIT - US Economic Research Service - Wool Situation

US LABOR STAT BUR - RETAIL FOOD PRICES - US Labor Statistics Bureau - Estimated Retail Food Prices by Cities

US LABOR STAT BUR - RETAIL PRICES FUELS & ELEC - US Labor Statistics Bureau - Retail Prices and Indexes of Fuels and Electricity

US LABOR STAT BUR - WHOLESALE PRICES & PRICE INDEXES - US Labor Statistics Bureau - Wholesale Prices and Price Indexes

US MKT NEWS SECT - COTTON LINTERS

ABBREVIATIONS OF PERIODICALS INDEXED

REV - US Market News Section -
  Monthly Cotton Linters Review
US MKT NEWS SECT - COTTON MKT
  REV - US Market News Section -
  Weekly Cotton Market Review
US STAT RPTG SER - AGRI PRICES -
  US Statistical Reporting Service -
  Agricultural Prices
US STAT RPTG SER - AGRI PRICES -
  ANNUAL SUMMARY - US Statistical Reporting Service - Agricultural
  Prices - Annual Summary
US STAT RPTG SER - DAIRY PROD -
  US Statistical Reporting Service -
  Dairy Products
US STAT RPTG SER WIS - AVERAGE
  PRICE MILK - US Statistical Reporting Service (Wisconsin) - Average
  Price Received by Farmers for Milk of
  Manufacturing Grade in the Minnesota-Wisconsin Area
US STAT RPTG SER WIS - PRICES
  RECEIVED - US Statistical Reporting
  Service (Wisconsin) - Prices Received
UTAH FARM - Utah Farmer-Stockman

WALL STREET J - Wall Street Journal
WASH FARM - Washington Farmer-Stockman
WEST LIVESTOCK J - Western Livestock Journal
WEST MINER - Western Miner
WEST PRODUCER - Western Producer
WIS BEV J - Wisconsin Beverage
  Journal
WK BUL LEATHER & SHOE - Weekly
  Bulletin of Leather and Shoe News
WOOL SACK - Wool Sack
WORLD WOOL DIG - World Wool
  Digest

COMMODITY PRICES

A

ABACA
J of Commerce - W - NY

ABIES SIBERICA OIL
Chem Mktg Rptr - W - NY

ACCELERATOR: 30, 40, 49, 108, 552, 808, 833, B
Rubber World - SA

ACETAL
J of Commerce - W - NY
Mod Pckg-Encyclo and Plan Guide - A - US

ACETALDEHYDE
Chem Mktg Rptr - W - US

ACETANILIDE
Chem Mktg Rptr - W - NY
J of Commerce - W - NY

ACETATE: FILAMENT YARN
US Labor Stat Bur - Wholesale Prices & Price Indexes - M

ACETATE: STAPLE FIBER
Mod Textiles Mag - M

ACETATE: TOW FIBER
Mod Textiles Mag - M

ACETATE RAYON
Dly News Rec - D

ACETATE SATIN
Wall Street J - D - NY

ACETATE SATIN GRAY GOODS
Dly News Rec - D
J of Commerce - W

ACETATE TRICOT
Dly News Rec - D
J of Commerce - W

US Labor Stat Bur - Wholesale Prices & Price Indexes - M

ACETATE YARN
Mod Textiles Mag - M

ACETIC ACID
Chem Mktg Rptr - W - East
J of Commerce - W - NY
Rubber World - SA
US Labor Stat Bur - Wholesale Prices & Price Indexes - M

ACETIC ANHYDRIDE
Chem Mktg Rptr - W - US
J of Commerce - W - NY

ACETIC GLACIAL ACID
J of Commerce - W - NY

ACETOACETANILIDE
Chem Mktg Rptr - W - NY

ACETOACET-O-CHLORANILIDE
Chem Mktg Rptr - W - NY

ACETOACET-O-TOLUIDIDE
Chem Mktg Rptr - W - NY

ACETOACET-O-XYLIDIDE
Chem Mktg Rptr - W - NY

ACETOMINOPHEN
J of Commerce - W - NY

ACETONE
Am Paint J - W
Chem Mktg Rptr - W - US
J of Commerce - W - NY
Rubber World - SA
US Labor Stat Bur - Wholesale Prices & Price Indexes - M

ACETONITRILE
Chem Mktg Rptr - W - NY

ACETOPHENETIDIN
Chem Mktg Rptr - W - NY
J of Commerce - W - NY
US Labor Stat Bur - Wholesale Prices & Price Indexes - M

COMMODITY PRICES

ACETOPHENONE
 Chem Mktg Rptr - W
 Rubber World - SA

N-ACETYL-P-AMINOPHENOL
 Chem Mktg Rptr - W - NY

ACETYLENE BLACK
 Can Chem Processing - M - Can
 Chem Mktg Rptr - W - NY

ACETYLENE TETRABROMIDE
 Chem Mktg Rptr - W

ACETYLSALICYLIC ACID
 Chem Mktg Rptr - W - NY
 J of Commerce - W - NY
 US Labor Stat Bur - Wholesale
  Prices & Price Indexes - M

ACETYLTRIBUTYL CITRATE
 Chem Mktg Rptr - W - East

ACETYLTRIETHYL CITRATE
 Chem Mktg Rptr - W - East

ACIDS
 See specific acids

ACINTENE DP DIPENTENE
 Rubber World - SA

A-C POLYETHYLENE: 6, 617
 Rubber World - SA

ACRAWAX
 Rubber World - SA

ACRAWAX: B, C
 Rubber World - SA

ACROLEIN
 Chem Mktg Rptr - W - NY

ACRYLAMIDE
 Chem Mktg Rptr - W - NY

ACRYLIC: CIRCULAR KNIT FABRICS
 US Labor Stat Bur - Wholesale
  Prices & Price Indexes - M

ACRYLIC ACID
 Chem Mktg Rptr - W - NY

ACRYLIC CARPET STAPLE
 US Labor Stat Bur - Wholesale
  Prices & Price Indexes - M

ACRYLIC FIBER: STAPLE
 Mod Textiles Mag - M

ACRYLIC FIBER: TOW
 Mod Textiles Mag - M
 US Labor Stat Bur - Wholesale
  Prices & Price Indexes - M

ACRYLIC RESIN EMULSION
 Am Paint J - W

ACRYLICS
 Mod Pckg-Encyclo & Plan Guide -
  A - US

ACRYLICS: MOLDING POWDERS
 J of Commerce - W - NY

ACRYLIC YARN: KNITTING
 US Labor Stat Bur - Wholesale
  Prices & Price Indexes - M

ACRYLONITRILE
 Chem Mktg Rptr - W - NY
 Purch World - M
 US Labor Stat Bur - Wholesale
  Prices & Price Indexes - M

ACRYLONITRILE - BUTADIENE - STYRENE
 J of Commerce - W - NY

ACRYSOL: ASE-60, ASE-75, GS
 Rubber World - SA

ACTAFOAM: F-2, R-3, XR34
 Rubber World - SA

ACTIVATOR DN
 Rubber World - SA

ADAPHAX: 758, 759
 Rubber World - SA

ADIPIC ACID
 Chem Mktg Rptr - W
 J of Commerce - W - NY

COMMODITY PRICES

AERO XANTHATE
  Rubber World - SA

AGAR
  Chem Mktg Rptr - W - NY
  J of Commerce - W - NY

AGARIC
  J of Commerce - W - NY

AGE RITE
  Rubber World - SA

AIR CONDITIONERS: WINDOW TYPE
  US Stat Rptg Ser - Agri Prices -
    Annual Summary - A

AIR HOSE: RUBBER
  US Labor Stat Bur - Wholesale
    Prices & Price Indexes - M

AKROCHEM PHENOLIC RESINS
  Rubber World - SA

AKROFLEX: AZ, CD, DAZ
  Rubber World - SA

AKROGEL
  Rubber World - SA

ALAMINE H26
  Rubber World - SA

ALBACER
  Rubber World - SA

ALCOHOL
  Alaska Bev Analyst - M - Alaska
  Bev News - M
  Ill Bev J - M - Ill
  Ky Bev J - M - Ky
  Md-Wash-Del Bev J - M - Md,
    DC, Del
  Wis Bev J - M - Wis

ALCOHOL: SYNTHETIC
  Chem Mktg Rptr - W - East

ALDRIN
  Chem Mktg Rptr - W - NY
  US Stat Rptg Ser Agri Prices -
    Annual Summary - A - US and by
    states

ALE
  Ariz Bev J - M - Ariz

ALETRIS
  J of Commerce - W - NY

ALFALFA
  Lancaster Farm - W - Lancaster
    Pa
        See also HAY

ALFALFA: DEHYDRATED
  Feed Bul - D - Boston, Chicago,
    Kansas City, Omaha, Toledo

ALFALFA: SUNCURED PELLETS
  Feedstuffs - W - Atlanta, Boston,
    Chicago, Ft. Worth, Kansas City,
    Los Angeles

ALFALFA MEAL
  Calif Farm - S - Los Angeles,
    San Francisco
  Feedstuffs - W
  US Econ Ser - Feed Sit - Q -
    Kansas City
  US Labor Stat Bur - Wholesale
    Prices & Price Indexes - M

ALFALFA MEAL: DEHYDRATED
  US Agri Mktg Ser - Feed Mkt
    News - W

ALFALFA MEAL: SUN-CURED
  US Agri Mktg Ser - Feed Mkt News
    - W - Buffalo, Denver, Kansas
    City, Los Angeles, Portland

ALFALFA SEED
  Seed World - A - US and by states
  US Labor Stat Bur - Wholesale
    Prices & Price Indexes - M
  US Stat Rptg Ser - Agri Prices - M -
    US and by states
  US Stat Rptg Ser - Agri Prices -
    Annual Summary - A - US and by
    states

ALGINS
  Am Paint J - W

COMMODITY PRICES

ALIQUAT 4
    Rubber World - SA

ALIZARINE
    J of Commerce - W - NY

ALIZARINE LAKE: RED
    Am Paint J - W

ALKALI BLUE
    Chem Mktg Rptr - W - US

ALKYDS
    J of Commerce - W - NY

ALLETHRIN
    Chem Mktg Rptr - W - NY

ALLSPICE
    J of Commerce - W - NY
    Natl Provision - W - Chicago

ALLSPICE OIL
    Chem Mktg Rptr - W - NY

ALLYL ALCOHOL
    Chem Mktg Rptr - W - NY

ALLYL BROMIDE
    Chem Mktg Rptr - W

ALLYL CAPROATE
    Chem Mktg Rptr - W - NY

ALLYL CHLORIDE
    Chem Mktg Rptr - W - NY

ALLYL ISOTHIOCYANATE
    Chem Mktg Rptr - W - NY

ALMOND OIL
    Chem Mktg Rptr - W - NY
    J of Commerce - W - NY

ALMONDS
    J of Commerce - W - NY

ALOE
    Chem Mktg Rptr - W - NY
    J of Commerce - W - NY

ALOIN
    Chem Mktg Rptr - W - NY
    J of Commerce - W - NY

ALROSOL
    Rubber World - SA

ALROWET D-65
    Rubber World - SA

ALSITE CLAY
    Rubber World - SA

ALTAX
    Rubber World - SA

ALTHEA ROOT
    J of Commerce - W - NY

ALUM: AMMONIA
    Chem Mktg Rptr - W
    J of Commerce - W - NY

ALUM: POTASH-CHROME
    Chem Mktg Rptr - W

ALUM: POTASSIUM
    Chem Mktg Rptr - W

ALUMINA: ACTIVATED
    Chem Mktg Rptr - W - NY

ALUMINA: CALCINED
    Can Chem Processing - M - Can

ALUMINUM
    Chem Mktg Rptr - W - NY
    Eng Min J - M
    Indus Wk - W
    Iron Age - W
    Met Wk - W
    North Miner - W - US
    UN Bul Stat - M - US
    West Miner - M - US

ALUMINUM: PRIMARY
    Am Met Mkt/Met News - D - US, Can

ALUMINUM: PRIMARY INGOT
    Foundry - M

COMMODITY PRICES

ALUMINUM: SECONDARY INGOT
   Foundry - M

ALUMINUM: SHEET
   Purch World - M

ALUMINUM: SMELTERS' ALLOYS
   Am Met Mkt/Met News - D - US, Can

ALUMINUM: SMELTERS' SCRAP
   Am Met Mkt/Met News - D - US

ALUMINUM ACETATE
   Chem Mktg Rptr - W

ALUMINUM ALLOYS
   Second Raw Materials - M

ALUMINUM AMMONIUM SULFATE
   Chem Mktg Rptr - W
   J of Commerce - W - NY

ALUMINUM CABLE
   US Labor Stat Bur - Wholesale
   Prices & Price Indexes - M

ALUMINUM CHLORIDE
   Chem Mktg Rptr - W

ALUMINUM FLUORIDE
   Chem Mktg Rptr - W
   US Labor Stat Bur - Wholesale
   Prices & Price Indexes - M

ALUMINUM FOIL
   Mod Pckg-Encyclo & Plan Guide -
   A - US

ALUMINUM FORMATE
   Chem Mktg Rptr - W

ALUMINUM HYDROXIDE
   Chem Mktg Rptr - W
   Rubber World - SA
   US Labor Stat Bur - Wholesale
   Prices & Price Indexes - M

ALUMINUM INGOT
   Barron's - W - NY
   Eng Min J - M
   J of Commerce - D - NY
   Min Rec - W

   NY Times - D - NY
   Purch World - M
   Wall Street J - D - NY

ALUMINUM OXIDE
   US Labor Stat Bur - Wholesale
   Prices & Price Indexes - M

ALUMINUM PASTE
   Chem Mktg Rptr - W - NY

ALUMINUM PHENOSULFONATE
   Chem Mktg Rptr - W - NY

ALUMINUM PIGMENT: PASTE
   US Labor Stat Bur - Wholesale
   Prices & Price Indexes - M

ALUMINUM PIGMENT: STANDARD
PASTE, STANDARD LINING PASTE,
EXTRA FINE LINING PASTE,
STANDARD POWDER, STANDARD
LINING POWDER, EXTRA FINE
LINING POWDER
   Am Paint J - W

ALUMINUM POWDER
   Am Met Mkt/Met News - D - US
   Can Chem Processing - M - Can
   Chem Mktg Rptr - W - NY

ALUMINUM RESINATE
   Chem Mktg Rptr - W - NY

ALUMINUM SCRAP
   Comm Bul - W
   Iron Age - W
   J of Commerce - W - NY
   Purch World - M - East
   Second Raw Materials - M -
     Montreal, Chicago, NY,
     Houston, Los Angeles, St. Louis,
     Toronto
   US Labor Stat Bur - Wholesale
   Prices & Price Indexes - M

ALUMINUM SHAPES
   US Labor Stat Bur - Wholesale
   Prices & Price Indexes - M

ALUMINUM SILICATE: HYDROUS,
C.L., SURFACE COATED
   Am Paint J - W

COMMODITY PRICES

ALUMINUM STEARATE
   Am Paint J – W
   Chem Mktg Rptr – W – NY
   Rubber World – SA

ALUMINUM SULFATE
   Can Chem Processing – M – Can
   Chem Mktg Rptr – W – NY
   J of Commerce – W – NY
   US Labor Stat Bur – Wholesale
     Prices & Price Indexes – M

ALUMINUM WIRE
   US Labor Stat Bur – Wholesale
     Prices & Price Indexes – M

AMAX AND AMAX I
   Rubber World – SA

AMBEREX
   Rubber World – SA

AMBERGRIS
   Chem Mktg Rptr – W – NY

AMBEROL
   Rubber World – SA

AMINOACETIC ACID
   Chem Mktg Rptr – W

p-AMINO ACID
   J of Commerce – W – NY

AMINOAZOTOLUENE BASE
   Chem Mktg Rptr – W – NY

2-AMINO-4-CHLOROPHENOL
   Chem Mktg Rptr – W – NY

AMINOETHYL ETHANOLAMINE
   Chem Mktg Rptr – W – NY

n-AMINOETHYLPIPERAZINE
   Chem Mktg Rptr – W – NY

2-AMINO-2-METHYL-1-PROPANOL
   Chem Mktg Rptr – W – NY

p-AMINOPHENOL
   Chem Mktg Rptr – W – East

AMINOPYRINE
   J of Commerce – W – NY

p-AMINOSALICYLIC ACID
   Chem Mktg Rptr – W – NY

AMINOX
   Rubber World – SA

AMMONIA
   Can Chem Processing – M – Can
   Chem Mktg Rptr – W – East
   J of Commerce – W – NY
   Purch World – M
   Rubber World – SA
   US Labor Stat Bur – Wholesale
     Prices & Price Indexes – M

AMMONIA: AQUEOUS
   US Labor Stat Bur – Wholesale
     Prices & Price Indexes – M

AMMONIA BICARBONATE
   J of Commerce – W – NY

AMMONIA BICHROMATE
   J of Commerce – W – NY

AMMONIAC
   J of Commerce – W – NY

AMMONIAC SAL
   Chem Mktg Rptr – W
     See also AMMONIUM
       CHLORIDE

AMMONIA NITRATE
   J of Commerce – W – NY

AMMONIA PERSULFATE
   J of Commerce – W – NY

AMMONIA SULFATE
   J of Commerce – W – NY

AMMONIUM ACETATE
   Chem Mktg Rptr – W – NY
   J of Commerce – W – NY

AMMONIUM BIBORATE
   Chem Mktg Rptr – W

COMMODITY PRICES

AMMONIUM BICARBONATE
 Chem Mktg Rptr - W

AMMONIUM BICHROMATE
 Chem Mktg Rptr - W

AMMONIUM BIFLUORIDE
 Chem Mktg Rptr - W

AMMONIUM BROMIDE
 Chem Mktg Rptr - W - NY
 J of Commerce - W - NY

AMMONIUM CHLORIDE
 Can Chem Processing - M - Can
 Chem Mktg Rptr - W

AMMONIUM CITRATE
 Chem Mktg Rptr - W - NY
 J of Commerce - W - NY

AMMONIUM FLUOBORATE
 Chem Mktg Rptr - W

AMMONIUM GLUCONATE
 Chem Mktg Rptr - W
 J of Commerce - W - NY

AMMONIUM LAURYL SULFATE
 Chem Mktg Rptr - W

AMMONIUM LIGNIN
 Chem Mktg Rptr - W

AMMONIUM MOLYBDATE
 Chem Mktg Rptr - W

AMMONIUM NITRATE
 Chem Mktg Rptr - W - NY
 US Labor Stat Bur - Wholesale
  Prices & Price Indexes - M

AMMONIUM OXALATE
 Chem Mktg Rptr - W - East
 J of Commerce - W - NY

AMMONIUM PENTABORATE
 Chem Mktg Rptr - W - NY

AMMONIUM PERSULFATE
 Chem Mktg Rptr - W

AMMONIUM SILICOFLUORIDE
 Chem Mktg Rptr - W

AMMONIUM SULFAMATE
 Chem Mktg Rptr - W

AMMONIUM SULFATE
 Chem Mktg Rptr - W
 Rubber World - SA
 US Labor Stat Bur - Wholesale
  Prices & Price Indexes - M

AMMONIUM SULFIDE
 Chem Mktg Rptr - W

AMMONIUM THIOCYANATE
 Chem Mktg Rptr - W

AMMONIUM THIOGLYCOLATE
 Chem Mktg Rptr - W - NY

AMMONIUM ZIRCONYL CARBONATE
 Chem Mktg Rptr - W - NY

AMMUNITION: SMALL ARMS
 US Labor Stat Bur - Wholesale
  Prices & Price Indexes - M

AMOCO 533 ANTIOXIDANT
 Rubber World - SA

d-AMPHETAMINE SULFATE
 Chem Mktg Rptr - W - NY

dl-AMPHETAMINE SULFATE
 Chem Mktg Rptr - W - NY

AMYL ACETATE
 J of Commerce - W - NY

AMYL ACETATE: EX FUSEL OIL,
PRIMARY & TECHNICAL
 Am Paint J - W
 Chem Mktg Rptr - W - East

AMYL ACETATE: EX PENTANE
 Am Paint J - W

AMYL ALCOHOL
 Am Paint J - W - Wyandotte
 Chem Mktg Rptr - W

COMMODITY PRICES

AMYL CINNAMIC ALDEHYDE
   Chem Mktg Rptr - W - NY
   J of Commerce - W - NY

p-tert-AMYLPHENOL
   Chem Mktg Rptr - W - NY

AMYL SALICYLATE
   Chem Mktg Rptr - W - NY
   J of Commerce - W - NY

AMYRIS OIL
   Chem Mktg Rptr - W - NY

ANETHOLE
   Chem Mktg Rptr - W - NY
   J of Commerce - W - NY

ANGELICA ROOT
   J of Commerce - W - NY

ANGELICA ROOT OIL
   Chem Mktg Rptr - W - NY

ANGOSTURA BARK
   J of Commerce - W - NY

ANILINE
   Chem Mktg Rptr - W - NY
   US Labor Stat Bur - Wholesale
     Prices & Price Indexes - M

ANILINE OIL
   J of Commerce - W - NY

ANILINE SALT
   Chem Mktg Rptr - W - NY

ANIMAL FAT
   Feedstuffs - W - Boston, Buffalo,
     Fort Worth, Kansas City
   US Agri Mktg Ser - Feed Mkt News
     - W - Chicago

ANISE OIL
   Chem Mktg Rptr - W - NY
   J of Commerce - W - NY

ANISE SEED
   Chem Mktg Rptr - W - NY
   J of Commerce - W - NY

ANISIC ALDEHYDE
   Chem Mktg Rptr - W - NY
   J of Commerce - W - NY

o-ANISIDINE
   Chem Mktg Rptr - W - NY
   J of Commerce - W - NY

p-ANISIDINE
   Chem Mktg Rptr - W

ANKLETS: GIRLS'
   US Stat Rptg Ser - Agri Prices -
     Annual Summary - A - US and by
     states

ANTHAQUINONE
   J of Commerce - W - NY

ANTHRACENE
   Chem Mktg Rptr - W
   J of Commerce - W - NY

ANTHRANILIC ACID
   Chem Mktg Rptr - W - NY
   J of Commerce - W - NY

ANTIDUST
   Rubber World - SA

ANTIFREEZE
   US Stat Rptg Ser - Agri Prices -
     Annual Summary - A - US and by
     states

ANTIMONIAL LEAD
   US Labor Stat Bur - Wholesale
     Prices & Price Indexes - M

ANTIMONY
   Am Met Mkt/Met News - D - Laredo,
     NY, Toronto, Montreal
   Chem Mktg Rptr - W
   Eng Min J - M - Laredo
   Iron Age - W - Tex
   J of Commerce - D - Laredo
   Met Wk - W
   Min Rec - W - Laredo
   NY Times - D - NY
   North Miner - W - Laredo, Toronto
   Purch World - M - Laredo
   US Labor Stat Bur - Wholesale
     Prices & Price Indexes - M

COMMODITY PRICES

ANTIMONY FLUOBORATE
  Chem Mktg Rptr - W

ANTIMONY ORE
  Eng Min J - M
  West Miner - M - US

ANTIMONY OXIDE
  Am Paint J - W
  Chem Mktg Rptr - W - East
  J of Commerce - W - NY

ANTIMONY POTASSIUM TARTRATE
  Chem Mktg Rptr - W
  J of Commerce - W - NY

ANTIMONY TRICHLORIDE
  Chem Mktg Rptr - W

ANTIOXIDANTS
  Rubber World - SA

ANTIOZONANT AFD
  Rubber World - SA

ANTISTATIC PLASTICIZER KA
  Rubber World - SA

ANTI-WEBBING J-524
  Rubber World - SA

ANTO$_3$: A-H
  Rubber World - SA

ANTOX SPECIAL
  Rubber World - SA

ANTOZITE: 1,2,67,67F
  Rubber World - SA

APERITIFS
  Alaska Bev Analyst - M - Alaska
  Ariz Bev J - M - Ariz
  Bev Media - M - NY
  Bev News - M
  Ill Bev J - M - Ill
  Mich Bev News - IR - Mich
  RI Bev J - M - RI
  Wis Bev J - M - Wis

APEX CLAY
  Rubber World - SA

APOMORPHINE HYDROCHLORIDE
  Chem Mktg Rptr - W - NY

APPAREL
  See also specific articles

APPAREL: INFANTS' & CHILDREN'S
  US Labor Stat Bur - Wholesale
    Prices & Price Indexes - M

APPAREL: MEN'S & BOYS'
  US Labor Stat Bur - Wholesale
    Prices & Price Indexes - M

APPAREL: WOMEN'S, MISSES',
JUNIORS'
  US Labor Stat Bur - Wholesale
    Prices & Price Indexes - M

APPLEJACK
  Md-Wash-Del Bev J - M - Md,
    DC, Del
  Patterson's - M - Calif

APPLE JUICE: CANNED
  US Labor Stat Bur - Wholesale
    Prices & Price Indexes - M

APPLES
  US Agri Mktg Ser - Fruit & Veg
    Prices - A - NY, Chicago, Mich,
    NC, Wash, W Va
  US Econ Ser - Mktg & Trans - Q -
    US
  US Labor Stat Bur - Retail Food
    Prices - M - US & 23 cities
  US Labor Stat Bur - Wholesale
    Prices & Price Indexes - M
  US Stat Rptg Ser - Agri Prices - M -
    US & by states
  US Stat Rptg Ser - Agri Prices -
    Annual Summary - A - US & by
    states

APPLES: CANNED
  J of Commerce - W

APPLES: FROZEN
  J of Commerce - W - NY, Mich

APPLESAUCE: CANNED
  J of Commerce - W

COMMODITY PRICES

US Labor Stat Bur - Wholesale
 Prices & Price Indexes - M

APRICOT KERNEL OIL
 Chem Mktg Rptr - W - NY

APRICOT OIL
 J of Commerce - W - NY

APRICOTS
 US Agri Mktg Ser - Fruit & Veg
  Prices - A - NY, Chicago,
  Calif, Wash

APRICOTS: CANNED
 J of Commerce - W
 US Labor Stat Bur - Wholesale Prices
  & Price Indexes - M

APRICOTS: DRIED
 J of Commerce - W

AQUAREX
 Rubber World - SA

ARABIC GUM
 Chem Mktg Rptr - W - NY
 J of Commerce - W - NY

ARANOX
 Rubber World - SA

ARAZATE
 Rubber World - SA

l-ARGININE: FREE BASE
 Chem Mktg Rptr - W - NY

l-ARGININE MONOHYDROCHLORIDE
 Chem Mktg Rptr - W - NY

ARIZONA
 Rubber World - SA

ARLEX
 Rubber World - SA

ARMEEN
 Rubber World - SA

ARMID HT
 Rubber World - SA

ARNEEL OD
 Rubber World - SA

ARNICA FLOWERS
 J of Commerce - W - NY

AROFENES
 Rubber World - SA

AROGEN 500
 Rubber World - SA

AROMATIC CHEMICALS
 J of Commerce - W

AROMATIC SOLVENTS
 J of Commerce - W - NY

ARQUADS: 12-50, T-50
 Rubber World - SA

ARROWROOT
 J of Commerce - W - NY

ARSENIC
 Chem Mktg Rptr - W - Tacoma,
  Mexican border
 Met Wk - W

ARSENIC PENTOXIDE
 Chem Mktg Rptr - W

ARSENIOUS TRIOXIDE
 Chem Mktg Rptr - W - Tacoma,
  Mexican border

ARUBREN CP
 Rubber World - SA

ASAFETIDA GUM
 J of Commerce - W - NY

ASBESTINE
 Chem Mktg Rptr - W - NY

ASBESTINE 3X
 Rubber World - SA

ASBESTOL SUPERFINE
 Rubber World - SA

COMMODITY PRICES

ASBESTOS
   Eng Min J - M - Que, North Vancouver, Morrisville Vt

ASBESTOS SHORTS
   Am Paint J - W - Can

ASBESTOS SIDING
   US Stat Rptg Ser - Agri Prices - Annual Summary - A - US & by states

ASCORBIC ACID
   Chem Mktg Rptr - W - NY
   J of Commerce - W - NY

ASH: BLACK
   Chem Mktg Rptr - W

ASH: NO. I COMMON
   US Labor Stat Bur - Wholesale Prices & Price Indexes - M

ASH (WOOD)
   Comm Bul - W

ASP: 106, 602
   Rubber World - SA

ASPARAGUS
   US Agri Mktg Ser - Fruit & Veg Prices - A - NY, Chicago, Calif, NJ
   US Labor Stat Bur - Retail Food Prices - M - US & 23 cities
   US Stat Rptg Ser - Agri Prices - M - US

ASPARAGUS: CANNED
   J of Commerce - W
   US Labor Stat Bur - Wholesale Prices & Price Indexes - M

ASPARAGUS: FROZEN
   J of Commerce - W

ASPHALT
   Chem Mktg Rptr - W

ASPHALT GILSONITE
   Chem Mktg Rptr - W - Craig Colo

ASPHALT PETROLEUM
   Chem Mktg Rptr - W - East Coast

ASPHALT ROOFING
   US Labor Stat Bur - Wholesale Prices & Price Indexes - M

ASPHALTUM
   Am Paint J - W - Craig Colo, NY, NJ

ASPIRIN
   Chem Mktg Rptr - W - NY, Philadelphia, Midland Mich, Chicago, St. Louis
   J of Commerce - W - NY
   US Labor Stat Bur - Wholesale Prices & Price Indexes - M

ASPIRIN ALUMINUM
   Chem Mktg Rptr - W

ATOMITE
   Rubber World - SA

ATRAZINE
   US Stat Rptg Ser - Agri Prices - Annual Summary - A - US & by states

ATROPINE SULFATE
   Chem Mktg Rptr - W - NY
   J of Commerce - W - NY

AUBEPINE
   Chem Mktg Rptr - W - NY
   J of Commerce - W - NY

AUTO RADIATORS: SCRAP
   Second Raw Materials - M - Chicago, Houston, Los Angeles, NY, St Louis, Toronto

AUTOMOBILES: NEW
   Auto Mkt Rpt - BW

AUTOMOBILES: USED
   Auto Mkt Rpt - BW
   Auto News - W

COMMODITY PRICES

AVOCADO OIL
  Chem Mktg Rptr - W - NY

AVOCADOS
  US Agri Mktg Ser - Fruit & Veg Prices - A - NY, Chicago

AXE: SINGLE BIT
  US Labor Stat Bur - Wholesale Prices & Price Indexes - M

AXES
  US Stat Rptg Ser - Agri Prices - Annual Summary - A - US & by states

AZELAIC ACID
  Chem Mktg Rptr - W - NY

AZO G YELLOW PIGMENT
  Chem Mktg Rptr - W - NY

AZO ORANGE
  Chem Mktg Rptr - W - NY

AZO YELLOW
  Chem Mktg Rptr - W - East

B

BABBIT: MIXED
  Comm Bul - W

BABBITT METAL: SCRAP
  Second Raw Materials - M - Chicago, Buffalo

BABY FOODS
  US Labor Stat Bur - Retail Food Prices - M - US & 23 cities

BACITRACIN
  Chem Mktg Rptr - W - NY

BACON
  See PORK CUTS: SMOKED

BAKING POWDER
  US Stat Rptg Ser - Agri Prices - Annual Summary - A - US & by states

BALERS: PICK-UP
  US Stat Rptg Ser - Agri Prices - Annual Summary - A - US and by states

BALMONY
  J of Commerce - W - NY

BALOGNA
  See SAUSAGES: DOMESTIC

BANANAS
  US Labor Stat Bur - Retail Food Prices - M - US & 23 cities
  US Labor Stat Bur - Wholesale Prices & Price Indexes - M
  US Stat Rptg Ser - Agri Prices - Annual Summary - A - US & by states

BARAK
  Rubber World - SA

BARBED WIRE: GALVANIZED
  US Stat Rptg Ser - Agri Prices - Annual Summary - A - US & by states

BARBERRY ROOT BARK
  J of Commerce - W - NY

BARBITAL-SODIUM
  Chem Mktg Rptr - W - NY

BARDEN: H CLAY, R CLAY
  Rubber World - SA

BARDOL B
  Rubber World - SA

BARIMITE
  Rubber World - SA

BARIMITE XF
  Rubber World - SA

BARIUM CARBONATE
  Chem Mktg Rptr - W - NY

COMMODITY PRICES

J of Commerce - W - NY
US Labor Stat Bur - Wholesale
　　Prices & Price Indexes - M

BARIUM CHLORATE
　Chem Mktg Rptr - W

BARIUM CHLORIDE
　Chem Mktg Rptr - W
　J of Commerce - W - NY
　US Labor Stat Bur - Wholesale
　　Prices & Price Indexes - M

BARIUM HYDRATE
　Chem Mktg Rptr - W - NY

BARIUM NITRATE
　Chem Mktg Rptr - W

BARIUM OXIDE
　Chem Mktg Rptr - W - NY

BARIUM PEROXIDE
　Chem Mktg Rptr - W

BARIUM STEARATE
　Chem Mktg Rptr - W - NY
　Rubber World - SA

BARIUM SULFATE
　Am Paint J - W
　Chem Mktg Rptr - W - NY
　J of Commerce - W - NY
　Rubber World - SA
　　See also BARYTES or BLANC FIXE

BARIUM SULFIDE
　Chem Mktg Rptr - W

BARLEY
　Comm Rev - W - US
　Dly Mkt Rec - D - Minneapolis, Winnipeg
　Feedstuffs - W - Los Angeles
　Fin Post - W - Winnipeg
　Free Press Farm - W - Winnipeg
　J of Commerce - D - Winnipeg, Chicago
　Lancaster Farm - W - Lancaster Pa
　US Labor Stat Bur - Wholesale
　　Prices & Price Indexes - M - Minneapolis

US Stat Rptg Ser - Agri Prices - M - US & by states
US Stat Rptg Ser - Agri Prices - Annual Summary - A - US & by states
US Stat Rptg Ser Wis - Prices Received - M - Wis
Wall Street J - D - Winnipeg, Minneapolis
West Producer - W - Winnipeg

BARLEY: FEED
　Dairyman - M - Los Angeles
　Feedstuffs - W - Atlanta, Boston, Buffalo, Chicago, Kansas City
　NY Times - D - Chicago
　US Econ Ser - Feed Sit - Q - Minneapolis

BARLEY: MALTING
　Dly Mkt Rec - D - Minneapolis
　NY Times - D - Chicago

BARLEY: NO. 2 MONTANA
　Mont Farm - S - Portland

BARLEY: NO. 2 WESTERN
　Calif Farm - S - Los Angeles, Stockton
　Ida Farm - S
　Ore Farm - S - Portland
　US Agri Mktg Ser - Grain Mkt News - W - Portland, Stockton, Los Angeles
　Utah Farm - S - Ogden Utah
　Wash Farm - S - Portland

BARLEY: NO. 3 OR BETTER
　US Agri Mktg Ser - Feed Mkt News - W - Los Angeles, Minneapolis, Portland
　US Agri Mktg Ser - Grain Mkt News - W - Minneapolis, Kansas City

BARLEY: SEED
　US Stat Rptg Ser - Agri Prices - Annual Summary - A - US & by states

BARRELS: STEEL
　US Labor Stat Bur - Wholesale
　　Prices & Price Indexes - M

COMMODITY PRICES

BARYTES
   Chem Mktg Rptr – W
   Eng Min J – M – Can, Gulf parts
   J of Commerce – W – NY

BARYTES: NO. 22
   Rubber World – SA

BARYTES: SOUTHERN OFF COLOR, DOMESTIC
   Am Paint J – W

BASIL
   J of Commerce – W – NY

BASIL: SWEET
   Natl Provision – W – Chicago

BASSWOOD
   Comm Bul – W
   US Labor Stat Bur – Wholesale Prices & Price Indexes – M

BATHTUBS: ENAMELED, CAST IRON
   US Stat Rptg Ser – Agri Prices – Annual Summary – A – US & by states

BATTERIES (MOTOR SUPPLIES)
   US Stat Rptg Ser – Agri Prices – Annual Summary – A – US & by states

BATTERY ACID
   Chem Mktg Rptr – W – East

BATTERY FENCE CHARGER
   US Stat Rptg Ser – Agri Prices – Annual Summary – A – US & by states

BATTERY PLATES: DRY
   Comm Bul – W

BATTERY PLATES: SCRAP
   Second Raw Materials – M – East, Chicago, Montreal, St Louis, San Francisco, Toronto

BAUXITE
   Can Chem Processing – M – Can
   Chem Mktg Rptr – W – Baltimore, Mobile
   Eng Min J – M – Baltimore, Mobile

BAYBERRY WAX
   Chem Mktg Rptr – W – NY

BAY LEAF
   Natl Provision – W – Chicago

BAY OIL
   Chem Mktg Rptr – W – NY
   J of Commerce – W – NY

BB TS
   Rubber World – SA

BEACONOL: M, S, T
   Rubber World – SA

BEANS: BLACKEYES
   US Agri Mktg Ser – Bean Mkt News – W – Calif

BEANS: BLACKEYES, DRY
   Calif Farm – S – Calif

BEANS: CANNED
   US Labor Stat Bur – Wholesale Prices & Price Indexes – M

BEANS: DRIED
   J of Commerce – W – NY
   US Labor Stat Bur – Retail Food Prices – M – US & 23 cities
   US Labor Stat Bur – Wholesale Prices & Price Indexes – M

BEANS: DRY EDIBLE
   US Stat Rptg Ser – Agri Prices – M – US & by states
   US Stat Rptg Ser – Agri Prices – Annual Summary – A – US & by states

BEANS: GREAT NORTHERN
   US Agri Mktg Ser – Bean Mkt News – W – Neb, Ida, Wyo

BEANS: GREAT NORTHERN, DRY
   Ida Farm – S – South Ida
   Mont Farm – S – Denver

COMMODITY PRICES

Neb Farm - S - Omaha
Ore Farm - S - South Ida
Utah Farm - S - Denver
Wash Farm - S - Denver

BEANS: GREEN, CANNED
J of Commerce - W
US Stat Rptg Ser - Agri Prices - Annual Summary - A - US & by states

BEANS: GREEN, FROZEN
J of Commerce - W

BEANS: KIDNEY, LIGHT RED
US Agri Mktg Ser - Bean Mkt News - W - Calif

BEANS: LIMA
US Agri Mktg Ser - Bean Mkt News - W - Calif
US Agri Mktg Ser - Fruit & Veg Prices - A - NY, Chicago, Fla

BEANS: LIMA, CANNED
J of Commerce - W

BEANS: LIMA, DRY
Calif Farm - S - Calif

BEANS: LIMA, FROZEN
J of Commerce - W

BEANS: NAVY
US Stat Rptg Ser - Agri Prices - Annual Summary - A - US & by states

BEANS: PINKS
US Agri Mktg Ser - Bean Mkt News - W - Ida, Calif

BEANS: PINKS, DRY
Calif Farm - S - Calif
Ida Farm - S - South Ida
Mont Farm - S - Denver
Ore Farm - S - South Ida
Utah Farm - S - Denver
Wash Farm - S - Denver

BEANS: PINTO
US Agri Mktg Ser - Bean Mkt News - W - Denver, Neb, Wyo, Ida

BEANS: PINTO, DRY
Ida Farm - S - South Ida
Mont Farm - S - Denver
Neb Farm - S - Omaha
Ore Farm - S - South Ida
Utah Farm - S - Denver
Wash Farm - S - Denver

BEANS: SMALL RED
US Agri Mktg Ser - Bean Mkt News - W - South Ida

BEANS: SMALL RED, DRY
Ida Farm - S - South Ida
Mont Farm - S - Denver
Ore Farm - S - South Ida
Utah Farm - S - Denver
Wash Farm - S - Denver

BEANS: SMALL WHITE
US Agri Mktg Ser - Bean Mkt News - W - Calif

BEANS: SMALL WHITE, DRY
Calif Farm - S - Calif

BEANS: SNAP
US Agri Mktg Ser - Fruit & Veg Prices - A - NY, Chicago, Fla, NC
US Labor Stat Bur - Wholesale Prices & Price Indexes - M
US Stat Rptg Ser - Agri Prices - M - US

BEANS: SNAP GREEN
US Econ Ser - Veg Sit - Q - NY

BEARFLEX: LPO, MPO
Rubber World - SA

BEDROOM SETS: WOOD, BED, DRESSER, CHEST OF DRAWERS
US Stat Rptg Ser - Agri Prices - Annual Summary - A - US & by states

COMMODITY PRICES

BEDSPREAD: COTTON
   US Labor Stat Bur - Wholesale
   Prices & Price Indexes - M

BEECH: NO. 2 COMMON
   US Labor Stat Bur - Wholesale
   Prices & Price Indexes - M

BEECH (WOOD)
   Comm Bul - W

BEEF
   US Labor Stat Bur - Wholesale
   Prices & Price Indexes - M

BEEF: BONELESS
   US Agri Mktg Ser - Livestock Mkt
   News - W - E Coast, Chicago,
   Colo, Los Angeles

BEEF: BONING CATTLE
   Natl Provision - W - Chicago

BEEF: BUTCHER CATTLE
   Natl Provision - W - Midwest River
   Points

BEEF: CHOICE
   US Econ Ser - Livestock Sit - BM -
   US
   US Econ Ser - Mktg & Trans - Q
   US

BEEF: COW
   US Agri Mktg Ser - Livestock Mkt
   News - W - E Coast, Chicago,
   Midwest, Colo, Los Angeles

BEEF: FRESH BONELESS
   Natl Provision - W - Chicago

BEEF: FROZEN BONELESS
   Natl Provision - W - Chicago

BEEF: FROZEN VARIETY MEATS
   Natl Provision - W - Chicago

BEEF: HEIFER
   Lancaster Farm - W - NY
   US Agri Mktg Ser - Livestock Mkt
   News - W - E Coast, Chicago,
   Midwest, Colo, Los Angeles

BEEF: HEIFER, CHOICE
   J of Commerce - D - Chicago
   US Econ Ser - Livestock Sit - BM -
   Chicago

BEEF: IMPORTED BONELESS
   J of Commerce - D - NY

BEEF: PRIMAL CUTS
   Natl Provision - W - Chicago

BEEF: SHELLS
   Dairyman - M - Modesto Calif,
   Phoenix

BEEF: STEER
   Calif Farm - S - Calif
   Lancaster Farm - W - NY
   Nation's Restaurant - S - E Coast,
   Midwest, Los Angeles
   US Agri Mktg Ser - Livestock Mkt
   News - W - E Coast, Chicago,
   Midwest, Colo, Los Angeles

BEEF ANIMALS
   See BULLS, CALVES, CANNERS &
   CUTTERS, HEIFERS, STEERS

BEEF CARCASS
   Neb Farm - S - Chicago

BEEF CATTLE
   US Stat Rptg Ser - Agri Prices -
   Annual Summary - A - US & by
   states

BEEF CATTLE: LIVE
   Fin Post - W - Chicago, Winnipeg
   Free Press Farm - W - Winnipeg,
   Chicago
   J of Commerce - D - Winnipeg
   NY Times - D

BEEF CATTLE CONCENTRATE FEED
   US Stat Rptg Ser - Agri Prices -
   Annual Summary - A - US & by
   states

BEEF CATTLE FEED
   Neb Farm - S
   US Econ Ser - Feed Sit - Q

COMMODITY PRICES

BEEF CUTS
    Lancaster Farm - W - NY
    Nation's Restaurant - S - E Coast, Los Angeles
    US Agri Mktg Ser - Livestock Mkt News - W - E Coast, Chicago, Midwest, Colo, Los Angeles
    US Labor Stat Bur - Retail Food Prices - M - US & 23 cities
    US Stat Rptg Ser - Agri Prices - Annual Summary - A - US & by states

BEEF TENDERLOINS
    Natl Provision - W - Chicago

BEEF TRIMMINGS
    See SAUSAGE MATERIALS

BEEF VARIETY MEATS
    US Agri Mktg Ser - Livestock Mkt News - W - East, Chicago, Denver, Mo River Points, West

BEER
    Alaska Bev Analyst - M - Alaska
    Ariz Bev J - M - Ariz
    Bev Media - M - NY
    Ill Bev J - M - Ill
    Md-Wash-Del Bev J - M - Md, DC, Del
    Patterson's - M - Calif
    US Stat Rptg Ser - Agri Prices - Annual Summary - A - US & by states

BEESWAX
    Chem Mktg Rptr - W - NY
    J of Commerce - W - NY
    US Agri Mktg Ser - Honey Mkt News - M - US

BEET PULP
    Dairyman - M - Los Angeles
    US Econ Ser - Feed Sit - Q - Los Angeles

BEET PULP: DRIED
    Dairynews - S - Buffalo, Philadelphia, NY, Boston
    Feedstuffs - W - Atlanta, Boston, Buffalo, Chicago, Kansas City, Memphis, Minneapolis-St Paul

BEET PULP: MOLASSES
    Calif Farm - S - Los Angeles, San Francisco
    US Agri Mktg Ser - Feed Mkt News - W - Chicago, Los Angeles, Portland

BEETS
    US Agri Mktg Ser - Fruit & Veg Prices - A - NY, Chicago

BEETS: CANNED
    J of Commerce - W
    US Labor Stat Bur - Retail Food Prices - M - US & 23 cities

BELLADONNA LEAVES
    Chem Mktg Rptr - W - NY
    J of Commerce - W - NY

BELTING: RUBBER
    US Labor Stat Bur - Wholesale Prices & Price Indexes - M

BELTS: CLOTHING
    Handbags - M - US

BENTONITE
    Am Paint J - W
    Chem Mktg Rptr - W

BENZALDEHYDE
    Chem Mktg Rptr - W - NY
    J of Commerce - W - NY

BENZENE
    Am Paint J - W
    Chem Mktg Rptr - W - Chicago, Cleveland, Houston, Catlettsburg Ky
    J of Commerce - W
    Rubber World - SA
    US Labor Stat Bur - Wholesale Prices & Price Indexes - M

BENZENE: PETROLEUM
    Purch World - M - Houston

BENZENE HEXACHLORIDE
    Chem Mktg Rptr - W

BENZIDINE ORANGE
    Am Paint J - W

COMMODITY PRICES

Chem Mktg Rptr - W - NY

BENZIDINE SULFATE
Chem Mktg Rptr - W - NY

BENZIDINE YELLOW
Am Paint J - W
Chem Mktg Rptr - W - NY

BENZOCAINE
Chem Mktg Rptr - W - NY

BENZODIHYDROPYRONE
Chem Mktg Rptr - W - NY

BENZOFLEX 9-88
Rubber World - SA

BENZOIC ACID
Chem Mktg Rptr - W - NY
J of Commerce - W - NY

BENZOIN GUM
Chem Mktg Rptr - W - NY
J of Commerce - W - NY

BENZOPHENONE
Chem Mktg Rptr - W - NY

BENZOTRIAZOLE
Chem Mktg Rptr - W - NY

BENZOTRICHLORIDE
Chem Mktg Rptr - W - NY

o-BENZOYLBENZOIC ACID
Chem Mktg Rptr - W

BENZOYL CHLORIDE
Chem Mktg Rptr - W - NY

BENZOYL PEROXIDE
Chem Mktg Rptr - W

BENZYL ACETATE
Chem Mktg Rptr - W - NY
J of Commerce - W - NY

BENZYL ALCOHOL
Chem Mktg Rptr - W - US

BENZYL BENZOATE
Chem Mktg Rptr - W - NY

J of Commerce - W - NY

BENZYL CHLORIDE
Chem Mktg Rptr - W - NY
J of Commerce - W - NY
Rubber World - SA

BENZYL CINNAMATE
Chem Mktg Rptr - W - NY

N-BENZYL-N, N-DIMETHYLAMINE
Chem Mktg Rptr - W - NY

BENZYL FORMATE
Chem Mktg Rptr - W - NY

BENZYLIDINE ACETONE
Chem Mktg Rptr - W - NY

BENZYL ISOEUGENOL
Chem Mktg Rptr - W - NY
J of Commerce - W - NY

BENZYL PROPIONATE
Chem Mktg Rptr - W - NY

BENZYL SALICYLATE
Chem Mktg Rptr - W - NY

BERGAMOT OIL
Chem Mktg Rptr - W - NY
J of Commerce - W - NY

BERYLLIUM
Eng Min J - M
Iron Age - W - Cleveland, Reading
Met Wk - W
Min Rec - W
Purch World - M

BERYLLIUM-ALUMINUM
Iron Age - W

BERYLLIUM-COPPER
Iron Age - W

BERYLLIUM POWDER
Am Met Mkt/Met News - D - US

BERYL ORE
Eng Min J - M

COMMODITY PRICES

BETANOX SPECIAL
    Rubber World - SA

BEUTENE
    Rubber World - SA

BEVEL SIDING
    US Stat Rptg Ser - Agri Prices -
       Annual Summary - A - US & by
       states

B-I-K
    Rubber World - SA

BIOTIN
    Chem Mktg Rptr - W - NY

BIRCH
    Comm Bul - W

BIRCH: NO. 1 COMMON
    US Labor Stat Bur - Wholesale
       Prices & Price Indexes - M

BIRCH: STANDARD PANEL
    US Labor Stat Bur - Wholesale
       Prices & Price Indexes - M

BIRCH SWEET OIL
    J of Commerce - W - NY

BIRCH TAR OIL
    J of Commerce - W - NY

BISMATE
    Rubber World - SA

BISMUTH
    Can Min J - IR - NY
    Chem Mktg Rptr - W - NY
    Eng Min J - M
    Iron Age - W
    J of Commerce - D - NY
    Met Wk - W
    North Miner - W
    West Miner - M - US, Can

BISMUTH NITRATE
    Chem Mktg Rptr - W - NY

BISMUTH OXYCHLORIDE
    Chem Mktg Rptr - W

BISMUTH SUBCARBONATE
    Chem Mktg Rptr - W
    J of Commerce - W - NY

BISMUTH SUBGALLATE
    Chem Mktg Rptr - W
    J of Commerce - W - NY

BISMUTH SUBNITRATE
    Chem Mktg Rptr - W
    J of Commerce - W - NY
    US Labor Stat Bur - Wholesale
       Prices & Price Indexes - M

BISMUTH SUBSALICYLATE
    Chem Mktg Rptr - W
    J of Commerce - W - NY

BISMUTH TRIOXIDE
    Chem Mktg Rptr - W

BISPHENOL-A
    Chem Mktg Rptr - W - NY

BITTERS
    Alaska Bev Analyst - M - Alaska
    Ariz Bev J - M - Ariz
    Bev Media - M - NY
    Ill Bev J - M - Ill
    Ky Bev J - M - Ky
    RI Bev J - M - RI

BLACKBERRIES
    US Agri Mktg Ser - Fruit & Veg
       Prices - A - NY

BLACKBERRIES: FROZEN
    J of Commerce - W

BLACKBERRY JAM OR PRESERVES
    US Labor Stat Bur - Wholesale
       Prices & Price Indexes - M

BLACK BIRD SULFUR
    Rubber World - SA

BLACK HAW ROOT BARK
    J of Commerce - W - NY

BLACK HAW TREE BARK
    J of Commerce - W - NY

COMMODITY PRICES

BLACK-OUT: BLACK, CLEAR, WHITE
   Rubber World - SA

BLACK WAX SDBA
   Rubber World - SA

BLANC FIXE
   Am Paint J - W
   Chem Mktg Rptr - W - Dallas, NY, Huntington
   J of Commerce - W - NY
   Rubber World - SA

BLANKETS
   US Stat Rptg Ser - Agri Prices - Annual Summary - A - US and by states

BLANKETS: WOOL
   US Labor Stat Bur - Wholesale Prices & Price Indexes - M

BLASTING CAPS: ELECTRIC
   US Labor Stat Bur - Wholesale Prices & Price Indexes - M

B-L-E: 25,75
   Rubber World - SA

BLENDED FABRIC: POLYESTER AND COTTON
   US Econ Ser - Stat Cotton - A - US

BLENDED FRUIT JUICES
   See FRUIT JUICES: BLENDED

BLEND JUICE: FROZEN
   J of Commerce - W - Fla

BLOOD: DRIED
   Chicago Hide - D - Midwest
   Fats & Oils - D - Midwest
   Feed Bul - D - Midwest

BLOOD MEAL
   Feedstuffs - W - Chicago, Kansas City, Memphis, Minneapolis - St Paul

BLOOD ROOT
   J of Commerce - W - NY

BLOUSES: WOMEN'S
   US Stat Rptg Ser - Agri Prices - Annual Summary - A - US and by states

BLUEBERRIES
   US Agri Mktg Ser - Fruit & Veg Prices - A - NY, Chicago, Mich, NJ

BLUEBERRIES: FROZEN
   J of Commerce - W - Me, Mich, Can

BOARDS: ROUGH, DRESSED
   US Stat Rptg Ser - Agri Prices - Annual Summary - A - US and by states

BOARS
   Free Press Farm - W - Winnipeg, Toronto
   Lancaster Farm - W - New Holland Pa

BOIS DE ROSE OIL
   Chem Mktg Rptr - W - NY
   J of Commerce - W - NY

BOLDO LEAVES
   J of Commerce - W - NY

BOLTS: MACHINE, CARRIAGE, MINE ROOF
   US Labor Stat Bur - Wholesale Prices & Price Indexes - M

BONDING AGENTS: M3, R-4, 6
   Rubber World - SA

BONDOGEN
   Rubber World - SA

BONE BLACK
   Am Paint J - W

BONEMEAL: STEAMED
   Chem Mktg Rptr - W - Midwest, Philadelphia
   Feedstuffs - W - Atlanta, Kansas City, Minneapolis-St Paul
   J of Commerce - W - NY

COMMODITY PRICES

BON RUBINE TONER
   Chem Mktg Rptr - W - NY

BOOK PAPER: NO. 2 PLAIN OFFSET
   US Bur Dom Comm - Pulp Q - Q
   US Labor Stat Bur - Wholesale
      Prices & Price Indexes - M

BOOK PAPER: A GRADE
   US Bur Dom Comm - Pulp Q - Q
   US Labor Stat Bur - Wholesale
      Prices & Price Indexes - M

BORAGE FLOWER
   J of Commerce - W - NY

BORAX
   Chem Mktg Rptr - W
   Eng Min J - M
   J of Commerce - W - NY

BORIC ACID
   Chem Mktg Rptr - W
   Finishers' Mgt - M
   J of Commerce - W - NY
   US Labor Stat Bur - Wholesale
      Prices & Price Indexes - M

BORON TRICHLORIDE
   Chem Mktg Rptr - W
   J of Commerce - W - NY

BORON TRIFLUORIDE
   Chem Mktg Rptr - W

BOURBON
   Ariz Bev J - M - Ariz
   Bev Media - M - NY
   Bev News - M
   Buck Bev J - M - Ohio
   Md-Wash-Del Bev J - M - Md, DC, Del
   Mich Bev News - IR - Mich
   NJ Bev J - M - NJ
   Patterson's - M - Calif
   RI Bev J - M - RI

BOURBON: FLAVORED
   Alaska Bev Analyst - M - Alaska
   Bev News - M

BOXBOARD: FOLDING
   Paperbd Pckg - A
   US Bur Dom Comm - Pulp Q - Q

BOXBOARD: FOLDING, CHIPBOARD, NORTH CENTRAL AND EASTERN
   US Labor Stat Bur - Wholesale
      Prices & Price Indexes - M

BOXBOARD: FOLDING, NEWSBACK, CENTRAL
   US Labor Stat Bur - Wholesale
      Prices & Price Indexes - M

BOXBOARD: SETUP
   US Bur Dom Comm - Pulp Q - Q

BOXBOARD: SETUP, CHIPBOARD, NORTH CENTRAL AND EASTERN
   US Labor Stat Bur - Wholesale
      Prices & Price Indexes - M

BOXES: SHIPPING CONTAINERS
   US Bur Dom Comm - Pulp Q - Q

BRAN
   US Labor Stat Bur - Wholesale
      Prices & Price Indexes - M
   US Stat Rptg Ser - Agri Prices - M - US and by states
   US Stat Rptg Ser - Agri Prices - Annual Summary - A - US and by states
   Wall Street J - D - Buffalo

BRAN: RED
   Dairyman - M - Los Angeles

BRAN: WHEAT
   US Econ Ser - Feed Sit - Q - Minneapolis, Buffalo

BRANDY: FLAVORED, UNFLAVORED
   Alaska Bev Analyst - M - Alaska
   Ariz Bev J - M - Ariz
   Bev Media - M - NY
   Bev News - M
   Buck Bev J - M - Ohio
   Ill Bev J - M - Ill
   Ky Bev J - M - Ky
   Md-Wash-Del Bev J - M - Md, DC, Del

COMMODITY PRICES

    Mich Bev News - IR - Mich
    NJ Bev J - M - NJ
    Patterson's - M - Calif
    RI Bev J - M - RI

BRASS
    Can Min J - IR - NY

BRASS: ANODE
    Finishers' Mgt - M

BRASS: LOW
    Iron Age - W

BRASS: NAVAL
    Iron Age - W

BRASS: RED
    Iron Age - W
    Purch World - M

BRASS: RED INGOT
    Foundry - M
    US Labor Stat Bur - Wholesale
      Prices & Price Indexes - M

BRASS: YELLOW
    Comm Bul - W
    Iron Age - W
    Purch World - M

BRASS FITTINGS
    US Labor Stat Bur - Wholesale
      Prices & Price Indexes - M

BRASSIERES: WOMEN'S, MISSES', & JUNIORS'
    US Labor Stat Bur - Wholesale
      Prices & Price Indexes - M

BRASS INGOT
    Am Met Mkt/Met News - D - US, Can
    J of Commerce - D - NY
    Second Raw Materials - M

BRASS INGOT MAKERS' SCRAP
    Am Met Mkt/ Met News - D - US

BRASS MILL SCRAP
    Am Met Mkt/ Met News - D - US
    Iron Age - W

    Second Raw Materials - M

BRASS PIPE
    Comm Bul - W

BRASS POWDER
    Am Met Mkt/Met News - D - US

BRASS RODS
    Comm Bul - W
    Iron Age - W

BRASS SCRAP
    Iron Age - W
    J of Commerce - W - NY
    Purch World - M - East
    Second Raw Materials - M - Montreal, Chicago, NY, Houston, St Louis, Los Angeles, Toronto

BRASS SCRAP: HEAVY YELLOW
    US Labor Stat Bur - Wholesale
      Prices & Price Indexes - M

BRASS SHAPES
    US Labor Stat Bur - Wholesale
      Prices & Price Indexes - M

BRAZE
    Rubber World - SA

BRAZIL NUTS
    J of Commerce - W - NY

BRAZIL OIL: NO. 1
    J of Commerce - D

BREAD
    US Econ Ser - Mktg & Trans Sit - Q - US
    US Econ Ser - Wheat Sit - Q - US
    US Labor Stat Bur - Retail Food Prices - M - US and 23 cities
    US Labor Stat Bur - Wholesale
      Prices & Price Indexes - M
    US Stat Rptg Ser - Agri Prices - Annual Summary - A - US and by states

BREWERS' DRIED GRAINS
    Dairynews - S - Buffalo, Philadelphia, NY, Boston

COMMODITY PRICES

Feedstuffs - W - Atlanta, Baltimore, Boston, Buffalo, Chicago, Memphis, Minneapolis-St Paul
US Agri Mktg Ser - Feed Mkt News - W - Baltimore, Boston, Buffalo, Chicago, Milwaukee, St Louis
US Econ Ser - Feed Sit - Q - Milwaukee

BREWERS DRIED YEAST
Feedstuffs - W - Atlanta, Boston, Baltimore, Buffalo, Chicago, St Paul

BREWERS' GRAINS
Feed Bul - D - St Louis, Milwaukee, Boston

BREWERS' STOCKS
J of Commerce - W

BREWS
Wis Bev J - M - Wis

BRICK
J of Commerce - W - NY
US Stat Rptg Ser - Agri Prices - Annual Summary - A - US and by states

BRICK: COMMON BACKING
Purch World - M - Chicago, NY

BRIJ 35
Rubber World - SA

BROADCLOTHS
See COTTON GRAY GOODS: BROADCLOTHS

BROCCOLI
Calif Farm - S - Salinas-Watsonville
US Agri Mktg Ser - Fruit & Veg Prices - A - NY, Chicago, Calif, Tex
US Econ Ser - Veg Sit - Q - NY, Chicago
US Stat Rptg Ser - Agri Prices - M - US

BROCCOLI: FROZEN
J of Commerce - W

US Labor Stat Bur - Retail Food Prices - M - US and 23 cities

BROENNER'S ACID
Chem Mktg Rptr - W - NY
J of Commerce - W - NY

BROILER GROWER FEED
US Econ Ser - Feed Sit - Q
US Stat Rptg Ser - Agri Prices - M - US and by states
US Stat Rptg Ser - Agri Prices - Annual Summary - A - US and by states

BROILERS
Poultry Times - W - Ga
US Agri Mktg Ser - Broiler Mktg Guide - Q - US
US Cons & Mktg Ser - Poultry Mkt Stat - A - East, Los Angeles, Pittsburgh, Seattle
US Econ Ser - Demand Sit - Q - US
US Econ Ser - Poultry & Egg Sit - 5/yr - US
See also CHICKENS; HENS

BROILERS: DRESSED
Wall Street J - D - NY

BROILERS: ICED
Dly Mkt Rec - D - Chicago
Free Press Farm - W - Chicago
J of Commerce - D - Chicago
Poultry & Egg Mktg - BW - Chicago
Poultry Times - W - Chicago
US Cons & Mktg Ser - Poultry Mkt Stat - A - Ga, Baltimore, Chicago, Denver, Los Angeles, NY, St Louis
Wall Street J - D - Chicago

BROILERS: LIVE
Agri Let - W - US
Lancaster Farm - W - Delmarva Man Co-op - W
US Stat Rptg Ser - Agri Prices - M - US and by states
US Stat Rptg Ser - Agri Prices - Annual Summary - A - US and by states

COMMODITY PRICES

BROMINE
    Chem Mktg Rptr - W - US
    J of Commerce - W - NY

BROMOCHLOROMETHANE
    Chem Mktg Rptr - W - NY

BROMOFORM
    Chem Mktg Rptr - W

BRONZE
    Iron Age - W

BRONZE INGOT
    Am Met Mkt/Met News - D - US, Can

BRONZE POWDER
    Am Met Mkt/Met News - D - US

BROOMS
    US Stat Rptg Ser - Agri Prices - Annual Summary - A - US and by states

BROWN FACTICE
    Rubber World - SA

BROWN VULCANIZED VEGETABLE OILS
    Rubber World - SA

BRUCINE ALKALOID
    Chem Mktg Rptr - W - NY
    J of Commerce - W - NY

BRUCINE SULFATE
    Chem Mktg Rptr - W - NY
    J of Commerce - W - NY

BRUSSELS SPROUTS
    US Agri Mktg Ser - Fruit & Veg Prices - A - NY, Chicago

BRUSSELS SPROUTS: FROZEN
    J of Commerce - W

BRV
    Rubber World - SA

BUCA CLAY
    Rubber World - SA

BUCHU LEAVES
    J of Commerce - W - NY

BUCKTHORN BARK
    J of Commerce - W - NY

BUILDING BOARD: HARDBOARD
    US Bur Dom Comm - Pulp Q - Q
    US Labor Stat Bur - Wholesale Prices & Price Indexes - M

BUILDING BOARD: INSULATION BOARD
    US Bur Dom Comm - Pulp Q - Q
    US Labor Stat Bur - Wholesale Prices & Price Indexes - M

BUILDING BOARD: PARTICLEBOARD
    US Bur Dom Comm - Pulp Q - Q

BUILDING MATERIALS
    J of Commerce - W
    Purch World - M

BUILDING PAPER AND BOARD: PLASTERBOARD
    Purch World - M - Philadelphia, San Francisco

BULLS
    Dairyman - M - Modesto, Phoenix
    Dakota Farm - M
    Kan Farm - S - Kan
    West Livestock J - W - US

BULLS: ANGUS
    Aber-Angus J - M - US

BULLS: BEEF
    Dairyman - M - ~~Corona Calif~~

BULLS: CHOICE
    Lancaster Farm - W - Lancaster Pa

BULLS: COMMERCIAL
    Dairyman - M - Pacific Northwest
    Lancaster Farm - W - Lancaster Pa, Peoria, Omaha
    US Agri Mktg Ser - Livestock Mkt News - W - Ga, Ill, Omaha, Sioux City, St Paul

COMMODITY PRICES

BULLS: DAIRY HEAVY, DAIRY LIGHT
    Dairyman - M - Corona Calif

BULLS: GOOD
    Lancaster Farm - W - Lancaster Pa
    US Agri Mktg Ser - Livestock Mkt
        News - W - Ga, Ill, Omaha,
        Sioux City, St Paul

BULLS: HEAVY BUTCHER, LIGHT BUTCHER
    Dairyman - M - San Joaquin Valley

BULLS: LIVE
    Livestock Breed J - M - US

BULLS: LIVESTOCK
    Farm & Dairy - W - Ohio
    Man Co-op - W
    Natl Provision - W - Chicago,
        Omaha, St Paul, Kansas City,
        Louisville

BULLS: RED POLL
    Red Poll News - SA - US

BULLS: SHORTHORN
    Shorthorn World - US - 16/yr

BULLS: SLAUGHTER
    Free Press Farm - W - Saskatoon,
        Winnipeg, Toronto, Montreal

BULLS: UTILITY
    Dairyman - M - Pacific Northwest
    Lancaster Farm - W - Lancaster Pa,
        Peoria, Omaha
    Mo Rural - S - Kansas City
    US Agri Mktg Ser - Livestock Mkt
        News - W - Ga, Ill, Omaha,
        Sioux City, St Paul

BUNAREX RESINS
    Rubber World - SA

BUNATAK: 210, N, U
    Rubber World - SA

BUNAWELD POLYMER 780
    Rubber World - SA

BUNNATOL: G, S
    Rubber World - SA

BURDOCK ROOT
    J of Commerce - W - NY

BURGESS ICEBERG
    Rubber World - SA

BURGUNDY
    Bev Media - M - NY
    Ill Bev J - M - Ill
    RI Bev J - M - RI
    Wis Bev J - M - Wis

BURLAP
    J of Commerce - D - NY
    Purch World - M - NY
    UN Bul Stat - M - US
    US Labor Stat Bur - Wholesale
        Prices & Price Indexes - M
    Wall Street J - D - NY

BUTADIENE
    Chem Mktg Rptr - W - NY
    US Labor Stat Bur - Wholesale
        Prices & Price Indexes - M

BUTADIENE STYRENE
    Am Paint J - W

BUTAZATE
    Rubber World - SA

BUTENE-1
    Chem Mktg Rptr - W - NY

BUTENE-2
    Chem Mktg Rptr - W - NY

BUTTER
    Calif Farm - S - San Francisco,
        Los Angeles
    Dairy Rec - M - NY
    Man Co-op - W
    US Cons & Mktg Ser - Dairy Mkt
        Stat - A - Chicago, NY, Los
        Angeles, Philadelphia
    US Econ Ser - Dairy Sit - 5/yr - US
    US Econ Ser - Fats & Oils Sit - 5/yr
        - US
    US Econ Ser - Mktg & Trans Sit - Q
        - US
    US Labor Stat Bur - Retail Food
        Prices - M - US and 23 cities

COMMODITY PRICES

US Labor Stat Bur - Wholesale
  Prices & Price Indexes - M
US Stat Rptg Ser - Agri Prices -
  Annual Summary - A - US and by
  states
Wall Street J - D - NY

BUTTER: A-92
  Barron's - W - NY

BUTTER: 92 SCORE
  NY Times - D - NY
  US Econ Ser - Fats & Oils Sit - 5/yr -
  Chicago, NY, San Francisco

BUTTERMILK: DRY
  Dairy Rec - M - NY, East, Midwest
  Feedstuffs - W - Chicago, Kansas
    City, Minneapolis-St Paul
  US Stat Rptg Ser - Dairy Prod - M -
    US

BUTYL ACETATE
  J of Commerce - W - NY

n-BUTYL ACETATE
  Am Paint J - W
  Chem Mktg Rptr - W - NY
  US Labor Stat Bur - Wholesale
    Prices & Price Indexes - M

sec-BUTYL ACETATE
  Am Paint J - W
  Chem Mktg Rptr - W - East

n-BUTYL ACRYLATE
  Chem Mktg Rptr - W - East

BUTYL ALCOHOL
  J of Commerce - W - NY
  US Labor Stat Bur - Wholesale
    Prices & Price Indexes - M

n-BUTYL ALCOHOL
  Am Paint J - W
  Chem Mktg Rptr - W - NY

sec-BUTYL ALCOHOL
  Am Paint J - W
  Chem Mktg Rptr - W - NY

tert-BUTYL ALCOHOL
  Am Paint J - W

Chem Mktg Rptr - W - East

tert-BUTYLAMINE
  Chem Mktg Rptr - W

BUTYLATED HYDROXYANISOLE
  Chem Mktg Rptr - W - NY

BUTYLATED HYDROXYTOLUENE
  Chem Mktg Rptr - W - NY

BUTYL BENZYL PHTHALATE
  Am Paint J - W
  Chem Mktg Rptr - W - NY
  Rubber World - SA

BUTYL CHLORIDE
  Chem Mktg Rptr - W - NY

BUTYL CYCLOHEXYL PHTHALATE
  Am Paint J - W
  Chem Mktg Rptr - W - NY

BUTYL EIGHT
  Rubber World - SA

1, 3 - BUTYLENE GLYCOL
  Chem Mktg Rptr - W - NY

n-BUTYL ETHER
  Chem Mktg Rptr - W

BUTYL ETHYLHEXYL PHTHALATE
  Am Paint J - W

BUTYL ISODECYL PHTHALATE
  Chem Mktg Rptr - W - NY

BUTYL LACTATE
  Chem Mktg Rptr - W - US

n-BUTYL LITHIUM
  Chem Mktg Rptr - W - NY

BUTYL METHACRYLATE
  Chem Mktg Rptr - W - NY

BUTYL NAMATE
  Rubber World - SA

BUTYL OCTYL PHTHALATE
  Chem Mktg Rptr - W - East

COMMODITY PRICES

BUTYL OLEATE
   Chem Mktg Rptr - W - NY
   Rubber World - SA

p-tert-BUTYLPHENOL
   Chem Mktg Rptr - W - NY

BUTYL STEARATE
   Rubber World - SA

BUTYL STEARATE: COSMETIC
   Chem Mktg Rptr - W - NY

BUTYL ZIMATE
   Rubber World - SA

BUTYL ZIMATE SLURRY
   Rubber World - SA

BUTYL ZIRAM: 0770, 0777
   Rubber World - SA

BUTYRALDEHYDE
   Chem Mktg Rptr - W - NY

BUTYRATE
   Mod Pckg-Encyclo & Plan Guide - A - US

BUTYRIC ACID
   Chem Mktg Rptr - W - NY

BUTYRIC ETHER
   Chem Mktg Rptr - W - NY

BUTYROLACTONE
   Chem Mktg Rptr - W

n-BUTYRONITRILE
   Chem Mktg Rptr - W - NY

B WAX: WHITE, YELLOW
   Rubber World - SA

BYRONIA ROOT
   J of Commerce - W - NY

C

CABBAGE
   Calif Farm - S - Imperial Valley
   US Agri Mktg Ser - Fruit & Veg Prices - A - NY, Chicago, Calif, Fla, NC, Tex
   US Econ Ser - Veg Sit - Q - NY, Chicago
   US Labor Stat Bur - Retail Food Prices - M - US and 23 cities
   US Labor Stat Bur - Wholesale Prices & Price Indexes - M
   US Stat Rptg Ser - Agri Prices - M - US
   US Stat Rptg Ser - Agri Prices - Annual Summary - A - US and by states

CABINETS: KITCHEN
   US Stat Rptg Ser - Agri Prices - Annual Summary - A - US and by states

CAB-O-SIL
   Rubber World - SA

CADE OIL
   J of Commerce - W - NY

CADMATE AMYL
   Rubber World - SA

CADMATE ETHYL
   Rubber World - SA

CADMIUM
   Am Met Mkt/Met News - D - Can
   Eng Min J - M
   Iron Age - W
   J of Commerce - D - NY
   Met Wk - W
   North Miner - W
   Purch World - M
   US Labor Stat Bur - Wholesale Prices & Price Indexes - M

COMMODITY PRICES

West Miner – M – US, Can

CADMIUM CHLORIDE
Chem Mktg Rptr – W

CADMIUM CP
Chem Mktg Rptr – W – East

CADMIUM FLUOBORATE
Chem Mktg Rptr – W

CADMIUM INGOT
Chem Mktg Rptr – W – NY

CADMIUM MERCURY LITHOPONE: ORANGE
Am Paint J – W
Chem Mktg Rptr – W – East

CADMIUM MERCURY LITHOPONE: RED, LIGHT, MEDIUM-LIGHT, MEDIUM, DARK, MAROON
Chem Mktg Rptr – W – East

CADMIUM MERCURY RED
Am Paint J – W

CADMIUM NITRATE
Chem Mktg Rptr – W

CADMIUM OXIDE
Finishers' Mgt – M

CADMIUM POWDER
Am Met Mkt/Met News – D – US

CADMIUM RED
Am Paint J – W

CADMIUM SELENIDE LITHOPONE: ORANGE
Am Paint J – W
Chem Mktg Rptr – W – East
J of Commerce – W – NY

CADMIUM SELENIDE LITHOPONE: RED, LIGHT, MEDIUM, DARK
J of Commerce – W – NY

CADMIUM SELENIDE LITHOPONE: RED, LIGHT, MEDIUM LIGHT, MEDIUM, DEEP, MAROON
Am Paint J – W

CADMIUM SELENIDE LITHOPONE: RED, LIGHT, MEDIUM LIGHT, MEDIUM, MAROON
Chem Mktg Rptr – W – NY

CADMIUM SELENIDE LITHOPONE: YELLOW
Chem Mktg Rptr – W – NY
J of Commerce – W – NY

CADMIUM STEARATE
Rubber World – SA

CADMIUM STICKS
Chem Mktg Rptr – W – NY

CADMIUM SULFATE
Chem Mktg Rptr – W

CADMIUM YELLOW
Am Paint J – W

CADMIUM YELLOW LITHOPONE
Am Paint J – W

CAFFEINE
Chem Mktg Rptr – W – NY
J of Commerce – W – NY

CAJUPUT OIL
J of Commerce – W – NY

CAKE MIX
US Stat Rptg Ser – Agri Prices – Annual Summary – A – US and by states

CAKES
US Stat Rptg Ser – Agri Prices – Annual Summary – A – US and by states

CALAMINE
Chem Mktg Rptr – W – NY

CALAMUS OIL
Chem Mktg Rptr – W – NY
J of Commerce – W – NY

CALAMUS ROOT
J of Commerce – W – NY

COMMODITY PRICES

CALCIUM
  Iron Age - W
  J of Commerce - W - NY
  Met Wk - W

CALCIUM ACETATE
  Chem Mktg Rptr - W - NY

CALCIUM BROMIDE
  J of Commerce - W - NY

CALCIUM CARBIDE
  Can Chem Processing - M - Can
  Chem Mktg Rptr - W - NY
  J of Commerce - W - NY
  US Labor Stat Bur - Wholesale
    Prices & Price Indexes - M

CALCIUM CARBONATE
  Am Paint J - W
  Chem Mktg Rptr - W
  J of Commerce - W
  Rubber World - SA
  US Labor Stat Bur - Wholesale
    Prices & Price Indexes - M

CALCIUM CHLORIDE
  Can Chem Processing - M - Can
  Chem Mktg Rptr - W - NY
  J of Commerce - W - NY
  Rubber World - SA
  US Labor Stat Bur - Wholesale
    Prices & Price Indexes - M

CALCIUM CITRATE
  Chem Mktg Rptr - W - NY
  J of Commerce - W - NY

CALCIUM CYANAMIDE
  Chem Mktg Rptr - W

CALCIUM GLUCONATE
  Chem Mktg Rptr - W - NY
  J of Commerce - W - NY

CALCIUM HYDRIDE
  Chem Mktg Rptr - W

CALCIUM HYPOCHLORITE
  Chem Mktg Rptr - W - East
  US Labor Stat Bur - Wholesale
    Prices & Price Indexes - M

CALCIUM HYPOPHOSPHITE
  Chem Mktg Rptr - W
  J of Commerce - W - NY

CALCIUM IODATE
  Chem Mktg Rptr - W - NY

CALCIUM IODIDE
  Chem Mktg Rptr - W

CALCIUM LACTATE
  Chem Mktg Rptr - W

CALCIUM MANDELATE
  Chem Mktg Rptr - W

CALCIUM NAPHTHENATE
  Am Paint J - W
  Chem Mktg Rptr - W - NY

CALCIUM OCTOATE
  Am Paint J - W

CALCIUM OXIDE
  Chem Mktg Rptr - W - NY
  US Labor Stat Bur - Wholesale
    Prices & Price Indexes - M

CALCIUM PANTOTHENATE
  J of Commerce - W - NY

d-CALCIUM PANTOTHENATE
  Chem Mktg Rptr - W - NY

dl-CALCIUM PANTOTHENATE: CHLORIDE COMPLEX, FEED GRADE
  Chem Mktg Rptr - W - NY

dl-CALCIUM PANTOTHENATE: FEED GRADE
  Chem Mktg Rptr - W - NY

CALCIUM PHOSPHATE: DIBASIC
  Chem Mktg Rptr - W
  US Labor Stat Bur - Wholesale
    Prices & Price Indexes - M

CALCIUM PHOSPHATE: MONOBASIC
  Chem Mktg Rptr - W - NY
  US Labor Stat Bur - Wholesale
    Prices & Price Indexes - M

COMMODITY PRICES

CALCIUM PHOSPHATE: TRIBASIC
   US Labor Stat Bur - Wholesale
     Prices & Price Indexes - M

CALCIUM PHYTATE
   Chem Mktg Rptr - W

CALCIUM PROPIONATE
   Chem Mktg Rptr - W - US
   J of Commerce - W - NY

CALCIUM SILICATE
   Am Paint J - W
   Chem Mktg Rptr - W

CALCIUM STEARATE
   Am Paint J - W
   Chem Mktg Rptr - W - NY
   Rubber World - SA

CALCIUM SULFATE
   Am Paint J - W
   Rubber World - SA

CALCIUM TALLATE
   Am Paint J - W

CALENDULA FLOWER
   J of Commerce - W - NY

CALF MEAT
   Lancaster Farm - W - NY

CALFSKINS
   Am Shoe - W
   Chicago Hide - D
   Hide & Leather Bul - D
   Natl Provision - W - Chicago
   US Labor Stat Bur - Wholesale
     Prices & Price Indexes - M

CALFSKINS: PACKER
   Leather & Shoes - W

CALIFLUX: 510, 550, GP, TT
   Rubber World - SA

CALOMEL
   Chem Mktg Rptr - W
   J of Commerce - W - NY

CALVES
   US Econ Ser - Livestock Sit - BM
   US Stat Rptg Ser - Agri Prices - M -
     US and by states
   US Stat Rptg Ser - Agri Prices -
     Annual Summary - A - US and by
     states
   US Stat Rptg Ser Wis - Prices
     Received - M - Wis
       See also CATTLE: LIVESTOCK

CALVES: ANGUS
   Aber-Angus J - M - US

CALVES: CHOICE STOCKERS & FEEDERS
   Neb Farm - S - Omaha

CALVES: HOLSTEIN BULL
   Dairyman - M - San Joaquin Valley

CALVES: LIVE
   Livestock Breed J - M - US

CALVES: LIVESTOCK
   Farm & Dairy - W - Ohio
   Man Co-op - W
   Natl Provision - W - Chicago,
     St Paul, Omaha, Sioux City
   US Labor Stat Bur - Wholesale
     Prices & Price Indexes - M

CALVES: SHORTHORN
   Shorthorn World - 16/yr - US

CALVES: SLAUGHTER
   Free Press Farm - W - Edmonton,
     Saskatoon, Winnipeg, Toronto,
     Montreal
   Lancaster Farm - W - New Holland,
     Lebanon Valley
   US Agri Mktg Ser - Livestock Mkt
     News - W - St Paul, Louisville,
     Ga, Portland, National
     Stockyards

CALVES: VEALERS
   Lancaster Farm - W - Lancaster Pa

CALWHITE
   Rubber World - SA

COMMODITY PRICES

CALWHITE T
   Rubber World - SA

CAMEL-CARB
   Rubber World - SA

CAMEL-TEX
   Rubber World - SA

CAMEL-WITE
   Rubber World - SA

CAMPHENE
   Chem Mktg Rptr - W - NY

CAMPHOR
   Chem Mktg Rptr - W - NY
   J of Commerce - W - NY

CAMPHOR OIL
   J of Commerce - W - NY

CAMPHOR OIL: SASSAFRASSY
   Chem Mktg Rptr - W - NY

CANANGA OIL
   Chem Mktg Rptr - W - NY
   J of Commerce - W - NY

CANARY SEED
   J of Commerce - W - NY

CANDELILLA WAX
   Chem Mktg Rptr - W - NY
   J of Commerce - W - NY

CANDY: NON-CHOCOLATE, WITHOUT NUTS
   US Stat Rptg Ser - Agri Prices - Annual Summary - A - US and by states

CANDY BAR: CHOCOLATE COVERED
   US Labor Stat Bur - Wholesale Prices & Price Indexes - M

CANNED FOODS
   J of Commerce - W

CANNERS AND CUTTERS
   J of Commerce - D - Chicago

CANS: COMPOSITE
   US Bur Dom Comm - Pulp Q - Q

CANS: METAL
   US Labor Stat Bur - Wholesale Prices & Price Indexes - M

CANTALOUPES
   US Agri Mktg Ser - Fruit & Veg Prices - A - NY, Chicago, Ariz, Calif, Mich, Tex
   US Econ Ser - Veg Sit - Q - NY, Chicago
   US Labor Stat Bur - Wholesale Prices & Price Indexes - M
   US Stat Rptg Ser - Agri Prices - M - US

CANTHARIDES
   Chem Mktg Rptr - W - NY

CAPONS
   Lancaster Farm - W - Fogelsville Pa

CAPRIC ACID
   Chem Mktg Rptr - W - NY

CAPRIC ALDEHYDE
   Chem Mktg Rptr - W - NY

CAPRIC FATTY ACID
   Rubber World - SA

CAPROLACTAM MONOMER
   Chem Mktg Rptr - W - NY

CAPRYL ALCOHOL
   Chem Mktg Rptr - W - NY
   Rubber World - SA

CAPRYLIC ACID
   Chem Mktg Rptr - W - NY

CAPRYLIC FATTY ACID
   Rubber World - SA

CAPS: BOYS'
   US Stat Rptg Ser - Agri Prices - Annual Summary - A - US and by states

CAPSICUM
   Chem Mktg Rptr - W - NY

COMMODITY PRICES

J of Commerce - W - NY

CAPSICUM OLEORESIN
Chem Mktg Rptr - W - NY
J of Commerce - W - NY

CAPTAX
Rubber World - SA

CAPTAX-TUADS BLENDS
Rubber World - SA

CARAWAY OIL
Chem Mktg Rptr - W - NY
J of Commerce - W - NY

CARAWAY SEED
Chem Mktg Rptr - W - NY
J of Commerce - W - NY
Natl Provision - W - Chicago

CARBARYL
U S Stat Rptg Ser - Agri Prices - Annual Summary - A - US and by states

CARBAZOLE
Chem Mktg Rptr - W - NY

CAR-BEL-LITE 1
Rubber World - SA

CAR-BEL-REZ C
Rubber World - SA

CARBIUM
Rubber World - SA

CARBIUM MM
Rubber World - SA

CARBON BLACK
Can Chem Processing - M - Can
Chem Mktg Rptr - W
J of Commerce - W - NY
Rubber World - SA

CARBON BLACK: CHANNELS, MEDIUM GRADE, HIGH COLOR, FURNACE
Am Paint J - W

CARBON BLACK OIL
Chem Mktg Rptr - W - Gulf refineries

CARBON DISULFIDE
Chem Mktg Rptr - W
J of Commerce - W - NY
US Labor Stat Bur - Wholesale Prices & Price Indexes - M

CARBON TETRACHLORIDE
Chem Mktg Rptr - W - NY
J of Commerce - W - NY
Rubber World - SA
US Labor Stat Bur - Wholesale Prices & Price Indexes - M

CARBOWAX POLYETHYLENE GLYCOL
Rubber World - SA

CARBOXYMETHYL CELLULOSE
Am Paint J - W
Chem Mktg Rptr - W - East

CARDAMON
J of Commerce - W - NY
Natl Provision - W - Chicago

CARDAMON OIL
Chem Mktg Rptr - W - NY
J of Commerce - W - NY

CARDAMON SEED
Chem Mktg Rptr - W - NY

CARMEL
J of Commerce - W

CARMINE
Chem Mktg Rptr - W - NY

CARMINE: NO. 40
J of Commerce - W - NY

CARNAUBA WAX
Chem Mktg Rptr - W - NY
J of Commerce - W - NY
Rubber World - SA

b-CAROTENE
Chem Mktg Rptr - W - NY

CARPET BACKING FABRIC
US Labor Stat Bur - Wholesale Prices & Price Indexes - M

COMMODITY PRICES

CARPETS: NYLON, WOOL, ACRYLIC FIBER
    US Stat Rptg Ser - Agri Prices - Annual Summary - A - US and by states

CARROTS
    Calif Farm - S - Coachella
    US Agri Mktg Ser - Fruit & Veg Prices - A - NY, Chicago, Calif, Fla, Mich, Tex
    US Econ Ser - Veg Sit - Q - NY, Chicago
    US Labor Stat Bur - Retail Food Prices - M - US and 23 cities
    US Labor Stat Bur - Wholesale Prices & Price Indexes - M
    US Stat Rptg Ser - Agri Prices - M

CARROTS: CANNED
    J of Commerce - W

CARROTS: FROZEN
    J of Commerce - W

CARTHAGE - 99 1/2
    Rubber World - SA

CARTONBOARD: FOLDING
    See BOXBOARD

d-CARVONE
    Chem Mktg Rptr - W - NY

l-CARVONE
    Chem Mktg Rptr - W - NY

CASCARA BARK
    J of Commerce - W - NY

CASCARA SAGRADA BARK
    Chem Mktg Rptr - W - NY

CASEIN
    Am Paint J - W
    Chem Mktg Rptr - W - NY
    Rubber World - SA

CASHEWS
    J of Commerce - W - NY

CASSELLA ACID
    Chem Mktg Rptr - W - NY

CASSIA
    Chem Mktg Rptr - W - NY
    J of Commerce - W - NY

CASSIA OIL
    J of Commerce - W - NY

CASTOREUM
    Chem Mktg Rptr - W - NY

CASTOR OIL
    Am Paint J - W - NY
    J of Commerce - D
    US Econ Ser - Fats & Oils Sit - 5/yr - NY
    US Labor Stat Bur - Wholesale Prices & Price Indexes - M

CASTOR OIL: A, AA-L
    Rubber World - SA

CASTOR OIL: ACIDS DEHYDRATED
    Chem Mktg Rptr - W - NY

CASTOR OIL: RAW
    Chem Mktg Rptr - W

CASTOR POMACE
    Chem Mktg Rptr - W - Plainview Tex

CASTORWAX
    Rubber World - SA

CATALIN ANTIOXIDANT CAO
    Rubber World - SA

CATALPO CLAY
    Rubber World - SA

CATALYZER C-7
    Rubber World - SA

CATNIP LEAVES
    J of Commerce - W - NY

CATSUP: TOMATO
    J of Commerce - W
    US Labor Stat Bur - Wholesale Prices & Price Indexes - M
    US Stat Rptg Ser - Agri Prices - Annual Summary - A - US and by states

COMMODITY PRICES

CATTLE
    Dly Mkt Rec - D - Chicago
    Fin Post - W
    Lancaster Farm - W - Lancaster Pa
    Mich Farm - S
    US Econ Ser - Demand Sit - Q - US
    Wall Street J - D - Chicago

CATTLE: FEEDER
    Dly Mkt Rec - D - Chicago
    Farm & Dairy - W - Ohio
    J of Commerce - D - Chicago
    US Econ Ser - Livestock Sit - BM - Kansas City

CATTLE: LIVE
    J of Commerce - D - Chicago
    Natl Livestock - M - Omaha

CATTLE: LIVESTOCK
    Farm & Dairy - W - Ohio
    Natl Provision - W - Indianapolis, St Joseph, Louisville, Peoria, Cincinnati

CATTLE FEED
    US Stat Rptg Ser - Agri Prices - M - US and by states

CAULIFLOWER
    US Agri Mktg Ser - Fruit & Veg Prices - A - NY, Chicago, Calif, Fla, Tex
    US Econ Ser - Veg Sit - Q - NY, Chicago
    US Stat Rptg Ser - Agri Prices - M - US

CAULIFLOWER: FROZEN
    J of Commerce - W

CAUSTIC POTASH
    Can Chem Processing - M - Can
    Chem Mktg Rptr - W - US
    J of Commerce - W - NY
    US Labor Stat Bur - Wholesale Prices & Price Indexes - M

CAUSTIC SODA
    Can Chem Processing - M - Can
    Chem Mktg Rptr - W - US
    Finishers' Mgt - M - NY
    J of Commerce - W - NY

Purch World - M
Rubber World - SA
US Labor Stat Bur - Wholesale Prices & Price Indexes - M

CAYTUR: 4, 7
    Rubber World - SA

CBTS
    Rubber World - SA

CEDAR: RED, WHITE
    Comm Bul - W

CEDAR LEAF OIL
    Chem Mktg Rptr - W - NY
    J of Commerce - W - NY

CEDAR LUMBER: BEVEL SIDING
    US Labor Stat Bur - Wholesale Prices & Price Indexes - M

CEDARWOOD OIL
    Chem Mktg Rptr - W - Tex, Va

CEDROL
    Chem Mktg Rptr - W - NY

CEDRYL ACETATE
    Chem Mktg Rptr - W - NY

CELEROSE DEXTROSE
    Natl Provision - W - Chicago

CELERY
    Calif Farm - S - Oxnard
    Nation's Restaurant - S - NY, Boston, Chicago
    US Agri Mktg Ser - Fruit & Veg Prices - A - NY, Chicago, Calif, Fla, Mich, Tex
    US Econ Ser - Veg Sit - Q - NY, Chicago
    US Labor Stat Ser - Retail Food Prices - M - US and 23 cities
    US Labor Stat Bur - Wholesale Prices & Price Indexes - M
    US Stat Rptg Ser - Agri Prices - M - US

CELERY SEED
    Chem Mktg Rptr - W - NY
    J of Commerce - W - NY
    Natl Provision - W - Chicago

COMMODITY PRICES

CELERY SEED OIL
  Chem Mktg Rptr - W - NY
  J of Commerce - W - NY

CELITES: 270 J-M, 292 J-M
  Rubber World - SA

CELLOPHANE
  Mod Pckg-Encyclo & Plan Guide -
    A - US

CELLULOSE ACETATE
  Am Paint J - W
  Chem Mktg Rptr - W - East
  J of Commerce - W - NY
  Mod Pckg-Encyclo & Plan Guide -
    A - US

CELLULOSE ACETATE BUTYRATE
  Am Paint J - W
  Chem Mktg Rptr - W - East
  J of Commerce - W - NY

CELLULOSE ACETATE SCRAP
  Purch World - M - NY

CELLULOSE GUM
  Chem Mktg Rptr - W
  U S Labor Stat Bur - Wholesale
    Prices & Price Indexes - M

CELLULOSE TRIACETATE
  Am Paint J - W

CELOGEN: AZ, OT
  Rubber World - SA

CEMENT
  J of Commerce - W - NY, Portland
  Purch World - M - Portland, New
    Orleans, NY

CEMENT: PORTLAND
  US Stat Rptg Ser - Agri Prices -
    Annual Summary - A - US and by
    states

CERESIN WAX
  Rubber World - SA

CERIT
  Rubber World - SA

CERIUM HYDRATE
  Chem Mktg Rptr - W

CERIUM OXIDE
  Chem Mktg Rptr - W - NY

CETYL ALCOHOL
  Chem Mktg Rptr - W - East

CHAIN SAWS: GASOLINE
  US Stat Rptg Ser - Agri Prices -
    Annual Summary - A - US and by
    states

CHAIRS: LOUNGE
  US Stat Rptg Ser - Agri Prices -
    Annual Summary - A - US and by
    states

CHALK
  Chem Mktg Rptr - W
  J of Commerce - W - NY

CHALLIS (ACRYLIC CREPE) GRAY GOODS
  Dly News Rec - D

CHALLIS (RAYON) GRAY GOODS
  Dly News Rec - D
  J of Commerce - W

CHAMOMILE FLOWERS
  Chem Mktg Rptr - W - NY
  J of Commerce - W - NY

CHAMOMILE OIL
  Chem Mktg Rptr - W - NY

CHAMPAGNE
  Alaska Bev Analyst - M - Alaska
  Ariz Bev J - M - Ariz
  Bev Media - M - NY
  Bev News - M
  Ill Bev J - M - Ill
  RI Bev J - M - RI
  Wis Bev J - M - Wis

CHAMPION HARD CLAY
  Rubber World - SA

CHARCOAL: HARDWOOD
  Chem Mktg Rptr - W

COMMODITY PRICES

CHEESE
    J of Commerce – D – NY

CHEESE: AMERICAN
    US Cons & Mktg Ser – Dairy Mkt Stat – A – Wis
    US Econ Ser – Mktg & Trans Sit – Q – US
    US Labor Stat Bur – Retail Food Prices – M – US and 23 cities
    US Stat Rptg Ser – Agri Prices – Annual Summary – A – US and by states

CHEESE: AMERICAN PROCESSED
    US Econ Ser – Dairy Sit – 5/yr – US

CHEESE: BARREL
    Dairy Rec – M – Wis
    US Labor Stat Bur – Wholesale Prices & Price Indexes – M

CHEESE: BLOCKS, MIDGETS
    Dairy Rec – M – Wis

CHEESE: BRICK
    US Cons & Mktg Ser – Dairy Mkt Stat – A – Chicago

CHEESE: CHEDDAR
    US Cons & Mktg Ser – Dairy Mkt Stat – A – Chicago, NY, Los Angeles, Portland

CHEESE: COTTAGE
    US Econ Ser – Dairy Sit – 5/yr – US
    US Stat Rptg Ser – Agri Prices – Annual Summary – A – US and by states

CHEESE: FOREIGN TYPES
    Dairy Rec – M – Chicago

CHEESE: FOREIGN TYPES, DOMESTICALLY MADE
    US Cons & Mktg Ser – Dairy Mkt Stat – A – Chicago, NY, San Francisco

CHEESE: IMPORTED
    US Cons & Mktg Ser – Dairy Mkt Stat – A – Chicago, NY, San Francisco

CHEESE: LONGHORN
    Dairy Rec – M – Wis

CHEESE: MUENSTER
    US Cons & Mktg Ser – Dairy Mkt Stat – A – Chicago, NY

CHEESE: SINGLE DAISIES
    Dairy Rec – M – Wis
    J of Commerce – D – NY
    US Labor Stat Bur – Wholesale Prices & Price Indexes – M

CHEESE: SWISS
    Dairy Rec – M – Wis
    J of Commerce – D – NY
    US Cons & Mktg Ser – Dairy Mkt Stat – A – Wisconsin, NY, Chicago, Philadelphia, Los Angeles

CHEESE CLOTH
    US Stat Rptg Ser – Agri Prices – Annual Summary – A – US and by states

CHEMANOX: 11, 21T, 22
    Rubber World – SA

CHEMICAL PULP
    See WOOD PULP

CHEMLINK METHACRYLATE MONOMERS
    Rubber World – SA

CHEMLOCK ADHESIVES
    Rubber World – SA

CHENOPODIUM OIL
    Chem Mktg Rptr – W – NY

CHERRIES
    US Agri Mktg Ser – Fruit & Veg Prices – A – NY, Chicago, Wash

CHERRIES: CANNED
    J of Commerce – W
    US Labor Stat Bur – Wholesale Prices & Price Indexes – M

CHERRIES: FROZEN
    J of Commerce – W – NY, Mich, Pa, Wis

COMMODITY PRICES

CHERRIES: MARASCHINO
    Alaska Bev Analyst - M - Alaska
    US Labor Stat Bur - Wholesale
    Prices & Price Indexes - M

CHERRY JAM OR PRESERVES
    U S Labor Stat Bur - Wholesale
    Prices & Price Indexes - M

CHERRY (LUMBER)
    Comm Bul - W
    US Labor Stat Bur - Wholesale
    Prices & Price Indexes - M

CHESTNUT EXTRACT
    J of Commerce - W - NY

CHEWING GUM
    US Labor Stat Bur - Wholesale
    Prices & Price Indexes - M

CHICAGO ACID
    Chem Mktg Rptr - W - NY

CHICKEN: FRYING
    US Econ Ser - Mktg & Trans Sit -
    Q - US

CHICKEN PARTS
    US Cons & Mktg Ser - Poultry Mkt
    Stat - A - NY, Pittsburgh,
    Portland, Seattle
    US Labor Stat Bur - Retail Food
    Prices - M - US and 23 cities

CHICKENS
    US Stat Rptg Ser Wis - Prices
    Received - M - Wis
        See also BROILERS, FOWL
                  HENS

CHICKENS: DRESSED
    J of Commerce - D - NY
    Man Co-op - W - Winnipeg

CHICKENS (EXCLUDING BROILERS):
LIVE
    US Stat Rptg Ser - Agri Prices - M -
    US and by states
    US Stat Rptg Ser - Agri Prices -
    Annual Summary - A - US and by
    states

CHICKS: BABY
    US Stat Rptg Ser - Agri Prices -
    Annual Summary - A - US and by
    states

CHICK STARTER FEED
    US Stat Rptg Ser - Agri Prices - M -
    US and by states
    US Stat Rptg Ser - Agri Prices - Annual
    Summary - A - US and by states

CHINCHONA BARK
    J of Commerce - W - NY

CHLORACETIC ACID
    J of Commerce - W - NY

CHLORAL
    Chem Mktg Rptr - W

CHLORALHYDRATE
    J of Commerce - W - NY

CHLORDANE
    Chem Mktg Rptr - W - NY

CHLORENDIC ANHYDRIDE
    Chem Mktg Rptr - W

CHLORINATED PARAFFIN
    Am Paint J - W

CHLORINATED PARAFFIN: PLASTICIZER
GRADE
    Chem Mktg Rptr - W

CHLORINATED RUBBER
    Am Paint J - W - Parlin & Bayonne
    NY
    Chem Mktg Rptr - W

CHLORINE
    Can Chem Processing - M - Can
    Chem Mktg Rptr - W - NY
    J of Commerce - W - NY
    Rubber World - SA
    US Labor Stat Bur - Wholesale
    Prices & Price Indexes - M

CHLOROACETIC ACID
    Chem Mktg Rptr - W

COMMODITY PRICES

2-CHLORO-4-AMINOTOLUENE
    Chem Mktg Rptr - W - NY

4-CHLORO-2-AMINOTOLUENE
    Chem Mktg Rptr - W - NY

6-CHLORO-2-AMINOTOLUENE
    Chem Mktg Rptr - W - NY

m-CHLOROANILINE
    Chem Mktg Rptr - W - NY
    J of Commerce - W - NY

o-CHLOROANILINE
    Chem Mktg Rptr - W - NY
    J of Commerce - W - NY

p-CHLOROANILINE
    Chem Mktg Rptr - W - NY
    J of Commerce - W - NY

o-CHLOROBENZALDEHYDE
    Chem Mktg Rptr - W

p-CHLOROBENZALDEHYDE
    Chem Mktg Rptr - W

o-CHLOROBENZOIC ACID
    Chem Mktg Rptr - W

p-CHLOROBENZOIC ACID
    Chem Mktg Rptr - W

CHLOROFORM
    Chem Mktg Rptr - W - NY
    J of Commerce - W - NY

2-CHLORO-4-NITROANILINE
    Chem Mktg Rptr - W - East

4-CHLORO-2-NITROANILINE
    Chem Mktg Rptr - W - East

4-CHLORO-2-NITROPHENOL
    Chem Mktg Rptr - W - NY

4 - CHLORO-2-NITROTOLUENE
    Chem Mktg Rptr - W - NY

6-CHLORO-2-NITROTOLUENE
    Chem Mktg Rptr - W - NY

o-CHLOROPHENOL
    Chem Mktg Rptr - W - NY

p-CHLOROPHENOL
    Chem Mktg Rptr - W - NY

CHLOROPHYL
    J of Commerce - W - NY

CHLOROPICRIN
    Chem Mktg Rptr - W - NY

CHLOROPRENE PEPTIZER CL-5
    Rubber World - SA

CHLOROSULFONIC ACID
    Chem Mktg Rptr - W - NY
    J of Commerce - W - NY

o-CHLOROTOLUENE
    Chem Mktg Rptr - W

CHLOROWAX: 40, 50, 70
    Rubber World - SA

CHOCOLATE BAR
    US Labor Stat Bur - Retail Food
    Prices - M - US and 23 cities

CHOCOLATE SYRUP
    US Labor Stat Bur - Retail Food
    Prices - M - US and 23 cities

CHOLINE BITARTRATE
    Chem Mktg Rptr - W - NY

CHOLINE CHLORIDE
    Chem Mktg Rptr - W - East

CHOLINE DIHYDROGEN CITRATE
    Chem Mktg Rptr - W - NY

CHROME
    Met Wk - W

CHROME GREEN
    Am Paint J - W
    Chem Mktg Rptr - W - US
    J of Commerce - W - NY

CHROME ORANGE
    Chem Mktg Rptr - W - US

COMMODITY PRICES

CHROME ORANGE: C P
    Am Paint J - W
    J of Commerce - W - NY

CHROME ORE
    Eng Min J - M - Atlantic ports

CHROME YELLOW
    Chem Mktg Rptr - W - US

CHROME YELLOW: C P
    Am Paint J - W
    J of Commerce - W - NY

CHROMIC ACID
    Chem Mktg Rptr - W
    Finishers' Mgt - M
    J of Commerce - W - NY

CHROMIUM
    Eng Min J - M
    Iron Age - W

CHROMIUM ACETATE
    Chem Mktg Rptr - W - NY

CHROMIUM FLUORIDE
    Chem Mktg Rptr - W

CHROMIUM OXIDE
    Am Paint J - W
    J of Commerce - W - NY

CHROMIUM OXIDE: HYDRATED
    Am Paint J - W
    Chem Mktg Rptr - W - NY

CIDER: HARD
    Alaska Bev Analyst - M - Alaska
    Bev Media - M - NY
    Ill Bev J - M - Ill
    Ky Bev J - M - Ky

CIGARETTES
    US Labor Stat Bur - Wholesale
        Prices & Price Indexes - M
    US Stat Rptg Ser - Agri Prices -
        Annual Summary - A - US
        and by states

CINNAMIC ALCOHOL
    Chem Mktg Rptr - W - NY

CINNAMIC ALDEHYDE
    Chem Mktg Rptr - W - NY

CINNAMON
    Chem Mktg Rptr - W - NY
    J of Commerce - W - NY

CINNAMON BARK OIL
    Chem Mktg Rptr - W - NY
    J of Commerce - W - NY

CINNAMON LEAF OIL
    Chem Mktg Rptr - W - NY
    J of Commerce - W - NY

CINNAMON OIL
    Chem Mktg Rptr - W - NY

CITRAL
    Chem Mktg Rptr - W - NY
    J of Commerce - W - NY

CITRIC ACID
    Chem Mktg Rptr - W - US
    J of Commerce - W - NY
    US Labor Stat Bur - Wholesale
        Prices & Price Indexes - M

CITRONELLAL
    Chem Mktg Rptr - W - NY

CITRONELLA OIL
    Chem Mktg Rptr - W - NY
    J of Commerce - W - NY
    US Labor Stat Bur - Wholesale
        Prices & Price Indexes - M

CITRONELLOL
    Chem Mktg Rptr - W - NY
    J of Commerce - W - NY

CITRONELLYL ACETATE
    Chem Mktg Rptr - W - NY

CITRONELLYL FORMATE
    Chem Mktg Rptr - W - NY

CITRUS PULP: DRIED
    Dairynews - S - Buffalo, Philadelphia, NY, Boston
    Feedstuffs - W - Atlanta, Boston, Buffalo, Los Angeles, Memphis

CIVET
    Chem Mktg Rptr - W - NY

CLAY
    Chem Mktg Rptr - W - Atlantic ports, Tennessee
        <u>See also</u> KAOLIN

COMMODITY PRICES

CLAY: CALCINED, WATER-WASHED, SURFACE MODIFIED
  Am Paint J - W - Ga

CLAY CHINA: ENGLISH, DOMESTICATED
  Am Paint J - W

CLEANER'S NAPHTHA
  Chem Mktg Rptr - W - NJ, NY, Houston

CLEVE'S ACID
  Chem Mktg Rptr - W - NY

CLOTHING
  See specific articles

CLOTHING: INFANTS', CHILDREN'S
  Earnshaw's - M - US

CLOTHS
  See specific kinds

CLOVE BUD OIL
  Chem Mktg Rptr - W - NY
  J of Commerce - W - NY

CLOVE LEAF OIL
  J of Commerce - W - NY

CLOVER
  Lancaster Farm - W

CLOVER SEED
  US Labor Stat Bur - Wholesale Prices & Price Indexes - M

CLOVER SEED: ALSIKE
  Seed World - A - US and by states
  US Stat Rptr Ser - Agri Prices - Annual Summary - A - US and by states

CLOVER SEED: CRIMSON
  Seed World - A - US and by states
  US Stat Rptg Ser - Agri Prices - Annual Summary - A - US and by states

CLOVER SEED: LADINO
  Seed World - A - US and by states
  US Stat Rptg Ser - Agri Prices - Annual Summary - A - US and by states

CLOVER SEED: RED
  Seed World - A - US and by states
  US Stat Rptg Ser - Agri Prices - M US and by states
  US Stat Rptg Ser - Agri Prices - Annual Summary - A - US and by states

CLOVER SEED: SWEET
  US Stat Rptg Ser - Agri Prices - Annual Summary - A - US and by states

CLOVER TOPS
  J of Commerce - W - NY

CLOVES
  Chem Mktg Rptr - W - NY
  J of Commerce - W - NY
  Natl Provision - W - Chicago

COAGULANT: CHA, WS
  Rubber World - SA

COAL
  UN Bul Stat - M - US, Can
  US Labor Stat Bur - Retail Prices
  Fuels & Elec - M

COAL: ANTHRACITE
  Comm Bul - W
  J of Commerce - W - NY
  US Labor Stat Bur - Wholesale Prices & Price Indexes - M

COAL: BITUMINOUS
  Comm Bul - W - Boston
  J of Commerce - W - Northern W Va
  US Labor Stat Bur - Wholesale Prices & Price Indexes - M

COALTAR
  Chem Mktg Rptr - W
  J of Commerce - W - NY

COALTAR CHEMICALS
  J of Commerce - W

COMMODITY PRICES

COALTAR PITCH
   Chem Mktg Rptr - W - NY
   US Labor Stat Bur - Wholesale
     Prices & Price Indexes - M

COATING RESINS
   J of Commerce - W - NY

COATS: MEN'S, SUBURBAN
   US Labor Stat Bur - Wholesale
     Prices & Price Indexes - M

COATS: MEN'S, WINTER
   US Stat Rptg Ser - Agri Prices -
     Annual Summary - A - US and by
     states

COATS: WOMEN'S, GIRLS'
   US Stat Rptg Ser - Agri Prices -
     Annual Summary - A - US and by
     states

COBALT
   Chem Mktg Rptr - W - NY, Chicago
   Eng Min J - M
   Iron Age - W
   Met Wk - W
   North Miner - W - NY, Chicago
   US Labor Stat Bur - Wholesale
     Prices & Price Indexes - M
   West Miner - M - US

COBALT ACETATE
   Chem Mktg Rptr - W - NY

COBALT BLUE
   Am Paint J - W

COBALT CARBONATE
   Chem Mktg Rptr - W - NY

COBALT CHLORIDE
   Chem Mktg Rptr - W - East

COBALT HYDRATE
   Chem Mktg Rptr - W - NY

COBALT NAPHTHENATE
   Chem Mktg Rptr - W - NY

COBALT NAPHTHENATE: LIQUID
   Am Paint J - W

COBALT NEODECANOATES
   Am Paint J - W

COBALT NITRATE
   Chem Mktg Rptr - W - NY

COBALT OCTOATE
   Am Paint J - W

COBALT OXIDE
   Chem Mktg Rptr - W - NY,
     Wilmington

COBALT PHOSPHATE
   Chem Mktg Rptr - W - NY

COBALT POWDER
   Am Met Mkt/Met News - D - US

COBALT RESINATE
   Chem Mktg Rptr - W - NY

COBALT SULFATE
   Chem Mktg Rptr - W - East

COBALT TALLATE
   Am Paint J - W
   Chem Mktg Rptr - W - NY

COBOSH ROOT
   J of Commerce - W - NY

COCAINE
   Chem Mktg Rptr - W

COCAINE HYDROCHLORIDE
   Chem Mktg Rptr - W

COCILLANA BARK
   Chem Mktg Rptr - W - NY
   J of Commerce - W - NY

COCKS AND FAUCETS: SCRAP
   Second Raw Materials - M - Pitts-
     burgh, NY, Buffalo, Detroit

COCKTAILS: PREPARED
   Alaska Bev Analyst - M - Alaska
   Ariz Bev J - M - Ariz
   Bev Media - M - NY
   Bev News - M
   Buck Bev J - M - Ohio

COMMODITY PRICES

   Ill Bev J – M – Ill
   Ky Bev J – M – Ky
   Md-Wash-Del Bev J – M – Md, DC, Del
   Mich Bev News – IR – Mich
   NJ Bev J – M – NJ
   Patterson's – M – Calif
   RI Bev J – M – RI
   Wis Bev J – M – Wis

COCOA
   Barron's – W – NY
   Fin Post – W
   J of Commerce – D – NY, West Coast
   NY Times – D – NY
   UN Bul Stat – M – US
   Wall Street J – D – NY

COCOA: BEANS
   US Labor Stat Bur – Wholesale Prices & Price Indexes – M

COCOA BUTTER
   Chem Mktg Rptr – W – NY
   J of Commerce – D – NY

COCOA: POWDERED SWEETENED
   US Labor Stat Bur – Wholesale Prices & Price Indexes – M

N-COCO MORPHOLINE: DISTILLED
   Rubber World – SA

COCONUT FATTY ACID
   Rubber World – SA

COCONUT OIL
   Am Paint J – W – NY
   Chem Mktg Rptr – W – Pacific, NY
   Chicago Hide – D – West Coast
   Fats & Oils – D – West Coast
   J of Commerce – D – Pacific, NY
   Natl Provision – W – Pacific Coast
   UN Bul Stat – M – US
   US Labor Stat Bur – Wholesale Prices & Price Indexes – M
   Wall Street J – D – Pacific Coast

COCONUT OIL: CRUDE
   US Econ Ser – Fats & Oils Sit – 5/yr – Pacific Coast, NY

COCONUT OIL: REFINED
   US Econ Ser – Fats & Oils Sit – 5/yr – NY

CODEINE HYDROCHLORIDE
   Chem Mktg Rptr – W – NY
   J of Commerce – W – NY

CODEINE PHOSPHATE
   Chem Mktg Rptr – W – NY
   J of Commerce – W – NY

CODEINE SULFATE
   Chem Mktg Rptr – W – NY
   J of Commerce – W – NY
   US Labor Stat Bur – Wholesale Prices & Price Indexes – M

CODLIVER OIL
   Chem Mktg Rptr – W – NY
   J of Commerce – W – NY
   US Econ Ser – Fats & Oils Sit – 5/yr – NY

COD OIL
   Chem Mktg Rptr – W – Gloucester Mass
   US Econ Ser – Fats & Oils Sit – 5/yr – NY

COFFEE
   Barron's – W – NY
   J of Commerce – D – NY
   NY Times – D – NY
   Tea & Coffee Trade J – M – US
   UN Bul Stat – M – US
   US Labor Stat Bur – Retail Food Prices – M – US and 23 cities
   US Stat Rptg Ser – Agri Prices – Annual Summary – A – US and by states
   Wall Street J – D – NY

COFFEE: GREEN
   Tea & Coffee Trade J – M – NY
   US Labor Stat Bur – Wholesale Prices & Price Indexes – M

COFFEE: ROASTED
   US Labor Stat Bur – Wholesale Prices & Price Indexes – M

COMMODITY PRICES

COGNAC: IMPORTED
  Alaska Bev Analyst - M - Alaska
  Ariz Bev J - M - Ariz
  Bev Media - M - NY
  Bev News - M
  Buck Bev J - M - Ohio
  Ill Bev J - M - Ill
  Ky Bev J - M - Ky
  Md-Wash-Del Bev J - M - Md, DC, Del
  Mich Bev News - IR - Mich
  Patterson's - M - Calif
  RI Bev J - M - RI
  Wis Bev J - M - Wis

COHEDUR: A, RL
  Rubber World - SA

COKE
  Comm Bul - W - Boston
  Foundry - M - Birmingham, Buffalo, Detroit, Milwaukee, Pittsburgh, St Louis, St Paul
  J of Commerce - W
  US Labor Stat Bur - Wholesale Prices & Price Indexes - M

COLA
  US Labor Stat Bur - Retail Food Prices - M - US and 23 cities
  US Stat Rptg Ser - Agri Prices - Annual Summary - A - US and by states

COLCHICINE
  Chem Mktg Rptr - W - NY

COLCHICUM ROOT
  J of Commerce - W - NY

COLCHICUM SEED
  J of Commerce - W - NY

COLITE CONCENTRATE
  Rubber World - SA

COLLODION
  Chem Mktg Rptr - W

COLLOIDAL SULFUR 95
  Rubber World - SA

COLOMBO ROOT
  J of Commerce - W - NY

COLTSFOOT LEAVES
  J of Commerce - W - NY

COLUMBITE ORE
  Eng Min J - M

COLUMBIUM
  Eng Min J - M
  Met Wk - W

COMBINES
  US Stat Rptg Ser - Agri Prices - Annual Summary - A - US and by states

COMFREY ROOT
  J of Commerce - W - NY

CONAC: NS, S
  Rubber World - SA

CONCRETE BLOCKS
  US Stat Rptg Ser - Agri Prices - Annual Summary - A - US and by states

CONCRETE INGREDIENTS
  US Labor Stat Bur - Wholesale Prices & Price Indexes - M

CONCRETE PRODUCTS
  US Labor Stat Bur - Wholesale Prices & Price Indexes - M

CONGO GUM: NOS, 1, 2, 3
  Am Paint J - W - NY

CONTAINERBOARD: CORRUGATED
  Paperbd Pckg - A
  US Labor Stat Bur - Wholesale Prices & Price Indexes - M

CONTAINERBOARD: CORRUGATED MEDIUM
  US Bur Dom Comm - Pulp Q - Q

CONTAINERBOARD: FIBRE DRUM
  Paperbd Pckg - A

COMMODITY PRICES

CONTAINERBOARD: FOLDING
   See BOXBOARD

CONTAINERBOARD: FOURDRINIER KRAFT LINERS
   Official Bd Mkts - W - US

CONTAINERBOARD: LINER
   US Bur Dom Comm - Pulp Q - Q
   US Labor Stat Bur - Wholesale Prices & Price Indexes - M

CONTAINERBOARD: SOLID FIBRE
   Paperbd Pckg - A

CONVECTORS: NONFERROUS
   US Labor Stat Bur - Wholesale Prices & Price Indexes - M

COOKIES
   US Labor Stat Bur - Retail Food Prices - M - US and 23 cities
   US Labor Stat Bur - Wholesale Prices & Price Indexes - M

COOKING OIL
   US Econ Ser - Fats & Oils Sit - 5/yr - US
   US Labor Stat Bur - Retail Food Prices - M - US and 23 cities

COPAIBA BALSAM
   Chem Mktg Rptr - W - NY
   J of Commerce - W - NY

COPAIBA OIL
   Chem Mktg Rptr - W - NY

COPAL CONGO GUM: NO. 3
   J of Commerce - W - NY

COPOLYMER
   Mod Pckg -Encyclo & Plan Guide - A - US

COPPER
   Am Met Mkt/Met News - D - US, Can
   Barron's - W
   Can Min J - M - NY
   Comm Bul - W
   Eng Min J - M

   Fin Post - W
   Fin Times Can - W - NY
   Indus Wk - W
   Iron Age - W
   J of Commerce - D
   Met Wk - W
   Min Rec - W
   UN Bul Stat - M - Can, US
   Wall Street J - D - NY
   West Miner - M - US, Can

COPPER: ANODE
   Finishers' Mgt - M

COPPER: CATHODE
   J of Commerce - D - NY

COPPER: CATHODE FULL PLATE
   Am Met Mkt/Met News - D - US

COPPER: ELECTROLYTIC
   Am Met Mkt/Met News - D
   NY Times - D - NY

COPPER: ELECTROLYTIC INGOT
   Foundry - M

COPPER: ELECTROLYTIC WIREBAR
   Chem Mktg Rptr - W - Valley
   Iron Age - W
   North Miner - W - US, Can
   Purch World - M

COPPER: FIRE REFINED
   Am Met Mkt/Met News - D

COPPER: LAKE
   Am Met Mkt/Met News - D
   Iron Age - W

COPPER: REFINED SCRAP
   Am Met Mkt/Met News - D - US

COPPER: SHEET
   Purch World - M

COPPER ACETATE
   Chem Mktg Rptr - W

COPPERAS
   Chem Mktg Rptr - W

COMMODITY PRICES

COPPER BROMIDE: CUPRIC
   Chem Mktg Rptr - W

COPPER CABLE
   US Labor Stat Bur - Wholesale
   Prices & Price Indexes - M

COPPER CARBONATE
   Chem Mktg Rptr - W
   J of Commerce - W - NY

COPPER CHLORIDE
   J of Commerce - W - NY

COPPER CHLORIDE: CUPRIC
   Chem Mktg Rptr - W

COPPER CYANIDE
   Chem Mktg Rptr - W - NY
   Finishers' Mgt - M
   J of Commerce - W - NY

COPPER FLUOBORATE
   J of Commerce - W - NY

COPPER FLUOBORATE: CUPRIC
   Chem Mktg Rptr - W

COPPER GLUCONATE
   Chem Mktg Rptr - W - NY

COPPER INHIBITOR 50
   Rubber World - SA

COPPER NAPHTHENATE
   Chem Mktg Rptr - W - NY

COPPER NICKEL TUBING
   Oil Dly - D - US

COPPER NITRATE: CUPRIC
   Chem Mktg Rptr - W

COPPER OLEATE
   Chem Mktg Rptr - W

COPPER OXIDE
   Am Paint J - W
   Chem Mktg Rptr - W

COPPER POWDER
   Am Met Mkt/Met News - D - US

   US Labor Stat Bur - Wholesale
   Prices & Price Indexes - M

COPPER-8-QUINOLINOLATE
   Chem Mktg Rptr - W - NY

COPPER RESINATE
   Chem Mktg Rptr - W - NY

COPPER SCRAP
   Fin Times Can - W
   Iron Age - W
   J of Commerce - W - NY
   Purch World - M - East
   Second Raw Materials - M -
     Montreal, Chicago, NY,
     Houston, Los Angeles, St Louis,
     Toronto
   US Labor Stat Bur - Wholesale
   Prices & Price Indexes - M
   Wall Street J - D - NY

COPPER SHAPES
   US Labor Stat Bur - Wholesale
   Prices & Price Indexes - M

COPPER SULFATE
   Chem Mktg Rptr - W
   Finishers' Mgt - M
   J of Commerce - W - NY
   US Labor Stat Bur - Wholesale
   Prices & Price Indexes - M

COPPER TUBING
   US Stat Rptg Ser - Agri Prices -
     Annual Summary - A - US and
     by states

COPPER WIRE
   Am Met Mkt/Met News - D - US
   Comm Bul - W
   US Labor Stat Bur - Wholesale
   Prices & Price Indexes - M

COPPER WIREBAR
   J of Commerce - D - NY
   US Labor Stat Bur - Wholesale
   Prices & Price Indexes - M

COPRA
   Calif Farm - S - Los Angeles
   US Econ Ser - Fats & Oils Sit -
     5/yr - Pacific coast

COMMODITY PRICES

COPRA MEAL
    Feedstuffs - W - Los Angeles
    US Econ Ser - Fats & Oils Sit -
       5/yr - Los Angeles

COPRA OIL
    J of Commerce - D

CORAX
    Rubber World - SA

CORDIALS
    Alaska Bev Analyst - M - Alaska
    Ariz Bev J - M - Ariz
    Bev Media - M - NY
    Bev News - M
    Buck Bev J - M - Ohio
    Ill Bev J - M - Ill
    Ky Bev J - M - Ky
    Md-Wash-Del Bev J - M - Md,
       DC, Del
    Mich Bev News - IR - Mich
    NJ Bev J - M - NJ
    Patterson's - M - Calif
    RI Bev J - M - RI
    Wis Bev J - M - Wis

CORDUROY: CARDED
    US Labor Stat Bur - Wholesale
       Prices & Price Indexes - M

CORIANDER
    Natl Provision - W - Chicago

CORIANDER OIL
    Chem Mktg Rptr - W - NY
    J of Commerce - W - NY

CORIANDER SEED
    J of Commerce - W - NY

CORN
    Agri Let - W - US
    Barron's - W - Chicago
    Comm Rev - W - US
    Dly Mkt Rec - D - Chicago
    Fin Post - W - Chicago
    Fin Times Can - W - Chicago
    Free Press Farm - W - Chicago
    J of Commerce - D - Chicago,
       NY, Toledo
    Lancaster Farm - W - Lancaster Pa
    NY Times - D - Chicago
    Poultry Times - W - Chicago
    US Stat Rptg Ser - Agri Prices -
       M - US and by states
    US Stat Rptg Ser - Agri Prices -
       Annual Summary - A - US and
       by states
    US Stat Rptg Ser Wis - Prices
       Received - M - Wis
    Wall Street J - D - Chicago

CORN: CANNED
    J of Commerce - W

CORN: CREAM STYLE, CANNED
    US Labor Stat Bur - Wholesale
       Prices & Price Indexes - M

CORN: FEED
    Feedstuffs - W

CORN: FROZEN
    J of Commerce - W

CORN: NO. 2
    US Labor Stat Bur - Wholesale
       Prices & Price Indexes - M -
       Chicago

CORN: NO. 2 GROUND
    Dairynews - S - Buffalo, Phila-
       delphia, NY, Boston

CORN: NO. 2 RED
    NY Times - D - Chicago

CORN: NO. 2 WHITE
    US Agri Mktg Ser - Grain Mkt
       News - W - Kansas City

CORN: NO. 2 YELLOW
    Calif Farm - S - Los Angeles,
       Stockton
    Mich Farm - S - Mich
    Mo Ruralist - S - US
    Neb Farm - S - Omaha
    NY Times - D - Chicago
    US Agri Mktg Ser - Feed Mkt
       News - W - Chicago, Kansas
       City, Omaha
    US Agri Mktg Ser - Grain Mkt
       News - W - Chicago, Kansas
       City, Minneapolis, Omaha,
       St. Paul, Toledo

COMMODITY PRICES

US Agri Mktg Ser - Livestock Mkt News - W - US

CORN: NO. 3 YELLOW
US Agri Mktg Ser - Grain Mkt News - W - Chicago
US Econ Ser - Feed Sit - Q - Chicago

CORN: SEED
US Stat Rptg Ser - Agri Prices - Annual Summary - A - US and by states

CORN: SWEET
US Agri Mktg Ser - Fruit & Veg Prices - A - NY, Chicago, Ala, Fla
US Labor Stat Bur - Wholesale Prices & Price Indexes - M
US Stat Rptg Ser - Agri Prices - M - US

CORN: WHOLE KERNEL, CANNED
US Labor Stat Bur - Wholesale Prices & Price Indexes - M

CORN EXTRACTIONS: CONDENSED FERMENTED
Feedstuffs - W - Chicago, Corpus Christi, Kansas

CORN FLAKES
US Econ Ser - Mkt & Trans Sit - Q - US
US Labor Stat Bur - Retail Food Prices - M - US and 23 cities
US Stat Rptg Ser - Agri Prices - Annual Summary - A - US and by states

CORN GLUTEN FEED
Dairynews - S - Buffalo, Philadelphia, NY, Boston
Feed Bul - D
Feedstuffs - W - Chicago, Kansas City, St Louis
US Labor Stat Bur - Wholesale Prices & Price Indexes - M

CORN GLUTEN MEAL
Feed Bul - D

Feedstuffs - W - Chicago, Kansas City, St Louis

CORN MEAL
US Stat Rptg Ser - Agri Prices - M - US and by states
US Stat Rptg Ser - Agri Prices - Annual Summary - A - US and by states

CORN OIL
Chem Mktg Rptr - W
Chicago Hide - D - Midwest
Fats & Oils - D - Midwest
Feed Bul - D
J of Commerce - D
Natl Provision - W
Wall Street J - D - Chicago

CORN OIL: CRUDE
US Econ Ser - Fats & Oils Sit - 5/yr - Midwest, NY
US Labor Stat Bur - Wholesale Prices & Price Indexes - M

CORN OIL: REFINED
US Econ Ser - Fats & Oils Sit - 5/yr - NY
US Labor Stat Bur - Wholesale Prices & Price Indexes - M

CORN OIL ACID
Chem Mktg Rptr - W - NY

CORN OIL MEAL
Feed Bul - D

CORN SILK
J of Commerce - W - NY

CORN SYRUP
Chem Mktg Rptr - W - NY
US Agri Stabil - Sugar Rpt - M - NY

CORN SYRUP: CONFECTIONERS'
US Labor Stat Bur - Wholesale Prices & Price Indexes - M

CORN TYPE FATTY ACID
Rubber World - SA

COMMODITY PRICES

CORROSIVE SUBLIMATE
   Chem Mktg Rptr - W - US
   J of Commerce - W - NY

CORTISONE ACETATE
   Chem Mktg Rptr - W - NY
   US Labor Stat Bur - Wholesale
     Prices & Price Indexes - M

CORUNDUM
   Eng Min J - M - US ports

COTTON
   Cotton Dig - W - NY
   Cotton-M Rev - M - US
   Dly News Rec - D
   J of Commerce - D - NY
   UN Bul Stat - M - US
   US Cons & Mktg Ser - Cotton
     Price Stat - M - US
   US Econ Ser - Cotton Sit - 5/yr -
     US
   US Econ Ser - Demand Sit - Q -
     US
   US Econ Ser - Stat Cotton - A -
     US
   US Mkt News Sect - Cotton Mkt
     Rev - W - US
   US Stat Rptg Ser - Agri Prices -
     M - US and by states
   Wall Street J - D - NY, Memphis

COTTON: AMERICAN MIDDLING WHITE
   US Econ Ser - Cotton Sit - 5/yr -
     US

COTTON: EXTRA-LONG STAPLE
   US Econ Ser - Stat Cotton -
     A - Tex, Ariz, Calif, Sea
     Island

COTTON: MIDDLING
   Calif Farm - S - Fresno
   Cotton Dig - W - US
   Cotton-M Rev - M - US
   Purch World - M - NY
   US Cons & Mktg Ser - Cotton
     Price Stat - M - US
   US Labor Stat Bur - Wholesale
     Prices & Price Indexes - M
   US Mkt News Sect - Cotton Mkt
     Rev - W - US

COTTON: RAW
   US Econ Ser - Stat Cotton - A -
     US

COTTON: UPLAND
   Cotton Dig - W - US

COTTON BROADWOVEN GOODS
   See COTTON GRAY GOODS

COTTON CLOTH
   See COTTON GRAY GOODS

COTTON FABRIC
   US Econ Ser - Cotton Sit - 5/yr -
     US

COTTON FIBER
   US Econ Ser - Stat Cotton -
     A - US

COTTON GINGHAM
   US Stat Rptg Ser - Agri Prices -
     Annual Summary - A - US and
     by states

COTTON GRAY GOODS
   UN Bul Stat - M - US

COTTON GRAY GOODS: BLENDED PRINT CLOTHS (POLYESTER/RAYON, POLYESTER/COTTON)
   Am Textile Rptr/Bul - M
   Dly News Rec - D

COTTON GRAY GOODS: BROADCLOTHS
   Am Textile Rptr/Bul - M
   Dly News Rec - D
   US Cons & Mktg Ser - Cotton
     Price Stat - M - US
   US Labor Stat Bur - Wholesale
     Prices & Price Indexes - M

COTTON GRAY GOODS: BROADCLOTHS, CARDED
   J of Commerce - D - Mills

COTTON GRAY GOODS: CHAFERS
   Dly News Rec - D

COMMODITY PRICES

COTTON GRAY GOODS: CORDUROY, CARDED
    US Labor Stat Bur - Wholesale Prices & Price Indexes - M

COTTON GRAY GOODS: DENIM
    US Labor Stat Bur - Wholesale Prices & Price Indexes - M

COTTON GRAY GOODS: DRAPERY CLOTH
    Dly News Rec - D
    US Labor Stat Bur - Wholesale Prices & Price Indexes - M

COTTON GRAY GOODS: DRAPERY SAILCLOTH
    Dly News Rec - D

COTTON GRAY GOODS: DRILLS
    Am Textile Rptr/Bul - M
    Dly News Rec - D
    Purch World - M - NY
    US Cons & Mktg Ser - Cotton Price Stat - M - US
    US Labor Stat Bur - Wholesale Prices & Price Indexes - M

COTTON GRAY GOODS: DUCKS
    Dly News Rec - D
    US Cons & Mktg Ser - Cotton Price Stat - M - US
    US Labor Stat Bur - Wholesale Prices & Price Indexes - M

COTTON GRAY GOODS: FLANNEL
    US Labor Stat Bur - Wholesale Prices & Price Indexes - M

COTTON GRAY GOODS: OSNABURGS
    Am Textile Rptr/Bul - M
    Dly News Rec - D
    J of Commerce - D - Mills
    US Cons & Mktg Ser - Cotton Price Stat - M - US
    US Labor Stat Bur - Wholesale Prices & Price Indexes - M

COTTON GRAY GOODS: PRINT CLOTHS
    Am Textile Rptr/Bul - M
    Barron's - W
    Dly News Rec - D
    J of Commerce - D - Mills
    NY Times - D - NY
    Purch World - M - NY
    US Cons & Mktg Ser - Cotton Price Stat - M - US
    US Labor Stat Bur - Wholesale Prices & Price Indexes - M
    Wall Street J - D - NY

COTTON GRAY GOODS: SATEENS
    US Cons & Mktg Ser - Cotton Price Stat - M - US

COTTON GRAY GOODS: SHEETINGS
    Am Textile Rptr/Bul - M
    Dly News Rec - D
    J of Commerce - D - Mills
    Purch World - M
    US Cons & Mktg Ser - Cotton Price Stat - M - US
    US Labor Stat Bur - Wholesale Prices & Price Indexes - M
    Wall Street J - D - NY

COTTON GRAY GOODS: TOBACCO CLOTHS
    Dly News Rec - D
    J of Commerce - D - Mills
    US Cons & Mktg Ser - Cotton Price Stat - M - US
    US Labor Stat Bur - Wholesale Prices & Price Indexes - M

COTTON GRAY GOODS: TWILLS
    Am Textile Rptr/Bul - M
    Dly News Rec - D
    J of Commerce - D - Mills
    US Cons & Mktg Ser - Cotton Price Stat - M - US
    US Labor Stat Bur - Wholesale Prices & Price Indexes - M

COTTON GRAY GOODS: UNFINISHED CLOTH
    US Econ Ser - Stat Cotton - A - US

COTTON GRAY GOODS: WIDE PRINT CLOTHS
    Am Textile Rptr/Bul - M
    Dly News Rec - D
    J of Commerce - D

COMMODITY PRICES

COTTON INDUSTRIAL FABRICS
  See COTTON GRAY GOODS

COTTON LINT
  US Stat Rptg Ser - Agri Prices - Annual Summary - A - US and by states

COTTON LINTERS
  US Econ Ser - Stat Cotton - A - US

COTTON LINTERS: GRADE AND STAPLE - FELTING 1-7
  US Mkt News Sect - Cotton Linters Rev - M - Atlanta, Memphis, Dallas, Los Angeles

COTTONROOT BARK
  J of Commerce - W - NY

COTTONSEED
  US Econ Ser - Fats & Oils Sit - 5/yr - US
  US Econ Ser - Stat Cotton - A - Ariz, Calif, Ga, La, NC, Okla, Tex
  US Labor Stat Bur - Wholesale Prices & Price Indexes - M
  US Stat Rptg Ser - Agri Prices - M - US and by states
  US Stat Rptg Ser - Agri Prices - Annual Summary - A - US and by states

COTTONSEED CAKE
  Dairyman - M - Los Angeles

COTTONSEED FATTY ACID
  Rubber World - SA

COTTONSEED MEAL
  Barron's - W - Memphis
  Calif Farm - S - Los Angeles, San Francisco
  Comm Rev - W - US
  Feed Bul - D - Mississippi Valley
  Feedstuffs - W - Atlanta, Boston, Chicago, Ft. Worth, Kansas City, Los Angeles, Memphis
  J of Commerce - D - Memphis
  US Agri Mktg Ser - Feed Mkt News - W

  US Agri Mktg Ser - Peanut Mkt News - W - US
  US Econ Ser - Fats & Oils Sit - 5/yr - Memphis, Chicago, Atlanta, Ft. Worth
  US Econ Ser - Feed Sit - Q - Memphis
  US Labor Stat Bur - Wholesale Prices & Price Indexes - M
  US Stat Rptg Ser - Agri Prices - M - US and by states
  US Stat Rptg Ser - Agri Prices - Annual Summary - A - US and by states
  Wall Street J - D - Memphis

COTTONSEED OIL
  Barron's - W - Mississippi Valley
  Chem Mktg Rptr - W
  Chicago Hide - D - Southeast, Valley, Tex
  Fats & Oils - D - Southeast, Valley, Texas
  Feed Bul - D - Mississippi Valley
  J of Commerce - D
  NY Times - D

COTTONSEED OIL: CRUDE
  Natl Provision - W - Valley, Tex
  US Econ Ser - Fats & Oils Sit - 5/yr - Valley, Texas, Southeast
  US Labor Stat Bur - Wholesale Prices & Price Indexes - M
  Wall Street J - D - Mississippi Valley

COTTONSEED OIL: REFINED
  US Econ Ser - Fats & Oils Sit - 5/yr - NY
  US Labor Stat Bur - Wholesale Prices & Price Indexes - M

COTTONSEED OIL ACIDS
  Chem Mktg Rptr - W - NY

COTTONSEED OILMEAL
  Chem Mktg Rptr - W - Memphis

COTTONWOOD
  Comm Bul - W

COMMODITY PRICES

COTTONWOOD: NO. 2 COMMON
   US Labor Stat Bur - Wholesale
     Prices & Price Indexes - M

COTTON WORK FABRICS
   See COTTON GRAY GOODS

COTTON YARNS
   Am Textile Rptr/Bul - M - NY
   J of Commerce - D - Mills
   UN Bul Stat - M - US
   US Econ Ser - Stat Cotton - A - US
   US Cons & Mktg Ser - Cotton Price Stat - M - US

COTTON YARNS: CARDED, KNITTING
   US Labor Stat Bur - Wholesale Prices & Price Indexes - M

COUMARIN
   Chem Mktg Rptr - W - NY
   J of Commerce - W - NY
   Rubber World - SA

COW BEEF
   J of Commerce - D - Chicago

COWS
   Dakota Farm - M
   Kan Farm - S - Kan
   US Stat Rptg Ser - Agri Prices - M - US and by states
   US Stat Rptg Ser - Agri Prices - Annual Summary - A - US and by states
   West Livestock J - W

COWS: ANGUS
   Aber-Angus J - M - US

COWS: CANNERS & CUTTERS
   Dairyman - M - Modesto, San Joaquin Valley, Phoenix
   Lancaster Farm - W - Lancaster Pa, Peoria, Omaha
   US Agri Mktg Ser - Livestock Mkt News - W - Ga, Ill, Omaha, Sioux City, St Paul
   US Econ Ser - Livestock Sit - BM - Omaha

COWS: COMMERCIAL
   J of Commerce - D - NY
   Lancaster Farm - W - Peoria, Omaha
   US Agri Mktg Ser - Livestock Mkt News - W - Ga, Ill, Omaha, Sioux City, St Paul
   US Econ Ser - Livestock Sit - BM - Omaha

COWS: CUTTER
   Calif Farm - S - Stockton
   Mo Rural - S - Kansas City

COWS: DAIRY
   Agri Let - W - US
   Lancaster Farm - W - New Holland Pa
   US Stat Rptg Ser - Agri Prices - Annual Summary - A - US and by states
   US Stat Rptg Ser Wis - Prices Received - M - Wis

COWS: HOLSTEIN
   Dairyman - M - Modesto, San Joaquin Valley, Phoenix

COWS: LIVE
   Livestock Breed J - M - US

COWS: LIVESTOCK
   Farm & Dairy - W - Ohio
   Man Co-op - W
   Natl Provision - W - Chicago, St Paul, Omaha, Kansas City, Louisville
   US Labor Stat Bur - Wholesale Prices & Price Indexes - M

COWS: RED POLL
   Red Poll News - SA - US

COWS: SHORTHORN
   Shorthorn World - 16/yr - US

COWS: SLAUGHTER
   Dairyman - M - Pacific Northwest
   Free Press Farm - W - Calgary, Edmonton, Saskatoon, Winnipeg, Toronto
   High Plains J - W - Kansas

COMMODITY PRICES

US Stat Rptg Ser Wis – Prices
  Received – M – Wis

COWS: UTILITY
  Calif Farm – S – Stockton
  Dairyman – M – Modesto, San
    Joaquin Valley
  Lancaster Farm – W – Lancaster Pa,
    Peoria, Omaha
  Mo Rural – S – Kansas City
  US Agri Mktg Ser – Livestock Mkt
    News – W – Ga, Ill, Omaha,
    Sioux City, St Paul
  US Econ Ser – Livestock Sit – BM –
    Omaha

C-P-B
  Rubber World – SA

CRABMEAT: CANNED
  J of Commerce – W

CRACKER MEAL
  US Labor Stat Bur – Retail Food
    Prices – M – US and 23 cities

CRACKERS
  US Stat Rptg Ser – Agri Prices –
    Annual Summary – A – US and
    by states
  US Labor Stat Bur – Wholesale
    Prices & Price Indexes – M

CRAMP BARK
  J of Commerce – W – NY

CRANBERRIES
  US Agri Mktg Ser – Fruit & Veg
    Prices – A – NY, Chicago

CRANBERRY SAUCE: CANNED
  US Labor Stat Bur – Wholesale
    Prices & Price Indexes – M

CREAM
  US Cons & Mktg Ser – Dairy Mkt
    Stat – A – Atlanta, New
    England, NY, Pa

CREAM: MILKFAT
  US Stat Rptg Ser – Agri Prices –
    M – Minn, Mo, Neb, Kan,
    Mont

US Stat Rptg Ser – Agri Prices –
  Annual Summary – A – US and
  by states

CREAM OF TARTAR
  Chem Mktg Rptr – W – NY
  J of Commerce – W – NY

CREOSOL
  J of Commerce – W – NY

CREOSOTE
  J of Commerce – W – NY

CREOSOTE COALTAR
  Chem Mktg Rptr – W

CREOSOTE OIL
  US Labor Stat Bur – Wholesale
    Prices & Price Indexes – M

CRESOL
  Chem Mktg Rptr – W – NY

m-CRESOL
  Chem Mktg Rptr – W – NY

m-p-CRESOL
  Chem Mktg Rptr – W – NY

o-CRESOL
  Chem Mktg Rptr – W – NY

p-CRESOL
  Chem Mktg Rptr – W – NY

CRESYLIC ACID
  Chem Mktg Rptr – W – NY
  J of Commerce – W – NY
  Purch World – M

CROTEN OIL
  J of Commerce – W – NY

CROTONIC ACID
  Chem Mktg Rptr – W – NY

CROWN CLAY
  Rubber World – SA

CRYOFLEX PLASTICIZER
  Rubber World – SA

COMMODITY PRICES

CRYOLITE
   Chem Mktg Rptr - W

CRYOVAC
   Mod Pckg-Encyclo & Plan Guide - A - US

CRYSTEX INSOLUBLE SULFUR
   Rubber World - SA

CRYSTEX OIL TREATED SULFUR
   Rubber World - SA

CUBEB BERRIES
   J of Commerce - W - NY

CUBEB OIL
   J of Commerce - W - NY

CUBE ROOT
   Chem Mktg Rptr - W
   J of Commerce - W - NY

CUCUMBERS
   US Agri Mktg Ser - Fruit & Veg Prices - A - Ariz, Chicago, Fla, NC, NY
   US Econ Ser - Veg Sit - Q - Chicago
   US Labor Stat Bur - Retail Food Prices - M - US and 23 cities
   US Stat Rptg Ser - Agri Prices - M - US

CULVERS ROOT
   J of Commerce - W - NY

CUMAR: MH, P-10, P-25, RH
   Rubber World - SA

CUMATE
   Rubber World - SA

CUMIN SEED
   Chem Mktg Rptr - W - NY
   J of Commerce - W - NY
   Natl Provision - W - Chicago

CUNIMENE: D-2681, - 2685-40, - 7286
   Rubber World - SA

CUNIPHEN: 2713, 7123
   Rubber World - SA

CUPRIC OXIDE
   J of Commerce - W - NY

CUPROUS OXIDE
   J of Commerce - W - NY

CUPS
   Rubber World - SA

CURTAINS: KITCHEN
   US Stat Rptg Ser - Agri Prices - Annual Summary - A - US and by states

CURTAINS: SHOWER, PLASTIC, VINYL
   US Labor Stat Bur - Wholesale Prices & Price Indexes - M

CYANAFLEX: 50, 100
   Rubber World - SA

CYANAMIDE
   Chem Mktg Rptr - W

CYANASET M
   Rubber World - SA

CYANOX: 8, LF, 53
   Rubber World - SA

CYANSOL: 18, 22
   Rubber World - SA

CYCLAMEN ALDEHYDE
   Chem Mktg Rptr - W - NY

1, 5, 9 - CYCLODODECATRIENE
   Chem Mktg Rptr - W - NY

CYCLOHEXANE
   Chem Mktg Rptr - W
   J of Commerce - W - NY
   Rubber World - SA
   US Labor Stat Bur - Wholesale Prices & Price Indexes - M

CYCLOHEXANOL
   Chem Mktg Rptr - W - NY

COMMODITY PRICES

Rubber World - SA

CYCLOHEXANONE
Chem Mktg Rptr - W - NY

CYCLOHEXYLAMINE
Chem Mktg Rptr - W

CYCLOLUBES
Rubber World - SA

1, 5 CYCLOOCTADIENE
Chem Mktg Rptr - W

CYCLOREXANE
Rubber World - SA

CYDAC
Rubber World - SA

CYPRESS LUMBER: C SELECT, NO. 2 COMMON
US Labor Stat Bur - Wholesale Prices & Price Indexes - M

CYPRESS (TIDEWATER RED)
Comm Bul - W - Boston

CYREZ: 711, 933, DCY, ZRT
Rubber World - SA

CYURAM: DS, MS, CYZATE M
Rubber World - SA

CYZONE DH
Rubber World - SA

D

2, 4 - D
US Labor Stat Bur - Wholesale Prices & Price Indexes - M
US Stat Rptg Ser - Agri Prices - Annual Summary - A - US and by states

2, 4 D ACID
Chem Mktg Rptr - W

DADI
Rubber World - SA

DAIRY FEED
US Econ Ser - Feed Sit - Q
US Stat Rptg Ser - Agri Prices - M - US and by states
US Stat Rptg Ser - Agri Prices - Annual Summary - A - US and by states

DAIRY FEED: MIXED
Neb Farm - S

DAIRY RATION: 16%
Dairynews - S - Buffalo, Philadelphia, NY, Boston

DAMIANA LEAVES
J of Commerce - W - NY

DAMMAR GUM
Am Paint J - W - NY

DAMMAR GUM: SINGAPORE
J of Commerce - W - NY

DANDELION ROOT
J of Commerce - W - NY

DARCO S-51
Rubber World - SA

DARVAN: 1, 2, 3, 6, 7
Rubber World - SA

DATES: DRIED
J of Commerce - W - NY

DAVENITE
Rubber World - SA

D-B-A
Rubber World - SA

2, 4 D BUTYL ESTER
Chem Mktg Rptr - W

DDD
Chem Mktg Rptr - W

2,4 D DIMETHYLAMINE SALT
Chem Mktg Rptr - W

COMMODITY PRICES

DDT
   Chem Mktg Rptr - W
   US Labor Stat Bur - Wholesale
     Prices & Price Indexes - M
   US Stat Rptg Ser - Agri Prices -
     Annual Summary - A - US and
     by states

tert-DECANOIC ACID
   Chem Mktg Rptr - W - NY

DECYL ALCOHOL
   Chem Mktg Rptr - W - NY

l-DECYL ALCOHOL
   Chem Mktg Rptr - W - East

DEER TONGUE LEAVES
   J of Commerce - W - NY

DEFLUORINATED PHOSPHATE
   Chem Mktg Rptr - W - US

DEGRAS
   Chem Mktg Rptr - W
   US Econ Ser - Fats & Oils Sit -
     5/yr - NY

DELAC: MOR, NS, S
   Rubber World - SA

DELVET 65
   Rubber World - SA

DENATURED ALCOHOL
   J of Commerce - W - NY
   US Labor Stat Bur - Wholesale
     Prices & Price Indexes - M

DENATURED ALCOHOL: ETHYL
   Chem Mktg Rptr - W - US

DENIM
   US Labor Stat Bur - Wholesale
     Prices & Price Indexes - M

DEODORANT: 64, 65, 66
   Rubber World - SA

DESI CAL
   Rubber World - SA

DESI CAL P
   Rubber World - SA

d-DESOXYEPHEDRINE HYDRO-
CHLORIDE
   Chem Mktg Rptr - W - NY

dl-DESOXYEPHEDRINE HYDRO-
CHLORIDE
   Chem Mktg Rptr - W - NY

DETERGENT ALKYLATE
   Chem Mktg Rptr - W - NY
   US Labor Stat Bur - Wholesale
     Prices & Price Indexes - M

DETERGENTS
   US Labor Stat Bur - Wholesale
     Prices & Price Indexes - M
   US Stat Rptg Ser - Agri Prices -
     Annual Summary - A - US and
     by states

DETONATING CORD
   US Labor Stat Bur - Wholesale
     Prices & Price Indexes - M

DEXTRIN
   J of Commerce - W - NY
   US Labor Stat Bur - Wholesale
     Prices & Price Indexes - M

DEXTRIN: CORN
   Chem Mktg Rptr - W

DEXTROSE
   Chem Mktg Rptr - W - NY
   US Agri Stabil - Sugar Rpt - M -
     NY

DFL NO. 3
   Rubber World - SA

DIACETONE ALCOHOL: ACETONE-
FREE
   Am Paint J - W
   Chem Mktg Rptr - W - NY

DIACETYL
   Chem Mktg Rptr - W - NY

DIAK: I-5
   Rubber World - SA

COMMODITY PRICES

DIAMMONIUM PHOSPHATE
  Chem Mktg Rptr - W - Fla

DIAMONDS
  J of Commerce - D - West Coast

2,4-DI-TERT-AMYLPHENOL
  Chem Mktg Rptr - W - NY

o-DIANISIDINE
  Chem Mktg Rptr - W - NY

DIARYLIDE YELLOW
  Chem Mktg Rptr - W - NY

DIATOMITE: WHITE
  Am Paint J - W

DIBENZO G-M-F
  Rubber World - SA

DIBENZO QDO
  Rubber World - SA

DIBENZYL SEBACATE
  Chem Mktg Rptr - W - East
  Rubber World - SA

p-DIBROMOBENZENE
  Chem Mktg Rptr - W - NY

DIBS
  Rubber World - SA

DIBUTYLAMINE
  Chem Mktg Rptr - W - NY

2,6 DI-TERT-BUTYL-P-CRESOL
  Chem Mktg Rptr - W - NY
  US Labor Stat Bur - Wholesale
    Prices & Price Indexes - M

DIBUTYL FUMARATE
  Chem Mktg Rptr - W - East

DIBUTYL MALEATE
  Chem Mktg Rptr - W - East

DIBUTYL PHTHALATE
  Am Paint J - W
  Chem Mktg Rptr - W - NY
  Rubber World - SA

DIBUTYL SEBACATE
  Chem Mktg Rptr - W - East
  Rubber World - SA

DICAPRYL PHTHALATE
  Chem Mktg Rptr - W - East
  Rubber World - SA

2-5 DICHLOROANILINE
  Chem Mktg Rptr - W

3,4 DICHLOROANILINE
  Chem Mktg Rptr - W

o-DICHLOROBENZENE
  Chem Mktg Rptr - W - NY
  J of Commerce - W - NY

p-DICHLOROBENZENE
  Chem Mktg Rptr - W - US
  J of Commerce - W - NY
  US Labor Stat Bur - Wholesale
    Prices & Price Indexes - M

DICHLOROBENZIDINE URETHANE GRADE
  Rubber World - SA

DICHLOROETHYL ETHER
  Rubber World - SA

DICHLOROISOCYANURIC ACID
  Chem Mktg Rptr - W - NY

2,6 DICHLORO-4-NITROANILINE
  Chem Mktg Rptr - W

DI-CUP: 40C, R, T
  Rubber World - SA

DICYCLOHEXYLAMINE
  Chem Mktg Rptr - W

DICYCLOHEXYL PHTHALATE
  Chem Mktg Rptr - W

DICYCLOPENTADIENE
  Chem Mktg Rptr - W

DI (N-DECYL) PHTHALATE
  Rubber World - SA

COMMODITY PRICES

DIELDRIN
  Chem Mktg Rptr - W- NY

DIESEL FUEL
  Comm Bul - W
  Oil Dly - D - Okla, North Tex
  Platt's - Okla, Ark, Buffalo, Los Angeles, San Francisco
  US Labor Stat Bur - Wholesale Prices & Price Indexes - M
  US Stat Rptg Ser - Agri Prices - Annual Summary - A - US and by states

DIESEL FUEL OIL
  Oil Dly - D - Tex, NM, Okla, Kan

DIETHANOLAMINE
  Chem Mktg Rptr - W - East
  Rubber World - SA

DIETHANOLAMINE LAURYL SULFATE
  Chem Mktg Rptr - W - NY

DIETHYLAMINE
  Am Paint J - W
  Chem Mktg Rptr - W - East
  Rubber World - SA

DIETHYLANILINE
  J of Commerce - W - NY

N, N-DIETHYLANILINE
  Chem Mktg Rptr - W - NY

DIETHYLBENZENE
  Chem Mktg Rptr - W - US

DIETHYL CARBONATE
  Chem Mktg Rptr - W - NY

DIETHYLENE GLYCOL
  Am Paint J - W
  Chem Mktg Rptr - W - East
  Rubber World - SA

DIETHYLENE GLYCOL DIETHYL ETHER
  Chem Mktg Rptr - W

DIETHYLENE GLYCOL MONOBUTYL ETHER
  Am Paint J - W
  Chem Mktg Rptr - W - East

DIETHYLENE GLYCOL MONOBUTYL ETHER ACETATE
  Chem Mktg Rptr - W - East

DIETHYLENE GLYCOL MONOETHYL ETHER
  Am Paint J - W
  Chem Mktg Rptr - W - East

DIETHYLENE GLYCOL MONOMETHYL ETHER
  Chem Mktg Rptr - W - NY

DIETHYLENE GLYCOL MONOMETHYL ETHER ACETATE
  Chem Mktg Rptr - W - East

DIETHYLENETRIAMINE
  Chem Mktg Rptr - W - East

DIETHYL ETHANOLAMINE
  Chem Mktg Rptr - W - NY

DI-2 ETHYLHEXYL AZETATE
  Rubber World - SA

DIETHYL OXALATE
  Chem Mktg Rptr - W

DIETHYL PHTHALATE
  Chem Mktg Rptr - W - NY
  Rubber World - SA

DIETHYSTILBESTROL
  Chem Mktg Rptr - W- NY

DIETHYL SULFATE
  Chem Mktg Rptr - W - East

DIETHYL THIOUREA
  Chem Mktg Rptr - W

DIETHYL TOLUAMIDE
  Chem Mktg Rptr - W

N, N-DIETHYL-M-TOLUIDINE
  Chem Mktg Rptr - NY

DIGITALIS LEAVES
  J of Commerce - W - NY

COMMODITY PRICES

DIGITOXIN
    Chem Mktg Rptr - W - NY

DIGLYCOL LAURATE
    Chem Mktg Rptr - W - NY
    Rubber World - SA

DIGLYCOL OLEATE
    Rubber World - SA

DIGLYCOL RICINOLEATE
    Rubber World - SA

DIGLYCOL STEARATE
    Chem Mktg Rptr - W - NY
    Rubber World - SA

DIHYDRAZINE SULFATE
    Chem Mktg Rptr - W - NY

DIHYDROSTREPTOMYCIN SULFATE
    Chem Mktg Rptr - W - NY

DIHYDROXYACETONE
    Chem Mktg Rptr - W

1,2-DIHYDROXY ANTHRAQUINONE
    Chem Mktg Rptr - W

2,2-DIHYDROXY-5-5-DICHLORO DIPHENYLMETHANE
    Chem Mktg Rptr - W - NY

DI-ISOBUTYLENE
    Chem Mktg Rptr - W - East

DI-ISOBUTYL KETONE
    Chem Mktg Rptr - W - US

DI-ISOBUTYL PHTHALATE
    Am Paint J - W
    Chem Mktg Rptr - W - East
    Rubber World - SA

DI-ISODECYL ADIPATE
    Rubber World - SA

DI-ISODECYL PHTHALATE
    Chem Mktg Rptr - W - NY
    Rubber World - SA
    US Labor Stat Bur - Wholesale Prices & Price Indexes - M

DI-ISONONYL PHTHALATE
    Chem Mktg Rptr - W - NY

DI-ISO-OCTYL AZELATE
    Chem Mktg Rptr - W - East

DI-ISO-OCTYL PHTHALATE
    Am Paint J - W
    Chem Mktg Rptr - W - NY

DI-ISOPROPANOLAMINE
    Chem Mktg Rptr - W - NY

DI-ISOPROPYLAMINE
    Chem Mktg Rptr - W - East

DILAURYL 3,3-THIODIPROPIONATE
    Chem Mktg Rptr - W - NY

DILL SEED
    J of Commerce - W - NY

DILLWEED OIL
    Chem Mktg Rptr - W - NY
    J of Commerce - W - NY

p-DIMETHOXYBENZENE
    Chem Mktg Rptr - W - NY

DIMETHYLACETAMIDE
    Chem Mktg Rptr - W

DIMETHYLAMINE
    Chem Mktg Rptr - W - NY

N,N-DIMETHYLANILINE
    Chem Mktg Rptr - W - NY

DIMETHYL ANTHRANILATE
    Chem Mktg Rptr - W - NY

DIMETHYL BENZYL CARBINYL ACETATE
    Chem Mktg Rptr - W - NY

DIMETHYL DICHLOROVINYL PHOSPHATE
    Chem Mktg Rptr - W - NY

DIMETHYL ETHANOLAMINES
    Chem Mktg Rptr - W - East

COMMODITY PRICES

DIMETHYL FORMAMIDE
Rubber World - SA

N,N-DIMETHYLFORMAMIDE
Chem Mktg Rptr - W

DIMETHYL PHTHALATE
Chem Mktg Rptr - W
J of Commerce - W - NY
Rubber World - SA

DIMETHYL SEBACATE
Chem Mktg Rptr - W - East
Rubber World - SA

DIMETHYL SULFATE
Chem Mktg Rptr - W

DIMETHYL SULFIDE
Chem Mktg Rptr - W

DIMETHYL SULFOXIDE
Chem Mktg Rptr - W

DINETTE SETS: TABLE & 4 CHAIRS
US Stat Rptg Ser - Agri Prices - Annual Summary - A - US and by states

DINING ROOM SETS: BUFFET, TABLE & 6 CHAIRS
US Stat Rptg Ser - Agri Prices - Annual Summary - A - US and by states

2,4-DINITROANILINE
Chem Mktg Rptr - W - NY

DINITROANILINE ORANGE
Am Paint J - W

DINITROANILINE ORANGE TONER
Chem Mktg Rptr - W - US

m-DINITROBENZENE
Chem Mktg Rptr - W - NY

2,4 DINITROCHLOROBENZENE
Chem Mktg Rptr - W - Charlotte NC

DINITROPHENOL
J of Commerce - W - NY

2,4-DINITROPHENOL
Chem Mktg Rptr - W - NY

2,4-DINITROTOLUENE
Chem Mktg Rptr - W

DIOCTYL ADIPATE
Chem Mktg Rptr - W - East
Rubber World - SA

DIOCTYL AZELATE
Chem Mktg Rptr - W - East

DIOCTYL PHTHALATE
Am Paint J - W
Chem Mktg Rptr - W - NY
J of Commerce - W - NY
Rubber World - SA
US Labor Stat Bur - Wholesale Prices & Price Indexes - M

DI (N-OCTYL) PHTHALATE
Rubber World - SA

DIOCTYL SEBACATE
Chem Mktg Rptr - W - East
Rubber World - SA

1,4 DIOXANE
Chem Mktg Rptr - W - US

DIPAC
Rubber World - SA

DIPENTAERYTHRITOL
Chem Mktg Rptr - W - East

DIPENTEINE 122
Rubber World - SA

DIPENTENE
Am Paint J - W - NY

DIPENTENE: STEAM
Chem Mktg Rptr - W - South, NY

DIPHENHYDRAMINE HYDROCHLORIDE
Chem Mktg Rptr - W - NY

DIPHENYL
Chem Mktg Rptr - W
J of Commerce - W - NY

COMMODITY PRICES

DIPHENYLAMINE
 Chem Mktg Rptr - W
 J of Commerce - W - NY

DIPHENYLGUANIDINE
 Chem Mktg Rptr - W - NY
 J of Commerce - W - NY

DIPHENYLHYDANTOIN-SODIUM
 Chem Mktg Rptr - W - NY

DIPHENYLMETHANE
 Chem Mktg Rptr - W - NY

DIPHENYL OXIDE
 Chem Mktg Rptr - W - NY

DIPHENYL PHTHALATE
 Chem Mktg Rptr - W

DIPROPYLENE GLYCOL
 Chem Mktg Rptr - W - NY

DIPROPYLENE GLYCOL DIBENZOATE
 Rubber World - SA

DIPROPYLENE GLYCOL MONOMETHYL ETHER
 Chem Mktg Rptr - W - NY

2,4 D ISO-OCTYL ESTER
 Chem Mktg Rptr - W

2,4 D ISOPROPYL ESTER
 Chem Mktg Rptr - W

DISPERSED BLACK NO. 25
 Rubber World - SA

DISPERSING OIL 10
 Rubber World - SA

DISPERSION 33
 Rubber World - SA

DISTILLATE: LIGHT, MIDDLE
 US Labor Stat Bur - Wholesale Prices & Price Indexes - M

DISTILLERS' DRIED FEEDS: GRAINS
 Feedstuffs - W - Atlanta, Boston, Buffalo, Chicago, Memphis

DISTILLERS' DRIED FEEDS: SOLUBLES
 Feedstuffs - W - Atlanta, Baltimore, Boston, Buffalo, Chicago

DISTILLERS' DRIED GRAINS
 Feedstuffs - W
 US Agri Mktg Ser - Feed Mkt News - W - Baltimore, Boston, Buffalo, Chicago, Cincinnati
 US Econ Ser - Feed Sit - Q - Cincinnati

DISTILLERS' DRIED GRAINS: CORN
 Dairynews - S - Buffalo, Philadelphia, NY, Boston

2,2-DITHIODIBENZOIC ACID
 Chem Mktg Rptr - W

DI-O-TOLYLGUANIDINE
 Chem Mktg Rptr - W - NY

DI-O-TOLYLTHIOUREA
 Chem Mktg Rptr - W - NY

DITRIDECYL PHTHALATE
 Chem Mktg Rptr - W - NY

DIVI-DIVI
 J of Commerce - W - NY

DIVINYLBENZENE
 Chem Mktg Rptr - W

DIXIE CLAY
 Rubber World - SA

l-DODECANOL
 Chem Mktg Rptr - W - NY

DODECENYL SUCCINIC ANHYDRIDE
 Chem Mktg Rptr - W - East

DODECYLBENZENE
 Chem Mktg Rptr - W - NY
 US Labor Stat Bur - Wholesale Prices & Price Indexes - M

DODECYLPHENOL
 Chem Mktg Rptr - W - US

DOGGRASS ROOT
 J of Commerce - W - NY

COMMODITY PRICES

DOGWOOD BARK
  J of Commerce - W - NY

DOORS: INTERIOR
  US Stat Rptg Ser - Agri Prices -
    Annual Summary - A - US and
    by states

DOTG
  Rubber World - SA

DOUGLAS FIR LUMBER
  J of Commerce - W - NY

DOUGLAS FIR LUMBER: DROP SIDINGS, DIMENSION BOARDS, TIMBERS
  US Labor Stat Bur - Wholesale
    Prices & Price Indexes - M

DOUGLAS FIR LUMBER: FRAMING LUMBER, FINISH
  Comm Bul - W

DOUGLAS FIR LUMBER: 2x4
  Purch World - M - Chicago

DOVER CLAY
  Rubber World - SA

DPESC
  Rubber World - SA

DPG
  Rubber World - SA

DPTT
  Rubber World - SA

DRAGON'S BLOOD
  J of Commerce - W - NY

DRAINAGE TILE
  US Stat Rptg Ser - Agri Prices -
    Annual Summary - A - US and
    by states

DRAKES
  Lancaster Farm - W - Fogelsville Pa

DRESIMATE: 214, 515, 2028, 2035, 945, 2030
  Rubber World - SA

DRESINOL: 40, 42, 155, 205, 210B, 215
  Rubber World - SA

DRESSES: GIRLS' KNIT
  US Labor Stat Bur - Wholesale
    Prices & Price Indexes - M

DRESSES: WOMEN'S, GIRLS'
  US Stat Rptg Ser - Agri Prices -
    Annual Summary - A - US and
    by states

DRIKALITE
  Rubber World - SA

DRILLS: ELECTRIC
  US Stat Rptg Ser - Agri Prices -
    Annual Summary - A - US and
    by states

DRI-LUBE
  Rubber World - SA

DRYERS, CLOTHES: ELECTRIC
  US Stat Rptg Ser - Agri Prices -
    Annual Summary - A - US and
    by states

DUCKS
  Lancaster Farm - W - Fogelsville Pa

DUCKS: READY TO COOK, FROZEN
  US Cons & Mktg Ser - Poultry Mkt
    Stat - A - NY, Boston, Los
    Angeles, Philadelphia

DUNGAREES: MEN'S
  US Labor Stat Bur - Wholesale
    Prices & Price Indexes - M

DURAL SCRAP
  Second Raw Materials - M - Montreal, Buffalo

DURAMITE
  Rubber World - SA

DURAX
  Rubber World - SA

DURENE
  Chem Mktg Rptr - W - NY

COMMODITY PRICES

DUREZ
  Rubber World - SA

DUROTEX 7665
  Rubber World - SA

DURUM
  West Producer - W - Saskatchewan

DYES
  US Labor Stat Bur - Wholesale Prices & Price Indexes - M

DYES, COALTAR: CLOTH DYEING
  Chem Mktg Rptr - W

DYES, COALTAR: FOOD, DRUGS & COSMETICS
  Chem Mktg Rptr - W

DYES, COALTAR: OIL SOLUBLE
  Chem Mktg Rptr - W

E

EARTH, DIATOMACEOUS
  Rubber World - SA

EASTERN SPRUCE: FRAMING LUMBER STRAPPING
  Comm Bul - W

EASTERN SPRUCE BOARDS
  Comm Bul - W - Boston

EASTERN WHITE PINE BOARDS
  Comm Bul - W

EASTERN WHITE PINE BOARDS: NO. 3
  US Labor Stat Bur - Wholesale Prices & Price Indexes - M

EAST INDIA GUM: BATER BOLD
  Am Paint J - W - NY
  J of Commerce - W - NY

EAST INDIA GUM: PALE NUBS, PALE CHIPS, BLACK BOLD SCRAPED, BLACK NUBS & CHIPS, BLACK UNSCRAPED, BATER NUBS & CHIPS
  Am Paint J - W - NY

EASTMAN 910 ADHESIVE
  Rubber World - SA

ECHIPACEA ROOT
  J of Commerce - W - NY

EGGNOG
  Ill Bev J - M - Ill
  Ky Bev J - M - Ky
  Md-Wash-Del Bev J - M - Md, DC, Del
  Patterson's - M - Calif

EGGPLANT
  US Agri Mktg Ser - Fruit & Veg Prices - A - NY, Chicago, Fla, Ariz

EGGS
  Agri Let - W - US
  Barron's - W - Chicago
  Calif Farm - S - San Francisco, Los Angeles, Fresno, Modesto
  Dly Mkt Rec - D - Chicago
  Fin Post - W
  Free Press Farm - W - Chicago
  J of Commerce - D - NY, Chicago, Pacific
  Lancaster Farm - W - US
  Man Co-op - W - Winnipeg
  Mich Farm - S - Detroit
  Mo Ruralist - S - Mo
  Neb Farm - S
  NY Times - D - Chicago, NY
  Pa Farm - S
  Poultry & Egg Mktg - BW - Chicago
  Poultry Times - W - Chicago, NY
  Poultry Trib - M - US
  US Agri Mktg Ser - Egg Mktg Guide - SA - NY
  US Cons & Mktg Ser - Poultry Mkt Stat - A - US
  US Econ Ser - Demand Sit - Q - US
  US Econ Ser - Mkt & Trans Sit - Q - US

COMMODITY PRICES

US Econ Ser - Poultry & Egg Sit -
  5/yr - US, Ga, Iowa
US Labor Stat Bur - Retail Food
  Prices - M - US and 23 cities
US Labor Stat Bur - Wholesale
  Prices & Price Indexes - M
US Stat Rptg Ser - Agri Prices - M
  - US and by states
US Stat Rptg Ser - Agri Prices -
  Annual Summary - A - US and
  by states
US Stat Rptg Ser Wis - Prices
  Received - M - Wis
Wall Street J - D - Chicago

EGGS: FROZEN
US Cons & Mktg Ser - Poultry Mkt
  Stat - A - Chicago, NY,
  Philadelphia, San Francisco

EGGS: FROZEN, DRIED
J of Commerce - W
US Labor Stat Bur - Wholesale
  Prices & Price Indexes - M

ELA
Rubber World - SA

ELASTOMAG
Rubber World - SA

ELDER FLOWERS
J of Commerce - W - NY

ELECTRIC CABLE: INDOOR
US Stat Rptg Ser - Agri Prices -
  Annual Summary - A - US and
  by states

ELECTRICITY
US Labor Stat Bur - Retail Prices
  Fuels & Elec - M

ELECTRIC POWER
US Labor Stat Bur - Wholesale
  Prices & Price Indexes - M

ELECTROTYPE: SCRAP
Second Raw Materials - M -
  Buffalo, Detroit

ELEMI GUM
Am Paint J - W - NY

J of Commerce - W - NY

ELM BARK
J of Commerce - W - NY

EL-SIXTY
Rubber World - SA

EMULVIN: S, W
Rubber World - SA

ENAMEL (PAINT)
US Labor Stat Bur - Wholesale
  Prices & Price Indexes - M

ENDIVE - CHICORY
US Agri Mktg Ser - Fruit & Veg
  Prices - A - NY

ENDOR
Rubber World - SA

ENDOX: 1IT, 2IT, 22
Rubber World - SA

ENDRIN
Chem Mktg Rptr - W - NY

ENGELMANN SPRUCE BOARDS
Comm Bul - W - US

ENGRAVERS' PLATES
Comm Bul - W

EPDM CATALYZER EC-10
Rubber World - SA

EPDM PEPTIZER EP-3, EP-4
Rubber World - SA

EPHEDRA HERB
J of Commerce - W - NY

EPHEDRINE
Chem Mktg Rptr - W - NY

EPHEDRINE HYDROCHLORIDE
Chem Mktg Rptr - W
J of Commerce - W - NY

EPHEDRINE SULFATE
Chem Mktg Rptr - W
J of Commerce - W - NY

COMMODITY PRICES

EPICHLOROHYDRIN
  Chem Mktg Rptr - W - NY

EPINEPHRINE BASE
  Chem Mktg Rptr - W - NY

EPOLENE: E-10, E-11, E-12, N-10, N-11
  Rubber World - SA

EPOXY RESINS
  Am Paint J - W

EPSOM SALTS
  Chem Mktg Rptr - W - US
  J of Commerce - W - NY
  US Labor Stat Bur - Wholesale
    Prices & Price Indexes - M

EPTAC 1
  Rubber World - SA

ERGOCALCIFEROL
  Chem Mktg Rptr - W

ERGOT
  Chem Mktg Rptr - W - NY
  J of Commerce - W - NY

ERIGERON OIL
  J of Commerce - W - NY

ERYTHORBIC ACID
  Chem Mktg Rptr - W - NY
  J of Commerce - W - NY

ESCAROLE
  US Agri Mktg Ser - Fruit & Veg
    Prices - A - NY, Fla

ESERINE SALICYLATE
  Chem Mktg Rptr - W - NY

E SPECIAL WHITE FACTICE
  Rubber World - SA

ESTER GUM
  Am Paint J - W

ESTER GUM: GUM-ROSIN TYPE, WOOD-ROSIN TYPE
  Chem Mktg Rptr - W

ESTER GUM 8L
  Rubber World - SA

ESTYNOX 408
  Rubber World - SA

ETHAZATE
  Rubber World - SA

ETHAZATE 50-D
  Rubber World - SA

ETHOMEEN 18/60
  Rubber World - SA

ETHYLAC
  Rubber World - SA

ETHYL ACETATE
  Am Paint J - W
  Chem Mktg Rptr - W - NY
  J of Commerce - W - NY
  US Labor Stat Bur - Wholesale
    Prices & Price Indexes - M

ETHYL ACETOACETATE
  Chem Mktg Rptr - W - NY

ETHYL ACRYLATE
  Chem Mktg Rptr - W - NY

ETHYL ALCOHOL
  Chem Mktg Rptr - W - East
  J of Commerce - W - NY

ETHYL ALCOHOL: SPECIAL NO. 1, SPECIAL NO. 2B
  Am Paint J - W

ETHYL AMINO ETHANOLS
  Am Paint J - W

ETHYL AMYL KETONE
  Am Paint J - W
  Chem Mktg Rptr - W - NY

n-ETHYLANILINE
  Chem Mktg Rptr - W - NY

ETHYL ANTIOXIDANT: 330, 702, 703, 736
  Rubber World - SA

COMMODITY PRICES

ETHYLBENZENE
Chem Mktg Rptr - W - US

ETHYL BENZOATE
Chem Mktg Rptr - W - NY

ETHYL BROMIDE
Chem Mktg Rptr - W - East
J of Commerce - W - NY

2-ETHYL BUTYL ALCOHOL
Chem Mktg Rptr - W

ETHYL BUTYL KETONE
Chem Mktg Rptr - W

ETHYL BUTYRATE
Chem Mktg Rptr - W - NY

ETHYL CARBAMATE
Chem Mktg Rptr - W

ETHYL CELLULOSE
Am Paint J - W
Chem Mktg Rptr - W - East
J of Commerce - W - NY

ETHYL CHLORIDE
Chem Mktg Rptr - W - NY

ETHYL CINNAMATE
Chem Mktg Rptr - W - NY

ETHYLENE
Chem Mktg Rptr - W - NY
J of Commerce - W - NY

ETHYLENE DIBROMIDE
Chem Mktg Rptr - W - NY

ETHYLENE DICHLORIDE
Am Paint J - W
Chem Mktg Rptr - W - US
Rubber World - SA

ETHYLENE GLYCOL
Am Paint J - W
Chem Mktg Rptr - W - East
J of Commerce - W - NY
Rubber World - SA
US Labor Stat Bur - Wholesale
  Prices & Price Indexes - M

ETHYLENE GLYCOL MONOBUTYL ETHER
Am Paint J - W
Chem Mktg Rptr - W - East

ETHYLENE GLYCOL MONOBUTYL ETHER ACETATE
Chem Mktg Rptr - W - East

ETHYLENE GLYCOL MONOETHYL ETHER
Am Paint J - W
Chem Mktg Rptr - W - East

ETHYLENE GLYCOL MONOETHYL ETHER ACETATE
Am Paint J - W
Chem Mktg Rptr - W - East

ETHYLENE GLYCOL MONOMETHYL ETHER
Chem Mktg Rptr - W - East

ETHYLENE GLYCOL MONOMETHYL ETHER ACETATE
Chem Mktg Rptr - W - East

ETHYLENE GLYCOL MONOSTEARATE
Chem Mktg Rptr - W - NY

ETHYLENE LACTATE
Rubber World - SA

ETHYLENE OXIDE
Chem Mktg Rptr - W

ETHYL ETHANOLAMINES
Chem Mktg Rptr - W - East

ETHYL ETHER
Am Paint J - W
Chem Mktg Rptr - W - NY
US Labor Stat Bur - Wholesale
  Prices & Price Indexes - M

ETHYL HEXANOATE
Chem Mktg Rptr - W - NY

2-ETHYLHEXOIC ACID
Chem Mktg Rptr - W - US

COMMODITY PRICES

2-ETHYLHEXYL ACRYLATE
Chem Mktg Rptr - W - East

2-ETHYLHEXYL ALCOHOL
Chem Mktg Rptr - W - NY

ETHYL IODIDE
Chem Mktg Rptr - W - NY

ETHYL LINALOOL
Chem Mktg Rptr - W - NY

ETHYL LINALYL ACETATE
Chem Mktg Rptr - W - NY

ETHYL METHACRYLATE
Chem Mktg Rptr - W - NY

ETHYL MORPHINE HYDROCHLORIDE
Chem Mktg Rptr - W - NY

n-ETHYL MORPHOLINE
Chem Mktg Rptr - W - NY

n-ETHYL-a-NAPHTHYLAMINE
Chem Mktg Rptr - W

ETHYL PARATHION
Chem Mktg Rptr - W - US

ETHYL SELENAC
Rubber World - SA

ETHYL SILICATE
Chem Mktg Rptr - W

ETHYL THIRAM
Rubber World - SA

N-ETHYL-M-TOLUIDINE
Chem Mktg Rptr - W - NY

N-ETHYL-O-TOLUIDINE
Chem Mktg Rptr - W - NY

ETHYL TUADS
Rubber World - SA

ETHYL TUEX
Rubber World - SA

ETHYL VANILLIN
Chem Mktg Rptr - W - NY

J of Commerce - W - NY

ETHYL ZIMATE
Rubber World - SA

ETHYL ZIMATE SLURRY
Rubber World - SA

ETHYL ZIRAM: 0671, 0677
Rubber World - SA

EUCALYPTOL
Chem Mktg Rptr - W - NY
J of Commerce - W - NY

EUCALYPTUS LEAVES
J of Commerce - W - NY

EUCALYPTUS OIL
Chem Mktg Rptr - W - NY
J of Commerce - W - NY

EUGENOL
Chem Mktg Rptr - W - NY
J of Commerce - W - NY

EUPHORBIA HERB
J of Commerce - W - NY

EWES
US Agri Mktg Ser - Livestock Mkt News - W - San Angelo, Omaha, Kansas City, Portland

EWES: SHORN
Natl Provision - W - Chicago, Kansas City, St Paul

EWES: SLAUGHTER
Lancaster Farm - W - Lancaster Pa

EXPANDEX THT
Rubber World - SA

EXTRUD-O-LUBE
Rubber World - SA

COMMODITY PRICES

F

FABRICS
See also Specific kinds of textile goods

FABRICS, INDUSTRIAL: SATEENS, BROKEN TWILLS, DRILLS, SHEETINGS, OSNABURGS, ARMY DUCK, ENAMELING, CHAFER FABRIC, 8 OZ DUCKS, KNITTED GOODS
J of Commerce - W - NY

FABRIFIL
Rubber World - SA

FANS
US Stat Rptg Ser - Agri Prices - Annual Summary - A - US and by states

FATTY ACIDS
J of Commerce - D
Rubber World - SA

FAUCETS: SINK, CHROME PLATED
US Stat Rptg Ser - Agri Prices - Annual Summary - A - US and by states

FEATHER MEAL
Chicago Hide - D - Kan, Minn, Iowa, Midsouth, Southeast
Fats & Oils - D - Kan, Minn, Iowa, Midsouth, Southeast
Feed Bul - D - Kan, Minn, Iowa, Delmarva, Mid-South
US Agri Mktg Ser - Feed Mkt News - W - Jackson Miss

FEATHER MEAL: HYDROLYZED
Feedstuffs - W - Atlanta, Boston, Ft Worth, Kansas City, Los Angeles, Memphis, Minneapolis

FEED: BULK MIXED
Dairyman - M - Los Angeles, Phoenix, San Joaquin

FEED GRAINS
US Econ Ser - Demand Sit - Q - US

FEEDING FATS, STABILIZED
Feed Bul - D - Northwest, Midwest, Mid-South, Delmarva

FELDSPAR
Eng Min J - M - NC, Ga, Conn

FELDSPAR C-6
Rubber World - SA

FELEX (FELDSPATHIC)
Rubber World - SA

FENCE: FIELD AND STOCK, WOVEN WIRE
US Stat Rptg Ser - Agri Prices - Annual Summary - A - US and by states

FENNEL OIL
Chem Mktg Rptr - W - NY
J of Commerce - W - NY

FENNEL SEED
Chem Mktg Rptr - W - NY
J of Commerce - W - NY

FENUGREEK SEED
Chem Mktg Rptr - W - NY

FERRIC-AMMONIUM CITRATE
Chem Mktg Rptr - W - NY

FERRIC-AMMONIUM OXALATE
Chem Mktg Rptr - W - East

FERRIC CHLORIDE
Chem Mktg Rptr - W - NY

FERRIC OXALATE
Chem Mktg Rptr - W
J of Commerce - W - NY

FERRIC PHOSPHATES
Chem Mktg Rptr - W - NY

COMMODITY PRICES

FERRIC PYROPHOSPHATE
    Chem Mktg Rptr - W - NY

FERRIC RESINATE
    Chem Mktg Rptr - W - NY

FERRIC SULFATE
    Chem Mktg Rptr - W

FERROALLOYS
    US Labor Stat Bur - Wholesale
      Prices & Price Indexes - M

FERROCHROME
    Eng Min J - M
    Met Wk - W

FERROCHROMIUM
    US Labor Stat Bur - Wholesale
      Prices & Price Indexes - M

FERROCOLUMBIUM
    Eng Min J - M
    Met Wk - W

FERROMANGANESE
    Eng Min J - M
    Met Wk - W
    US Labor Stat Bur - Wholesale
      Prices & Price Indexes - M

FERROMOLYBDENUM
    Eng Min J - M
    Met Wk - W

FERRONICKEL
    Eng Min J - M

FEUROPHOSPHOROUS
    Met Wk - W

FERROSILICON
    Eng Min J - M
    Met Wk - W
    US Labor Stat Bur - Wholesale
      Prices & Price Indexes - M

FERROTITANIUM
    Eng Min J - M

FERROTUNGSTEN
    Eng Min J - M

    Met Wk - W

FERROUS FLUOBORATE
    Chem Mktg Rptr - W

FERROUS GLUCONATE
    Chem Mktg Rptr - W - East
    J of Commerce - W - NY

FERROUS NAPHTHENATE
    Chem Mktg Rptr - W - NY

FERROUS SULFATE
    Chem Mktg Rptr - W

FERROVANADIUM
    Eng Min J - M
    Met Wk - W

FERTILIZERS: MIXED
    US Stat Rptg Ser - Agri Prices -
      Annual Summary - A - US and
      by states

FESCUE SEED
    Seed World - A - US and by states
    US Stat Rptg Ser - Agri Prices -
      Annual Summary - A - US and
      by states

FIBERS: HARD
    J of Commerce - W

FIBRENE C-400
    Rubber World - SA

FIGS: DRIED
    J of Commerce - W - NY

FILBERTS: TURKISH
    J of Commerce - W - NY

FILE FLATS
    US Labor Stat Bur - Wholesale
      Prices & Price Indexes - M

FILFLOC
    Rubber World - SA

FINE CHEMICALS
    J of Commerce - **W**

COMMODITY PRICES

FIR: DROP SIDING
   US Stat Rptg Ser - Agri Prices -
     Annual Summary - A - US and
     by states

FIR: FLOORING
   Comm Bul - W
   US Stat Rptg Ser - Agri Prices -
     Annual Summary - A - US and
     by states

FIR: FRAMING LUMBER
   Comm Bul - W
   US Stat Rptg Ser - Agri Prices -
     Annual Summary - A - US and
     by states

FIR: GUTTER, STEPPING
   Comm Bul - W

FIR BALSAM
   Chem Mktg Rptr - W - Can, Ore

FIR OIL
   Chem Mktg Rptr - W - Can

FIR PLYWOOD
   Purch World - M

FISH
   See also Specific kinds

FISH BLOCKS: FROZEN
   US Labor Stat Bur - Wholesale
     Prices & Price Indexes - M

FISHLIVER OIL
   Chem Mktg Rptr - W - NY

FISH MEAL
   Calif Farm - S - Los Angeles,
     Stockton
   Chem Mktg Rptr - W - Atlantic
     & Gulf Ports
   Comm Rev - W - US
   Feed Bul - D - East Coast, West
     Coast, Gulf Coast
   Feedstuffs - W - Atlanta, Boston,
     Chicago, Ft Worth, Kansas City,
     Los Angeles
   NY Times - D
   US Econ Ser - Fats & Oils Sit -
     5/yr - NY, Los Angeles

   US Agri Mktg Ser - Feed Mkt
     News - W
   US Econ Ser - Feed Sit - Q
   US Labor Stat Bur - Wholesale
     Prices & Price Indexes - M

FISH OIL
   Chem Mktg Rptr - W - NY
   J of Commerce - D

FISH PORTIONS: FROZEN
   US Labor Stat Bur - Wholesale
     Prices & Price Indexes - M

FISHSCRAP
   Chem Mktg Rptr - W - Atlantic
     & Gulf Coasts

FISH SOLUBLES, CONDENSED
   Feedstuffs - W - Atlanta, Boston,
     Chicago, Kansas City, Los Angeles

FISH STICKS: FROZEN
   US Labor Stat Bur - Wholesale
     Prices & Price Indexes - M

FLANNEL
   US Labor Stat Bur - Wholesale
     Prices & Price Indexes - M

FLAX
   Dly Mkt Rec - D - Winnipeg
   Fin Post - W - Winnipeg
   Fin Times Can - W - Winnipeg
   Free Press Farm - W - Winnipeg
   West Producer - W - Winnipeg

FLAXSEED
   Am Paint J - W - Ft William,
     Rotterdam
   Barron's - W - Minneapolis
   Fats & Oils Sit - 5/yr - US
   J of Commerce - D - Winnipeg
   Wall Street J - D - Winnipeg,
     Minneapolis
   US Stat Rptg Ser - Agri Prices -
     M - US and by states
   US Stat Rptg Ser - Agri Prices -
     Annual Summary - A - US and
     by states
   US Labor Stat Bur - Wholesale
     Prices & Price Indexes - M

COMMODITY PRICES

FLAXSEED: NO. 1
   US Agri Mktg Ser - Grain Mkt
   News - W - Minneapolis
   US Econ Ser - Fats & Oils Sit -
   5/yr - Minneapolis

FLAXSEED OIL
   J of Commerce - D

FLECTOL: H, ODP
   Rubber World - SA

FLEXAMINE
   Rubber World - SA

FLEXICHEM CS
   Rubber World - SA

FLEXOL PLASTICIZERS
   Rubber World - SA

FLEXONE
   Rubber World - SA

FLEXO WAX: C, CLT
   Rubber World - SA

FLEXRICIN: 13, P-1, P-4, P-8, P-6
   Rubber World - SA

FLOUNDER FILLETS: FROZEN
   US Labor Stat Bur - Wholesale
   Prices & Price Indexes - M

FLOUR
   Comm Rev - W - US
   Dly Mkt Rec - D - Minneapolis
   UN Bul Stat - M - US, Can
   US Econ Ser - Wheat Sit - Q -
   Kansas City, Minneapolis
   US Labor Stat Bur - Retail Food
   Prices - M - US and 23 cities
   US Labor Stat Bur - Wholesale
   Prices & Price Indexes - M
   US Stat Rptg Ser - Agri Prices -
   Annual Summmary - A - US and
   by states

FLOUR: DURUM
   J of Commerce - W - NY

FLOUR: FANCY CAKE
   J of Commerce - W - NY

FLOUR: HARD WINTER
   Barron's - W - NY
   Wall Street J - D - NY

FLOUR: RYE
   J of Commerce - W - NY

FLOUR: SEMOLINA
   J of Commerce - W - NY

FLOUR: SPRING
   J of Commerce - W - NY
   NY Times - D - NY

FLOUR: WINTER
   J of Commerce - W - NY

FLOUR BASE MIXES & DOUGHS
   US Labor Stat Bur - Wholesale
   Prices & Price Indexes - M

FLUOBORIC ACID
   Chem Mktg Rptr - W

FLUOROCARBON FIBERS ("TEFLON")
   Mod Textiles Mag - M

FLUOROHALOCARBON
   Mod Pckg-Encyclo & Plan Guide -
   A - US

FLUORSPAR
   Eng Min J - M - Ill, Ky

FLUXOL
   Rubber World - SA

FOAMNIX
   Rubber World - SA

FOENGREEK SEED
   J of Commerce - W - NY

FOIL-ACETATE
   Mod Pckg-Encyclo & Plan Guide -
   A - US

FOLDING CARTONBOARD
   See BOXBOARD

COMMODITY PRICES

FOLDING CONTAINERBOARD
See BOXBOARD

FOLIC ACID
J of Commerce - W - NY

FOOTWEAR: CHILDREN'S & INFANTS'
US Labor Stat Bur - Wholesale Prices & Price Indexes - M

FOOTWEAR: MEN'S & BOYS'
US Stat Rptg Ser - Agri Prices - Annual Summary - A - US and by states
US Labor Stat Bur - Wholesale Prices & Price Indexes - M

FOOTWEAR: MEN'S OVERSHOES & RUBBER BOOTS
US Stat Rptg Ser - Agri Prices - Annual Summary - A - US and by states

FOOTWEAR: MEN'S, WORK
US Stat Rptg Ser - Agri Prices - Annual Summary - A - US and by states

FOOTWEAR: WOMEN'S & GIRLS'
US Stat Rptg Ser - Agri Prices - Annual Summary - A - US and by states

FOOTWEAR: WOMEN'S & MISSES'
US Labor Stat Bur - Wholesale Prices & Price Indexes - M

FOOTWEAR: WOMEN'S & MISSES', IMPORTED
US Labor Stat Bur - Wholesale Prices & Price Indexes - M

FORMALDEHYDE
Chem Mktg Rptr - W - NY
J of Commerce - W - NY
Purch World - M
Rubber World - SA
US Labor Stat Bur - Wholesale Prices & Price Indexes - M

FORMAMIDE
Chem Mktg Rptr - W - Belle, W Va

FORMIC ACID
Chem Mktg Rptr - W
J of Commerce - W - NY
Rubber World - SA

FORMOPON
Rubber World - SA

FORTEX: 1-5, 6-10, 11-20
Rubber World - SA

FOWL
See also BROILERS; CHICKEN; TURKEY

FOWL: LIVE
Man Co-op - W - Winnipeg

FRANKFURTERS
US Stat Rptg Ser - Agri Prices - Annual Summary - A - US and by states

FREEZERS: FOOD
US Stat Rptg Ser - Agri Prices - Annual Summary - A - US and by states

FRICTION TAPE
US Labor Stat Bur - Wholesale Prices & Price Indexes - M

FRINGE TREE
J of Commerce - W - NY

FRUCTOSE
Chem Mktg Rptr - W

FRUIT
See also specific fruits

FRUIT: DRIED
J of Commerce - W

FRUIT COCKTAIL: CANNED
J of Commerce - W
US Labor Stat Bur - Retail Food Prices - M - US and 23 cities
US Labor Stat Bur - Wholesale Prices & Price Indexes - M

COMMODITY PRICES

FRUIT DRINK: CARBONATED
   US Labor Stat Bur - Retail Food
      Prices - M - US and 23 cities

FRUIT JUICE: BLENDED, CANNED
   J of Commerce - W

FRUITS: FROZEN
   J of Commerce - W

FRUITS: MIXED
   J of Commerce - W

FRYERS
   Calif Farm - S - delivered Los
      Angeles from Southern States
   Poultry Times - W - Ga
   US Cons & Mktg Ser - Poultry Mkt
      Stat - A - East, Los Angeles,
      San Francisco, Seattle
   US Stat Rptg Ser - Agri Prices -
      Annual Summary - A - US and
      by states

FRYERS: ICED
   US Cons & Mktg Ser - Poultry Mkt
      Stat - A - Ga, Chicago,
      Denver, Los Angeles, NY,
      Philadelphia, St Louis

FRYERS: LIVE
   Lancaster Farm - W - Delmarva

F SALT
   Chem Mktg Rptr - W - NY

FUEL: BUNKER C
   Platt's - D - Atlantic and Gulf
      coast, Houston, Buffalo, Detroit,
      Los Angeles

FUEL: HEAVY
   Natl Petro News - M - Los
      Angeles, Gulf, Chicago

FUEL: HEAVY (PS 400)
   Purch World - M - Los Angeles

FUEL: NO. 2
   Natl Petro News - M - Los
      Angeles, Gulf, Chicago

FUEL: RESIDUAL
   Oil & Gas J - W
   US Labor Stat Bur - Wholesale
      Prices & Price Indexes - M

FUEL OIL
   J of Commerce - D
   US Labor Stat Bur - Retail Prices
      Fuels & Elec - M
   US Stat Rptg Ser - Agri Prices -
      Annual Summary - A - US and
      by states

FUEL OIL: BUNKER C
   Oil Dly - D - NY, Baltimore,
      Southeast, Gulf Coast

FUEL OIL: DISTILLATE
   Oil Dly - D - West Coast

FUEL OIL: KERO
   Oil Dly - D - Gulf Coast, Kan,
      Tex, NM

FUEL OIL: LIGHT, HEAVY
   Platt's - D - Los Angeles, San
      Francisco

FUEL OIL: RESIDUAL
   Oil Dly - D - West Coast, Kan,
      Minn

FUEL OIL NO. 1
   Comm Bul - W
   Oil Dly - D - Chicago, Philadelphia,
      Baltimore, Boston, Kan, Neb,
      Minn, Carolinas
   Platt's - D - Okla, Ark, Buffalo, Detroit

FUEL OIL NO. 2
   Barron's - W - Mid-continent
   Comm Bul - W - Boston
   NY Times - D - NY
   Oil Dly - D - Gulf Coast, Chicago,
      NY, Kan, Minn, Carolinas
   Platt's - D - Gulf Coast, Atlantic,
      St Louis, Chicago, Okla, Buffalo
   US Labor Stat Bur - Retail Prices
      Fuels & Elec - M
   Wall Street J - D - Mid-continent

COMMODITY PRICES

FUEL OIL NO. 4
    Comm Bul - W - Boston
    Oil Dly - D - NY, Philadelphia, Carolinas, Va
    Platt's - D - Atlantic and Gulf Coast

FUEL OIL NO. 5
    Oil Dly - D - Chicago, NY, Philadelphia, Va, Carolinas
    Platt's - D - Atlantic and Gulf Coast, St Louis, Chicago, Okla, Buffalo

FUEL OIL NO. 6
    Comm Bul - W - NY, Boston, Providence
    Oil Dly - D - Chicago, NY, Philadelphia, Okla, Carolinas
    Platt's - D - Atlantic and Gulf Coast, St Louis, Chicago, Okla, Buffalo
    Purch World - M - Gulf, NY

FUMARIC ACID
    Am Paint J - W
    Chem Mktg Rptr - W - US
    J of Commerce - W - NY

FURA-TONE NC-1008
    Rubber World - SA

FURFURAL
    Chem Mktg Rptr - W - Cedar Rapids Iowa

FURFURYL ALCOHOL
    Chem Mktg Rptr - W - Memphis, Omaha

FURNACE OIL
    Oil Dly - D - Chicago

FURNACES & ATTACHMENTS
    US Labor Stat Bur - Wholesale Prices & Price Indexes - M

FUSTIC EXTRACT
    J of Commerce - W - NY

G

G 2401
    Rubber World - SA

GALBANUM GUM
    J of Commerce - W - NY

GALLIC ACID
    Chem Mktg Rptr - W - NY
    J of Commerce - W - NY

GALLIUM
    Eng Min J - M
    Met Wk - W

GALLNUTS
    J of Commerce - W - NY

GAMACO
    Rubber World - SA

GAMACO-T
    Rubber World - SA

GAMAKAL
    Rubber World - SA

GAMBOGE GUM
    J of Commerce - W - NY

GAMMA ACID
    J of Commerce - W - NY

GARLIC OIL
    J of Commerce - W - NY

GAS
    US Labor Stat Bur - Retail Prices Fuels & Elec - M

GAS: LIQUIFIED PETROLEUM
    Purch World - M - Okla
    US Stat Rptg Ser - Agri Prices - Annual Summary - A - US and by states

COMMODITY PRICES

GAS: NATURAL
    US Labor Stat Bur - Wholesale
    Prices & Price Indexes - M

GAS: PROPANE
    US Labor Stat Bur - Wholesale
    Prices & Price Indexes - M

GAS BURNER
    US Labor Stat Bur - Wholesale
    Prices & Price Indexes - M

GASOLINE
    Barron's - W - Mid-continent
    Oil & Gas J - W
    US Labor Stat Bur - Wholesale
    Prices & Price Indexes - M

GASOLINE: 92 OCTANE
    Wall Street J - D - Mid-continent

GASOLINE: PREMIUM
    Oil Dly - D - Gulf Coast, NY,
    Baltimore, West Coast, Chicago,
    Ark, NM
    Platt's - D - NY, Gulf Coast,
    Chicago, Ark, Los Angeles,
    Seattle, Atlantic
    Super Ser Station - M - Birmingham,
    Chicago, Houston, Kansas City,
    NY, Stamford

GASOLINE: REGULAR
    Natl Petro News - M - Los
    Angeles, Gulf, Chicago
    Oil & Gas J - W
    Oil Dly - D - Gulf Coast, NY,
    Baltimore, West Coast, Chicago,
    Tex
    Platt's - D - NY, Gulf Coast,
    Atlantic, Chicago, Los Angeles,
    Seattle
    Purch World - M - Los Angeles,
    Chicago
    Super Ser Station - M - Birmingham,
    Chicago, Houston, NY, Seattle,
    Stamford
    US Stat Rptg Ser - Agri Prices -
    Annual Summary - A - US and
    by states

GAS TANKS
    NY Times - D - NY

GELATIN
    Chem Mktg Rptr - W - NY

GELATIN: EDIBLE
    US Labor Stat Bur - Wholesale
    Prices & Price Indexes - M

GELATIN & GLUE STOCKS
    Natl Provision - W - Chicago,
    Midwest

GELATIN DESSERT
    US Stat Rptg Ser - Agri Prices -
    Annual Summary - A - US and
    by states

GELSEMIUM ROOT
    J of Commerce - W - NY

GENTIAN ROOT
    J of Commerce - W - NY

GERANIOL
    Chem Mktg Rptr - W - NY
    J of Commerce - W - NY

GERANIUM OIL
    Chem Mktg Rptr - W - NY
    J of Commerce - W - NY

GERANYL ACETATE
    Chem Mktg Rptr - W - NY
    J of Commerce - W - NY

GERANYL FORMATE
    Chem Mkt'g Rptr - W - NY

GERMANIUM
    Eng Min J - M
    Iron Age - W - Miami, Okla
    Met Wk - W

GHATTI GUM
    J of Commerce - W - NY

GIN
    Alaska Bev Analyst - M - Alaska
    Ariz Bev J - M - Ariz
    Bev Media - M - NY
    Bev News - M
    Buck Bev J - M - Ohio
    Ill Bev J - M - Ill
    Ky Bev J - M - Ky

COMMODITY PRICES

Md-Wash-Del Bev J - M - Md, DC, Del
Mich Bev News - IR - Mich
NJ Bev J - M - NJ
Patterson's - M
RI Bev J - M - RI
Wis Bev J - M - Wis

GIN: FLAVORED
Ariz Bev J - M - Ariz
Ill Bev J - M - Ill
Ky Bev J - M - Ky
Patterson's - Calif

GINGER
Chem Mktg Rptr - W - NY
J of Commerce - W - NY
Natl Provision - W - Chicago

GINGER OIL
Chem Mktg Rptr - W - NY
J of Commerce - W - NY

GINGER OLEORESIN
Chem Mktg Rptr - W - NY
J of Commerce - W - NY

GIN SPECIALTIES
Bev Media - M - NY
Md-Wash-Del Bev J - M - Md, DC, Del

GIRDLES: MISSES', JUNIORS'
US Labor Stat Bur - Wholesale Prices & Price Indexes - M

GIRDLES: WOMEN'S
US Labor Stat Bur - Wholesale Prices & Price Indexes - M
US Stat Rptg Ser - Agri Prices - Annual Summary - A - US and by states

GK SOFT CLAY
Rubber World - SA

GLASS: WINDOW
US Labor Stat Bur - Wholesale Prices & Price Indexes - M

GLASSINE
Mod Pckg-Encyclo & Plan Guide - A - US

GLOMAX: HE, LL, PVR
Rubber World - SA

GLOVES: MEN'S
US Labor Stat Bur - Wholesale Prices & Price Indexes - M

GLOVES: MEN'S, CANVAS
US Stat Rptg Ser - Agri Prices - Annual Summary - A - US and by states

GLOVES: WOMEN'S, MISSES', & JUNIORS'
US Labor Stat Bur - Wholesale Prices & Price Indexes - M

GLUCONIC ACID
Chem Mktg Rptr - W - NY
J of Commerce - W - NY

GLUE: BONE EXTRACTED
Chem Mktg Rptr - W - NY
J of Commerce - W - NY
Rubber World - SA

GLUE: HIDE
Chem Mktg Rptr - W - NY
J of Commerce - W - NY
US Labor Stat Bur - Wholesale Prices & Price Indexes - M

l-GLUTAMIC ACID
Chem Mktg Rptr - W - NY

GLUTEN FEED
Feedstuffs - W
US Agri Mktg Ser - Feed Mkt News - W
US Econ Ser - Feed Sit - Q - Chicago

GLUTEN MEAL
US Agri Mktg Ser - Feed Mkt News - W - Buffalo, Chicago, Kansas City, Memphis, Minneapolis

GLUTEN MEAL: 60%
Feedstuffs - W

GLYCERIN
Am Paint J - W

COMMODITY PRICES

Chem Mktg Rptr - W - NY
J of Commerce - W - NY
Purch World - M
Rubber World - SA
US Econ Ser - Fats & Oils Sit -
  5/yr - NY
US Labor Stat Bur - Wholesale
  Prices & Price Indexes - M

GLYCERIZED LIQUID LUBRICANT
CONCENTRATE
Rubber World - SA

GLYCEROPHOSPHATES
J of Commerce - W - NY

GLYCERYL GUALACOLATE
Chem Mktg Rptr - W - NY

GLYCOINITRILE AQUEOUS
Chem Mktg Rptr - W

GLYCOLIC ACID
Rubber World - SA

GLYCO WAX S932
Rubber World - SA

GLYOXAL
Chem Mktg Rptr - W - Taft La,
  Charleston W Va

GLYSO-LUBE
Rubber World - SA

G-M-F
Rubber World - SA

GOATSKINS
Am Shoe - W
US Labor Stat Bur - Wholesale
  Prices & Price Indexes - M

GOLD
Am Met Mkt/Met News - D - US
Eng Min J - M
Fin Times Can - W
Finishers' Mgt - M
Free Press Farm - W - Winnipeg
Iron Age - W
J of Commerce - D - Winnipeg
Met Wk - W

Min Rec - W - US
North Miner - W - London,
  Ottawa
Oil Dly - D - US
West Miner - M - US, Can

GOLD: REFINED
US Labor Stat Bur - Wholesale
  Prices & Price Indexes - M

GOLDENSEAL ROOT
J of Commerce - W - NY

GOOD-RITE: 3I4, 3300X2, VULTROL
Rubber World - SA

GRAIN SORGHUM
Calif Farm - S - Los Angeles,
  Stockton
Comm Rev - W - US
Feedstuffs - W
Neb Farm - S - Omaha
US Econ Ser - Feed Sit - Q -
  Kansas City
US Stat Rptg Ser - Agri Prices -
  M - US and by states
US Stat Rptg Ser - Agri Prices -
  Annual Summary - A - US and
  by states

GRAIN SORGHUM: NO. 2 YELLOW
US Agri Mktg Ser - Grain Mkt News
  - W - Kansas City, Los Angeles,
  Tex

GRAPEFRUIT
Calif Farm - S - Coachella
Fla Field Rpt - W - Fla
US Agri Mktg Ser - Fruit & Veg
  Prices - A - NY, Chicago, Tex
US Labor Stat Bur - Retail Food
  Prices - M - US and 23 cities
US Labor Stat Bur - Wholesale Prices
  & Price Indexes - M
US Stat Rptg Ser - Agri Prices - M -
  US, Fla, Tex, Ariz, Calif

GRAPEFRUIT JUICE
Alaska Bev Analyst - M - Alaska

GRAPEFRUIT JUICE: CANNED
J of Commerce - W
US Labor Stat Bur - Wholesale
  Prices & Price Indexes - M

COMMODITY PRICES

GRAPEFRUIT JUICE: FROZEN
   J of Commerce - W

GRAPEFRUIT OIL
   Chem Mktg Rptr - W
   J of Commerce - W - NY

GRAPEFRUIT SEGMENTS: CANNED
   J of Commerce - W

GRAPE JELLY
   US Labor Stat Bur - Wholesale Prices & Price Indexes - M

GRAPE JUICE
   Ky Bev J - M - Ky

GRAPE JUICE: CANNED
   US Labor Stat Bur - Wholesale Prices & Price Indexes - M

GRAPES
   Calif Farm - M - Kern Central San Joaquin Valley
   US Agri Mktg Ser - Fruit & Veg Prices - A - NY, Chicago, Calif, Mich
   US Labor Stat Bur - Retail Food Prices - M - US and 23 cities
   US Labor Stat Bur - Wholesale Prices & Price Indexes - M

GRAPHITE
   Chem Mktg Rptr - W - US
   Eng Min J - M

GRAPHITE: FLAKE
   Am Paint J - W

GRAVEL: FOR CONCRETE
   US Labor Stat Bur - Wholesale Prices & Price Indexes - M

GREASE
   Chem Mktg Rptr - W - NY
   Natl Provision - W - Chicago
   US Econ Ser - Fats & Oils Sit - 5/yr - NY, Chicago
   US Labor Stat Bur - Wholesale Prices & Price Indexes - M

GREASE: INEDIBLE
   Chicago Hide - D - Chicago
   Fats & Oils - D - Chicago

GREASE: YELLOW
   Feedstuffs - W - Atlanta, Boston, Chicago, Ft. Worth, Los Angeles
   J of Commerce - D - NY

GREASE GUNS
   US Stat Rptg Ser - Agri Prices - Annual Summary - A - US and by states

GREASE (MOTOR SUPPLIES)
   US Stat Rptg Ser - Agri Prices - Annual Summary - A - US and by states

GREASE OIL
   US Econ Ser - Fats & Oils Sit - 5/yr - Chicago

GRINDELIA ROBUSTA
   J of Commerce - W - NY

GRITS
   J of Commerce - W

GROUND: AMORPHOUS
   Am Paint J - W

GROUNDNUTS
   UN Bul Stat - M - US

G SALT
   Chem Mktg Rptr - W - NY
   J of Commerce - W - NY

GT-25
   Rubber World - SA

GUAIAC GUM
   J of Commerce - W - NY

GUAIACWOOD OIL
   Chem Mktg Rptr - W - NY
   J of Commerce - W - NY

GUARANA
   J of Commerce - W - NY

COMMODITY PRICES

GUAR GUM
    Chem Mktg Rptr – W.
    J of Commerce – W – NY

GUINEAS
    Lancaster Farm – W – Fogelsville

GUM: NO. 1 COMMON, NO. 2 COMMON
    US Labor Stat Bur – Wholesale Prices
        & Price Indexes – M

GUM ARABIC
    US Labor Stat Bur – Wholesale Prices
        & Price Indexes – M

GUM ROSIN
    Am Paint J – W – NY
    J of Commerce – D – NY
    US Labor Stat Bur – Wholesale Prices
        & Price Indexes – M

GUM (WOOD): RED, SAP
    Comm Bul – W

G-WHITE
    Rubber World – SA

GYPSUM PRODUCTS
    US Labor Stat Bur – Wholesale Prices
        & Price Indexes – M

GYPSUM BOARD
    US Stat Rptg Ser – Agri Prices –
        Annual Summary – A – US and
        by states

H

H ACID
    Chem Mktg Rptr – W – NY

HACKBERRY
    Comm Bul – W

HACKSAW BLADES
    US Labor Stat Bur – Wholesale Prices
        & Price Indexes – M

HADDOCK: FROZEN
    US Stat Rptg Ser – Agri Prices –
        Annual Summary – A – US and
        by states

HADDOCK: UNPROCESSED
    US Labor Stat Bur – Wholesale Prices
        & Price Indexes – M

HADDOCK FILLETS: FRESH
    US Labor Stat Bur – Wholesale Prices
        & Price Indexes – M

HADDOCK FILLETS: FROZEN
    US Labor Stat Bur – Retail Food
        Prices – M – US and 23 cities
    US Labor Stat Bur – Wholesale Prices
        & Price Indexes – M

HAKUENKA CC
    Rubber World – SA

HALIBUT: UNPROCESSED
    US Labor Stat Bur – Wholesale Prices
        & Price Indexes – M

HALLCO
    Rubber World – SA

HAM
    See PORK CUTS: SMOKED

HAMMERS
    US Stat Rptg Ser – Agri Prices –
        Annual Summary – A – US and
        by states

HANDBAGS
    Handbags – M – US
    US Stat Rptg Ser – Agri Prices –
        Annual Summary – A – US and
        by states

HANSA YELLOW
    Am Paint J – W

HARD HYDROCARBON
    Rubber World – SA

HARDWARD: BUILDERS'
    US Labor Stat Bur – Wholesale Prices
        & Price Indexes – M

COMMODITY PRICES

HARROWS: DISK
   US Stat Rptg Ser - Agri Prices - Annual Summary - A - US and by states

HARWICK CLAY
   Rubber World - SA

HATS: MEN'S FELT
   US Stat Rptg Ser - Agri Prices - Annual Summary - A - US and by states

HAWKEYE SOAP FLAKES & POWDER
   Rubber World - SA

HAY
   Dairyman - M - Antelope Valley, Imperial Valley, Sacramento Valley, Petaluma
   Natl Wool - M - US states (varies)
   US Econ Ser - Feed Sit - Q
   US Stat Rptg Ser - Agri Prices - M - US and by states
   US Stat Rptg Ser - Agri Prices - Annual Summary - A - US and by states

HAY: ALFALFA
   Calif Farm - S - Chino Valley, Los Angeles, Petaluma
   Ida Farm - S - central Washington state
   Ore Farm - S - central Washington state
   US Econ Ser - Feed Sit - Q
   US Labor Stat Bur - Wholesale Prices & Price Indexes - M
   US Stat Rptg Ser - Agri Prices - M - US and by states
   US Stat Rptg Ser - Agri Prices - Annual Summary - A - US and by states
   US Stat Rptg Ser Wis - Prices Received - M - Wis
   Utah Farm - S - central Washington state
   Wash Farm - S - central Washington state

HAY: CLOVER-TIMOTHY
   US Stat Rptg Ser - Agri Prices - Annual Summary - A - US and by states

HAY: GREEN ALFALFA
   Ida Farm - S - central Washington state
   Mont Farm - S - central Washington state
   Ore Farm - S - central Washington state
   Utah Farm - S - central Washington state
   Wash Farm - S - central Washington state

HAY: LESPEDEZA
   US Stat Rptg Ser - Agri Prices - Annual Summary - A - US and by states

HAY: MIXED
   Lancaster Farm - W - Lancaster Pa

HAY: PEANUTVINE
   US Stat Rptg Ser - Agri Prices - Annual Summary - A - US and by states

HAY: WILD
   US Stat Rptg Ser - Agri Prices - Annual Summary - A - US and by states

HC: 75 CLAY, 100 CLAY
   Rubber World - SA

HEATER OIL
   Oil Dly - D - Chicago

HEATERS: UNIT
   US Labor Stat Bur - Wholesale Prices & Price Indexes - M

HEATING BOILERS
   US Labor Stat Bur - Wholesale Prices & Price Indexes - M

COMMODITY PRICES

HEATING EQUIPMENT
 US Labor Stat Bur - Wholesale Prices & Price Indexes - M
 <u>See also</u> specific types

HEATING OIL
 Platt's - D - NY

HEATING OIL: NO. 2
 Fueloil & Oil - M - Baltimore, Boston, Chicago, Seattle
 Purch World - M - Chicago, NY

HEAVY CHEMICALS
 J of Commerce - W

1-D HEAVY OIL
 Rubber World - SA

HEELS: RUBBER
 US Labor Stat Bur - Wholesale Prices & Price Indexes - M

HEIFER BEEF
 Lancaster Farm - W - NY
 US Agri Mktg Ser - Livestock Mkt News - W - Chicago, Colorado, East Coast, Los Angeles, Midwest

HEIFER BEEF: CHOICE
 J of Commerce - D - Chicago
 US Econ Ser - Livestock Sit - BM - Chicago

HEIFERS
 Agri Let - W - US
 Dairyman - M - Modesto, Phoenix, San Joaquin Valley
 Dakota Farm - M
 Mo Rural - S - Kansas City
 US Stat Rptg Ser - Agri Prices - M - US and by states
 US Stat Rptg Ser - Agri Prices - Annual Summary - A - US and by states
 US Stat Rptg Ser Wis - Prices Received - M - Wis
 West Livestock J - W - US

HEIFERS: ANGUS
 Aber-Angus J - M - US

HEIFERS: FEEDER
 Dairyman - M - Pacific Northwest
 High Plains J - W - Kansas
 US Agri Mktg Ser - Livestock Mkt News - W - Amarillo, Kansas City, Omaha, Sioux City

HEIFERS: LIVE
 Livestock Breed J - M - US

HEIFERS: LIVESTOCK
 Farm & Dairy - W - Ohio
 Man Co-op - W
 Natl Provision - W - Chicago, Louisville, Kansas City, Omaha

HEIFERS: RED POLL
 Red Poll News - SA - US

HEIFERS: SHORTHORN
 Shorthorn world - 16/yr - US

HEIFERS: SLAUGHTER
 Dairyman - M - Pacific Northwest
 Free Press Farm - W - Edmonton, Saskatoon, Toronto, Winnipeg
 High Plains J - W - Kansas
 Lancaster Farm - W - Lancaster, Omaha, Peoria
 US Agri Mktg Ser - Livestock Mkt News - W - Ga, Ill, Omaha, St. Paul

HELIOTROPIN
 Chem Mktg Rptr - W - NY
 J of Commerce - W - NY

HELIOZONE
 Rubber World - SA

HEMATINE EXTRACT
 J of Commerce - W - NY

HEMLOCK: FINISH
 Comm Bul - W

HEMLOCK: GUTTER
 Comm Bul - W

HEMLOCK: 2 X 4
 Purch World - M - NY

COMMODITY PRICES

HEMLOCK-FIR COASTAL LUMBER: DIMENSION
   US Labor Stat Bur - Wholesale Prices & Price Indexes - M

HEMLOCK-FIR INLAND LUMBER: DIMENSION
   US Labor Stat Bur - Wholesale Prices & Price Indexes - M

HEMLOCK-FIR LUMBER: FRAMING LUMBER
   Comm Bul - W

HEMLOCK OIL
   J of Commerce - W - NY

HEMP
   See MANILA HEMP

HENBANE LEAVES
   J of Commerce - W - NY

HENNA POWDER
   J of Commerce - W - NY

HENS
   See CHICKENS, BROILERS, TURKEYS

HENS: HEAVY
   Lancaster Farm - W - Fogelsville
   Mo Rural - S - Mo
   Poultry Times - W - Ga
   US Cons & Mktg Ser - Poultry Mkt Stat - A - Mo, New England, NC, Seattle

HENS: LIGHT
   Calif Farm - S - central Calif
   Mo Rural - S - Mo
   Poultry Times - W - Ga
   US Cons & Mktg Ser - Poultry Mkt Stat - A - Calif, Iowa, NJ, NC Ohio, Seattle

HENS: LIVE
   Lancaster Farm - W - eastern Pa and NJ

HENS: READY-TO-COOK, FRESH AND FROZEN
   US Cons & Mktg Ser - Poultry Mkt Stat - A - Boston, Los Angeles, Seattle

HENS: READY-TO-COOK, ICED
   US Cons & Mktg Ser - Poultry Mkt Stat - A - Chicago, NY, Ohio, Philadelphia

HEPTACHLOR
   Chem Mktg Rptr - W - NY

HEPTANE
   Chem Mktg Rptr - W - NJ, NY, Houston
   Rubber World - SA

tert-HEPTANOIC ACID
   Chem Mktg Rptr - W - NY

HEPTEEN BASE
   Rubber World - SA

HERCOLYN
   Rubber World - SA

HERIBANE LEAVES
   Chem Mktg Rptr - W - NY

HEXACHLOROPHENE
   Chem Mktg Rptr - W

1 - HEXADECANOL
   Chem Mktg Rptr - W - East

HEXALIN
   Rubber World - SA

HEXAMETHYLENETETRAMINE
   Chem Mktg Rptr - W - Ford NJ, NY
   J of Commerce - W - NY
   US Labor Stat Bur - Wholesale Prices & Price Indexes - M

HEXANE
   Chem Mktg Rptr - W - NJ, NY, Houston
   Rubber World - SA

COMMODITY PRICES

I - HEXANOL
  Chem Mktg Rptr - W - East

HEXYL ALCOHOL
  Chem Mktg Rptr - W - NY

HEXYLENE GLYCOL
  Chem Mktg Rptr - W - US

p-HEXYL METHACRYLATE
  Chem Mktg Rptr - W

HEXYLRESORCINOL
  Chem Mktg Rptr - W - NY

HIDES
  Fin Post - W

HIDES: BIG PACKER SLUNKS
  Leather & Shoes - W

HIDES: BULLS
  J of Commerce - D - NY

HIDES: BUTT BRANDED
  NY Times - D - NY
  US Agri Mktg Ser - Livestock Mkt
    News - W - Chicago, Denver,
    East, Mo River points

HIDES: CALF-KIP
  Am Shoe - W

HIDES: COLORADO BRANDED,
BRANDED COW
  US Agri Mktg Ser - Livestock Mkt
    News - W - Chicago, Denver,
    East, Mo River points

HIDES: COUNTRY
  Am Shoe - W
  Leather & Shoes - W

HIDES: COW
  J of Commerce - D - NY
  Purch World - M - Chicago

HIDES: HEAVY NATIVE
  US Agri Mktg Ser - Livestock Mkt
    News - W - Chicago, Denver,
    East, Mo River points

HIDES: LAMB SHEARLINGS
  Natl Provision - W - Chicago

HIDES: LIGHT COW
  Barron's - W - Chicago
  NY Times - D - NY

HIDES: LIGHT NATIVE
  US Agri Mktg Ser - Livestock Mkt
    News - W - Chicago, Denver,
    East, Mo River points
  Purch World - M - Chicago

HIDES: LIGHT NATIVE COWS
  Wall Street J - D - Chicago

HIDES: OUTSIDE
  Chicago Hide - D
  Hide & Leather Bul - D

HIDES: PACKER
  Chicago Hide - D
  Hide & Leather Bul - D
  Leather & Shoes - W
  Natl Provision - W - Chicago
  Purch World - M - Chicago
  US Labor Stat Bur - Wholesale Prices
    & Price Indexes - M

HIDES: PACKER, CHICAGO
  Am Shoe - W

HIDES: SMALL PACKER
  Am Shoe - W
  Leather & Shoes - W
  Natl Provision - W - Chicago

HIDES: STEER
  J of Commerce - D - NY

HINGES: BUTT
  US Labor Stat Bur - Wholesale Prices
    & Price Indexes - M

HI-SIL: 233, EP
  Rubber World - SA

HODAG ANTIFOAM: FD-82, PV-48, TBX
  Rubber World - SA

COMMODITY PRICES

HOES
    US Labor Stat Bur - Wholesale Prices & Price Indexes - M
    US Stat Rptg Ser - Agri Prices - Annual Summary - A - US and by states

HOG FEED
    Neb Farm - S
    US Econ Ser - Feed Sit - Q
    US Stat Rptg Ser - Agri Prices - M - US and by states
    US Stat Rptg Ser - Agri Prices - Annual Summary - A - US and by states

HOG FEED SUPPLEMENT
    US Stat Rptg Ser - Agri Prices - Annual Summary - A - US and by states

HOGS
    Agri Let - W - US
    Barron's - W - Omaha
    Dly Mkt Rec - D - Chicago
    Fin Post - W
    Free Press Farm - W - Edmonton, Saskatoon, Toronto, Winnipeg
    Hog Farm Mgt - M - US
    J of Commerce - D
    Mich Farm - S
    Neb Farm - S - Omaha
    Pa Farm - S
    US Econ Ser - Demand Sit - Q - US
    US Stat Rptg Ser - Agri Prices - M - US and by states
    US Stat Rptg Ser - Agri Prices - Annual Summary - A - US and by states
    US Stat Rptg Ser Wis - Prices Received - M - Wis
    Wall Street J - D - Chicago, Omaha

HOGS: BARROWS & GILTS
    Calif Farm - S - Stockton
    Ida Farm - S - Spokane
    Lancaster Farm - W - Lancaster, Peoria, St. Louis
    Mo Rural - S - Kansas City
    Mont Farm - S - Spokane
    Natl Livestock - M - US
    Natl Provision - W - Chicago
    Ore Farm - S - Spokane
    Utah Farm - S - Omaha
    Wash Farm - S - Spokane
    US Agri Mktg Ser - Broiler Mktg Guide - Q - US
    US Agri Mktg Ser - Livestock Mkt News - W - Baltimore, Kansas City, Omaha, Peoria
    US Agri Mktg Ser - Turkey Mktg Guide - A - US
    US Econ Ser - Livestock Sit - BM
    US Labor Stat Bur - Wholesale Prices & Price Indexes - M

HOGS: LIVE
    Free Press Farm - W - Chicago
    J of Commerce - D - Chicago
    NY Times - D

HOGS: LIVESTOCK
    Farm & Dairy - W - Ohio
    Man Co-op - W
    Natl Provision - W - Chicago, Kansas City, Louisville, Omaha

HOMATROPINE HYDROBROMIDE
    Chem Mktg Rptr - W - NY

HOMATROPINE METHYLBROMIDE
    Chem Mktg Rptr - W - NY

HOMINY FEED
    Dairynews - S - Boston, Buffalo, NY, Philadelphia
    Feedstuffs - W - Atlanta, Boston, Chicago, Los Angeles
    US Agri Mktg Ser - Feed Mkt News - W
    US Econ Ser - Feed Sit - Q - Chicago

HONEY: EXTRACTED, CREAMED, BULK COMB, SECTION COMB
    US Agri Mktg Ser - Honey Mkt News - M - US

HONEYDEWS
    US Agri Mktg Ser - Fruit & Veg Prices - A - Chicago, NY

HOPS
    J of Commerce - W

COMMODITY PRICES

HOREHOUND HERB
  Chem Mktg Rptr – W – NY
  J of Commerce – W – NY

HORSES
  Lancaster Farm – W – New Holland

HORSES: SLAUGHTER
  Free Press Farm – W – Winnipeg

HOSIERY: CHILDREN'S, ANKLETS
  US Labor Stat Bur – Wholesale Prices
    & Price Indexes – M

HOSIERY: MEN'S
  US Labor Stat Bur – Wholesale Prices
    & Price Indexes – M

HOSIERY: WOMEN'S, NYLON
  US Labor Stat Bur – Wholesale Prices
    & Price Indexes – M
  US Stat Rptg Ser – Agri Prices –
    Annual Summary – A – US and
    by states

HOUSE FURNISHINGS
  See specific items

HVA-2
  Rubber World – SA

HYDRANGEA ROOT
  J of Commerce – W – NY

HYDRAZINE HYDRATE
  Chem Mktg Rptr – W – NY

HYDRIOIC ACID
  Chem Mktg Rptr – W

HYDRITE: 10S, FLAT D, PXS, RS
  Rubber World – SA

HYDROABIETYL ALCOHOL
  Chem Mktg Rptr – W

HYDROBROMIC ACID
  Chem Mktg Rptr – W – NY

HYDROCHLORIC ACID
  Can Chem Processing – M – Can
  Chem Mktg Rptr – W – NY
  J of Commerce – W – NY
  Rubber World – SA
  US Labor Stat Bur – Wholesale Prices
    & Price Indexes – M

HYDROCORTISONE
  J of Commerce – W – NY

HYDROCORTISONE ACETATE
  Chem Mktg Rptr – W – NY

HYDROCORTISONE ALCOHOL
  Chem Mktg Rptr – W – NY

HYDROFLUORIC ACID
  Can Chem Processing – M – Can
  Chem Mktg Rptr – W
  J of Commerce – W – NY
  US Labor Stat Bur – Wholesale Prices
    & Price Indexes – M

HYDROFLUOSILICIC ACID
  Chem Mktg Rptr – W

HYDROFOL GLYCERIDE: 50-51, 200
  Rubber World – SA

HYDROGEN BROMIDE
  Chem Mktg Rptr – W

HYDROGEN CHLORIDE
  Chem Mktg Rptr – W

HYDROGEN CYANIDE
  Chem Mktg Rptr – W

HYDROGEN FLOURIDE
  Chem Mktr Rptr – W – NY

HYDROGEN PEROXIDE
  Chem Mktg Rptr – W – NY
  US Labor Stat Bur – Wholesale Prices
    & Price Indexes – M

HYDROGEN SULFIDE
  Chem Mktg Rptr – W

COMMODITY PRICES

HYDROQUINONE
   Chem Mktg Rptr - W - NY
   J of Commerce - W - NY

HYDROQUINONE-DI(B-HYDROXY-
ETHYL)ETHER
   Rubber World - SA

HYDROXYACETIC ACID
   Chem Mktg Rptr - W - Belle W Va,
     Chicago, Philadelphia

HYDROXYCITRONELLAL
   Chem Mktr Rptr - W - NY
   J of Commerce - W - NY

HYDROXYCITRONELLAL DIMETHYL
ACETAL
   Chem Mktg Rptr - W - NY

HYDROXYETHYLCELLULOSE
   Am Paint J - W
   Chem Mktg Rptr - W - East

8-HYDROXYQUINOLINE BASE
   Chem Mktg Rptr - W - NY

8-HYDROXYQUINOLINE SULFATE
   Chem Mktg Rptr - W - NY

HYDROXYSTEARIC ACID
   Rubber World - SA

HYDRO-ZINC
   Rubber World - SA

HYONIC PE-90
   Rubber World - SA

HYPALON PEPTIZER: H-20, H-40
   Rubber World - SA

HYPERNIC EXTRACT
   J of Commerce - W - NY

HYPOPHOSPHOROUS ACID
   Chem Mktg Rptr - W

HYSTL B SERIES RESINS: -1000,
-2000, -3000
   Rubber World - SA

HYTROL O CYCLOHEXANONE
   Rubber World - SA

I

ICE CREAM
   US Econ Ser - Dairy Sit - 5/yr - US
   US Labor Stat Bur - Retail Food
     Prices - M - US and 23 cities
   US Labor Stat Bur - Wholesale Prices
     & Price Indexes - M
   US Stat Rptr Ser - Agri Prices -
     Annual Summary - A - US and
     by states

ICHTHAMMOL
   Chem Mktg Rptr - W - NY

IDAHO WHITE PINE BOARDS
   Comm Bull - W

IMINODIACETIC ACID
   Chem Mktg Rptr - W

IML: -1, -2
   Rubber World - SA

INDANTHRONE BLUE LAKE
   Am Paint J - W

INDIAN RED: AMERICAN PURE,
AMERICAN COMMERCIAL
   Am Paint J - W

INDIUM
   Finishers' Mgt - M
   Iron Age - W
   Met Wk - W

INDIUM INGOT
   Eng Min J - M

INDOLE
   Chem Mktg Rptr - W - NY

INDOPOL: H-100, H-300, L-10
   Rubber World - SA

COMMODITY PRICES

INDUSOIL L-5
   Rubber World - SA

INDUSTRIAL
   Rubber World - SA

INDUSTRIAL YARNS
   Mod Textiles Mag - M

INGOT MOLDS
   US Labor Stat Bur - Wholesale Prices
   & Price Indexes - M

INOSITOL
   Chem Mktg Rptr - W

INSECTICIDES
   US Stat Rptg Ser - Agri Prices -
   Annual Summary - A - US and
   by states

INSULATING SHEATHING
   US Stat Rptg Ser - Agri Prices -
   Annual Summary - A - US and
   by states

IODINE
   Chem Mktg Rptr - W
   J of Commerce - W - NY

IODOCHLOROHYDROXYQUINOLINE
   Chem Mktg Rptr - W - NY

IODOFORM
   Chem Mktg Rptr - W

IONOMER
   Mod Pckg-Encyclo & Plan Guide -
   A - US

IONOMER RESIN
   J of Commerce - W - NY

a-IONONE
   Chem Mktg Rptr - W - NY

b-IONONE
   Chem Mktg Rptr - W - NY

a-b IONONES
   J of Commerce - W - NY

IPECAC ROOT
   Chem Mktg Rptr - W - NY
   J of Commerce - W - NY

IRGANOX: 565, 1093, 1010, 1076
   Rubber World - SA

IRGASAN DP 300
   Rubber World - SA

IRGASTAB 2002
   Rubber World - SA

IRIDIUM
   Am Met Mkt/Met News - D - US
   Eng Min J - M
   Iron Age - W
   Met Wk - W

IRISH MOSS
   Chem Mktg Rptr - W - NY
   J of Commerce - W - NY

IRON
   Chem Mktg Rptr - W - NY
   Comm Bul - W
   NY Times - D - Midwest

IRON: PIG
   UN Bul Stat - M - US
   US Labor Stat Bur - Wholesale Prices
   & Price Indexes - M

IRON: PIG (BASIC)
   Purch World - M - Valley

IRON: PIG (BESSEMER)
   Purch World - M - Pittsburgh

IRON: PIG (FOUNDRY)
   Foundry - M - Birmingham, Buffalo,
   Chicago, Pittsburgh

IRON: PIG (MALLEABLE)
   Foundry - M - Birmingham, Buffalo,
   Chicago, Pittsburgh

IRON BLUE
   Chem Mktg Rptr - W - US
   J of Commerce - W - NY

COMMODITY PRICES

IRON BLUE: PRUSSIAN
   Am Paint J - W

IRON NAPHTHENATE
   Am Paint J - W

IRON OCTOATE
   Am Paint J - W

IRON ORE
   Eng Min J - M
   Met Wk - W
   North Miner - W
   UN Bul Stat - M - US
   US Labor Stat Bur - Wholesale Prices & Price Indexes - M

IRON OXIDE
   J of Commerce - W - NY
   US Labor Stat Bur - Wholesale Prices & Price Indexes - M

IRON OXIDE: BLACK
   Chem Mktg Rptr - W - NY
   J of Commerce - W - NY

IRON OXIDE: BLACK, SYNTHETIC
   Am Paint J - W

IRON OXIDE: BROWN
   Chem Mktg Rptr - W - NY

IRON OXIDE: METALLIC BROWN
   Chem Mktg Rptr - W - NY

IRON OXIDE: RED
   Am Paint J - W
   Chem Mktg Rptr - W - NY

IRON OXIDE: YELLOW
   Am Paint J - W
   Chem Mktg Rptr - W - NY
   J of Commerce - W - NY

IRON OXIDE: YELLOW, SYNTHETIC
   Am Paint J - W

IRON PIPE: GALVANIZED
   US Stat Rptg Ser - Agri Prices - Annual Summary - A - US and by states

IRON POWDERS
   Am Met Mkt/Met News - D - US

IRONS
   US Stat Rptg Ser - Agri Prices - Annual Summary - A - US and by states

IRON SCRAP
   Foundry - M - Birmingham, Chicago, Houston, Los Angeles, NY, St. Louis
   Second Raw Materials - M - Birmingham, Chicago, Houston, Los Angeles, Montreal, NY, St. Louis
   UN Bul Stat - M - US
   US Labor Stat Bur - Wholesale Prices & Price Indexes - M - Birmingham, Chicago, Philadelphia, San Francisco

IRON TALLATE
   Am Paint J - W

ISOAMYL ALCOHOL
   Chem Mktg Rptr - W - East

ISOAMYL SALICYLATE
   Chem Mktg Rptr - W - NY
   J of Commerce - W - NY

ISOBORNEOL
   Chem Mktg Rptr - W - NY

ISOBORNYL ACETATE
   Chem Mktg Rptr - W - NY

ISOBUTYL ACETATE
   Am Paint J - W
   Chem Mktg Rptr - W - NY
   J of Commerce - W - NY

ISOBUTYL ACETATE 95%
   Rubber World - SA

ISOBUTYL ACRYLATE
   Chem Mktr Rptr - W - East

ISOBUTYL ALCOHOL
   Am Paint J - W
   Chem Mktg Rptr - W - NY

COMMODITY PRICES

ISOBUTYLENE
   Chem Mktg Rptr – W – NY

ISOBUTYL ISOBUTYRATE
   Chem Mktg Rptr – W – NY

ISOBUTYL METHACRYLATE
   Chem Mktg Rptr – W – NY

ISOBUTYL PHENYLACETATE
   Chem Mktg Rptr – W – NY

ISOBUTYL SALICYLATE
   Chem Mktg Rptr – W – NY

ISOBUTYRALDEHYDE
   Chem Mktg Rptr – W – NY

ISOBUTYRIC ACID
   Chem Mktg Rptr – W – NY

ISOBUTYRONITRILE
   Chem Mktg Rptr – W – NY

ISO DECYL ADIPATE
   Am Paint J – W

ISOEUGENOL
   Chem Mktg Rptr – W – NY
   J of Commerce – W – NY

ISONIAZID
   Chem Mktg Rptr – W – NY
   US Labor Stat Bur – Wholesale Prices
     & Prices Indexes – M

ISONONYL ALCOHOL
   Chem Mktg Rptr – W – NY

ISO-OCTYL ALCOHOL
   Chem Mktg Rptr – W – NY

ISO-OCTYL ISODECY PHTHALATE
   Chem Mktg Rptr – W – NY

ISOPHORONE
   Am Paint J – W
   Chem Mktg Rptr – W – US

ISOPHTHALIC ACID
   Am Paint J – W
   Chem Mktg Rptr – W – NY

ISOPRENE ANTIOXIDANT IROX-4
   Rubber World – SA

ISOPROPYL ACETATE
   Am Paint J – W
   Chem Mktg Rptr – W – NY
   J of Commerce – W – NY

ISOPROPYL ACETATE 95%
   Rubber World – SA

ISOPROPYL ALCOHOL
   Am Paint J – W
   Chem Mktg Rptr – W – NY
   J of Commerce – W – NY
   US Labor Stat Bur – Wholesale Prices
     & Price Indexes – M

ISOPROPYL ETHER
   Chem Mktg Rptr – W – NY

ISOPROPYL MYRISTATE
   Chem Mktg Rptr – W – East

ISOQUINOLINE
   Chem Mktg Rptr – W

ISOSTEARIC ACID
   Rubber World – SA

ITACONIC ACID
   Chem Mktg Rptr – W

IVORY CHIPS
   Rubber World – SA

J

JABORANDI LEAVES
   J of Commerce – W – NY

J ACID
   Chem Mktg Rptr – W

JACKETS: BOYS'
   US Stat Rptg Ser – Agri Prices –
     Annual Summary – A – US and
     by states

COMMODITY PRICES

JALAP ROOT
   J of Commerce – W – NY

JAPAN WAX
   Chem Mktg Rptr – W – NY
   J of Commerce – W – NY

JARS: 1 QUART FRUIT
   US Stat Rptg Ser – Agri Prices –
     Annual Summary – A – US and
     by states

JELLY: GRAPE
   US Labor Stat Bur – Retail Food
     Prices – M – US and 23 cities

JEWELRY
   Handbags – M – US

JUICE
   See specific entries

JUNIPER BERRIES
   J of Commerce – W – NY

JUNIPER BERRY OIL
   Chem Mktg Rptr – W – NY
   J of Commerce – W – NY

JUTE
   UN Bul Stat – M – US
   US Labor Stat Bur – Wholesale Prices
     & Price Indexes – M

JUTE: RAW
   J of Commerce – W

J-SERIES DISPERSIONS
   Rubber World – SA

J-851 WAX EMULSION
   Rubber World – SA

JZF
   Rubber World – SA

K

KALE
   US Agri Mktg Ser – Fruit & Veg Prices –
     A – NY

KALMAC
   Rubber World – SA

KAMALA
   J of Commerce – W – NY

KAOLIN
   Chem Mktg Rptr – W

KAOLIN: CALCINED
   J of Commerce – W – NY

KAOLLOID
   Rubber World – SA

KAPOK
   J of Commerce – W

KARAYA GUM
   Chem Mktg Rptr – W – NY
   J of Commerce – W – NY

K-78 CLAY
   Rubber World – SA

KEMPORES
   Rubber World – SA

KENFLEX: A, A30 & L, N
   Rubber World – SA

KEN-MAG
   Rubber World – SA

KENPLAST: G, H, PRO, RD, RDN, VR
   Rubber World – SA

KENTUCKY BLUEGRASS SEED
   Seed World – A – US and by state
   US Stat Rptg Ser – Agri Prices –
     Annual Summary – A – US and
     by state

COMMODITY PRICES

KEROSENE
    Oil Dly - D - Chicago
    Platt's - D - Atlantic coast, Gulf coast, Arkansas, Detroit, Oklahoma
    US Labor Stat Bur - Wholesale Prices & Price Indexes - M
    US Stat Rptg Ser - Agri Prices - Annual Summary - A - US and by states

KEROSENE: DISTILLATE
    Oil & Gas J - W

KING CLAY
    Rubber World - SA

KIPSKINS
    Chicago Hide - D
    Hide & Leather Bul - D
    Natl Provision - W - Chicago
    US Labor Stat Bur - Wholesale Prices & Price Indexes - M

KIPSKINS: PACKER
    Leather & Shoes - W

KNIT GOODS
    See ACETATE TRICOT, NYLON TRICOT

KO-BLEND I S
    Rubber World - SA

KOCH ACID
    Chem Mktg Rptr - W - NY

KOKABACE
    Rubber World - SA

KOLA NUTS
    Chem Mktg Rptr - W - NY
    J of Commerce - W - NY

KORESIN
    Rubber World - SA

KP-140
    Rubber World - SA

KROMER 95-S
    Rubber World - SA

KRONIFLEX TOF
    Rubber World - SA

KRONITEX: AA, I, K-3, MX, 100
    Rubber World - SA

K-STAY G
    Rubber World - SA

KURE-BLEND M T
    Rubber World - SA

KYANITE
    Eng Min J - M - Ga

L

LABEL STOCK
    Mod Pckg-Encyclo & Plan Guide - A - US

L ACID
    Chem Mktg Rptr - W

LACQUER DILUENT
    Am Paint J - W - NY

LACQUER DILUENT: PETROLEUM
    Chem Mktg Rptr - W - NJ, NY, Houston

LAC SPECIAL WHITE FACTICE
    Rubber World - SA

LACTIC ACID
    Chem Mktg Rptr - W - NY
    J of Commerce - W - NY

LACTOSE
    Chem Mktg Rptr - W - NY

LADY SLIPPER ROOT
    J of Commerce - W - NY

LAKE C, RED TONER
    Chem Mktg Rptr - W - NY

COMMODITY PRICES

LAMB
    J of Commerce - D - NY
    US Agri Mktg Ser - Livestock Mkt
        News - W - Chicago, East Coast,
        Colorado, Midwest, Los Angeles
    US Labor Stat Bur - Wholesale Prices
        & Price Indexes - M

LAMB: CHOICE
    Calif Farm - S - Calif
    Lancaster Farm - W - NY
    US Econ Ser - Livestock Sit - BM
    US Econ Ser - Mktg & Trans Sit -
        Q - US

LAMB: PRIME
    Calif Farm - S - Calif
    US Econ Ser - Livestock Sit - BM

LAMB: SPRING, CHOICE & PRIME
    Nation's Restaurant - S - East
        Coast, Los Angeles

LAMB CHOPS
    US Labor Stat Bur - Retail Food
        Prices - M - US and 23 cities

LAMBS
    Mo Rural - S - Kansas City
    US Econ Ser - Demand Sit - Q - US
    See also SHEEP & LAMBS

LAMBS: CHOICE
    Natl Livestock - M - San Angelo

LAMBS: FEEDER
    Neb Farm - S - Omaha
    US Agri Mktg Ser - Livestock Mkt
        News - W - Kansas City, Omaha,
        Portland, San Angelo
    US Econ Ser - Livestock Sit - BM -
        San Angelo

LAMBS: LIVESTOCK
    US Labor Stat Bur - Wholesale Prices
        & Price Indexes - M

LAMBS: SHORN
    Natl Provision - W - Chicago,
        Omaha, St. Paul

LAMBS: SLAUGHTER
    Calif Farm - S - Dixon
    Neb Farm - S - Omaha
    US Agri Mktg Ser - Livestock Mkt
        News - W - Kansas City, Omaha,
        Portland, San Angelo
    US Econ Ser - Livestock Sit - BM -
        San Angelo

LAMBSKINS
    US Labor Stat Bur - Wholesale Prices
        & Price Indexes - M

LAMINAR
    Rubber World - SA

LAMINAR: 5, 35
    Rubber World - SA

LAMPBLACK
    J of Commerce - W - NY

LAMPS: FLOOR
    US Stat Rptg Ser - Agri Prices -
        Annual Summary - A - US and
        by states

LANOLIN
    Chem Mktg Rptr - W
    J of Commerce - W - NY

LARCH: FRAMING LUMBER
    Comm Bul - W

LARCH-DOUGLAS FIR LUMBER: DIMENSION
    US Labor Stat Bur - Wholesale Prices
        & Price Indexes - M

LARD
    Barron's - W - Chicago
    Chem Mktg Rptr - W - Chicago
    J of Commerce - D - NY
    Natl Provision - W - Chicago
    US Agri Mktg Ser - Livestock Mkt
        News - W - Chicago, East, Mo
        River points, West
    US Econ Ser - Fats & Oils Sit - 5/yr -
        Chicago
    US Labor Stat Bur - Wholesale Prices
        & Price Indexes - M

COMMODITY PRICES

US Stat Rptg Ser - Agri Prices -
  Annual Summary - A - US and
  by states
Wall Street J - D - Chicago

LARD: REFINED
  Natl Provision - W - Chicago

LARD OIL
  Chem Mktg Rptr - W
  J of Commerce - D

LARKSPUR SEED
  J of Commerce - W - NY

LATEX
  J of Commerce - W - NY

LATEX PLASTICIZER: A-12, W-617
  Rubber World - SA

LAUREL
  J of Commerce - W - NY

LAURENT'S ACID
  Chem Mktg Rptr - W - NY

LAUREX
  Rubber World - SA

LAURIC ACID
  Chem Mktg Rptr - W - NY
  Rubber World - SA

LAURIC ALDEHYDE (ALDEHYDE C-12)
  Chem Mktg Rptr - W - NY

n-LAURYL METHACRYLATE
  Chem Mktg Rptr - W

LAVANDIN OIL
  Chem Mktg Rptr - W - NY
  J of Commerce - W - NY

LAVENDER FLOWER OIL
  Chem Mktg Rptr - W - NY

LAVENDER FLOWERS
  Chem Mktg Rptr - W - NY
  J of Commerce - W - NY

LAVENDER OIL
  J of Commerce - W - NY
  US Labor Stat Bur - Wholesale Prices
    & Price Indexes - M

LAYING FEED
  US Econ Ser - Feed Sit - Q
  US Stat Rptg Ser - Agri Prices - M - US
  US Stat Rptg Ser - Agri Prices -
    Annual Summary - A - US and
    by states

LEAD
  Am Met Mkt/Met News - D - US,
    Can
  Barron's - W - NY
  Can Min J - M - NY
  Chem Mktg Rptr - W - NY
  Comm Bul - W
  Eng Min J - M
  Fin Times Can - W - NY
  Indus Wk - W
  Iron Age - W
  J of Commerce - D - NY
  Met Wk - W
  Min Rec - W - NY
  North Min - W - US, Can
  NY Times - D - NY
  UN Bul Stat - M - US, Can
  UN Lead & Zinc Stat - M - US, Can
  Wall Street J - D - NY
  West Miner - M - US, Can

LEAD: BASIC SILICO CHROMATE
  Am Paint J - W

LEAD: COMMON
  Purch World - M - NY

LEAD: PIG, COMMON
  US Labor Stat Bur - Wholesale Prices
    & Price Indexes - M

LEAD: RED
  Chem Mktg Rptr - W - US
  J of Commerce - W - NY
  Rubber World - SA

LEAD: RED, DRY
  Am Paint J - W

COMMODITY PRICES

LEAD: SMELTERS' SCRAP
   Am Met Mkt/Met News - D - US

LEAD: WHITE
   Chem Mktg Rptr - W - NY
   J of Commerce - W - NY
   US Labor Stat Bur - Wholesale Prices
     & Price Indexes - M

LEAD: WHITE, BASIC CARBONATE,
BASIC SILICATE, BASIC SULFATE
   Am Paint J - W

LEAD ACETATE
   Chem Mktg Rptr - W - US
   J of Commerce - W - NY

LEAD ARSENATE
   Chem Mktg Rptr - W - NY
   J of Commerce - W - NY
   US Stat Rptg Ser - Agri Prices -
     Annual Summary - A - US and
     by states

LEAD BLUE
   Chem Mktg Rptr - W - NY

LEAD CHLORIDE
   Chem Mktg Rptr - W - US

LEAD FLUOBORATE
   Chem Mktg Rptr - W

LEAD MONOSILICATE
   Chem Mktg Rptr - W - US

LEAD NAPHTHENATE
   Chem Mktg Rptr - W - NY
   US Labor Stat Bur - Wholesale Prices
     & Price Indexes - M

LEAD NAPHTHENATE: LIQUID
   Am Paint J - W

LEAD NEODECANOATE
   Am Paint J - W

LEAD NITRATE
   Chem Mktg Rptr - W - US

LEAD OCTOATE
   Am Paint J - W

LEAD PEROXIDE
   Chem Mktg Rptr - W - US

LEAD PHTHALATE
   Chem Mktg Rptr - W - US

LEAD PIPE
   US Labor Stat Bur - Wholesale Prices
     & Price Indexes - M

LEAD POWDER
   Am Met Mkt/Met News - D - US

LEAD RESINATE
   Chem Mktg Rptr - W - NY

LEAD SALICYLATE
   Chem Mktg Rptr - W - US

LEAD SCRAP
   Iron Age - W
   J of Commerce - W - NY
   Purch World - M - East
   Second Raw Materials - M - Chicago,
     Houston, Los Angeles, Montreal,
     NY, St. Louis, Toronto

LEAD SILICOCHROMATE
   Chem Mktg Rptr - W
   J of Commerce - W - NY

LEAD STEARATE
   Rubber World - SA

LEAD STEARATE: PRECIPITATED
   Am Paint J - W

LEAD TALLATE
   Am Paint J - W
   Chem Mktg Rptr - W - NY

LEATHER: BELLIES
   Leather & Shoes - W

LEATHER: CALF
   Leather & Shoes - W

LEATHER: EXTREMES
   Leather & Shoes - W

LEATHER: INDUSTRIAL BELTING
   US Labor Stat Bur - Wholesale Prices
     & Price Indexes - M

COMMODITY PRICES

LEATHER: KID
   Leather & Shoes - W

LEATHER: KIDSKINS
   Am Shoe - W

LEATHER: KID SUEDE
   Leather & Shoes - W

LEATHER: KIPS
   Leather & Shoes - W

LEATHER: LAMB
   US Labor Stat Bur - Wholesale Prices
     & Price Indexes - M

LEATHER: LIGHT NATIVE STEERS
   Leather & Shoes - W

LEATHER: PATENT
   Am Shoe - W
   Leather & Shoes - W

LEATHER: SHEEPSKINS
   Am Shoe - W
   Leather & Shoes - W

LEATHER: SHOULDERS
   Leather & Shoes - W

LEATHER: SIDE
   Am Shoe - W

LEATHER: SOLE
   Am Shoe - W
   Leather & Shoes - W

LEATHER: SPLIT
   Am Shoe - W
   Leather & Shoes - W

LEATHER: WELTING
   Leather & Shoes - W

LEATHER: WORK ELK
   Leather & Shoes - W

LEBCOL T-40
   Rubber World - SA

LECITHIN
   Am Paint J - W
   Chem Mktg Rptr - W

LEDATE
   Rubber World - SA

LEEGEN
   Rubber World - SA

LEMONADE: FROZEN CONCENTRATE
   US Labor Stat Bur - Retail Food
     Prices - M - US and 23 cities

LEMONGRASS OIL
   Chem Mktg Rptr - W - NY
   J of Commerce - W - NY
   US Labor Stat Bur - Wholesale Prices
     & Price Indexes - M

LEMON OIL
   Chem Mktg Rptr - W
   J of Commerce - W - NY
   US Labor Stat Bur - Wholesale Prices
     & Price Indexes - M

LEMON PEEL
   J of Commerce - W - NY

LEMONS
   Calif Farm - S - Southern Calif
   US Agri Mktg Ser - Fruit & Veg
     Prices - A - Calif, Chicago, NY
   US Labor Stat Bur - Wholesale Prices
     & Price Indexes - M
   US Stat Rptg Ser - Agri Prices - M -
     Ariz, Calif, US

LEMONSEED, DRIED
   Chem Mktg Rptr - W - NY

LENTIL
   J of Commerce - W - NY

LESPEDEZA SEED
   US Stat Rptg Ser - Agri Prices - M -
     US and by states
   US Stat Rptg Ser - Agri Prices -
     Annual Summary - A - US and
     by states

COMMODITY PRICES

LETTUCE
    Calif Farm - S - Imperial Valley
    Nation's Restaurant - S - Boston, Chicago, NY
    US Econ Ser - Mktg & Trans Sit - Q - US
    US Labor Stat Bur - Retail Food Prices - M - US and 23 cities
    US Labor Stat Bur - Wholesale Prices & Price Indexes - M
    US Stat Rptg Ser - Agri Prices - M - US
    US Stat Rptg Ser - Agri Prices - Annual Summary - A - US and by states

LETTUCE: ICEBERG
    US Agri Mktg Ser - Fruit & Veg Prices - A - Ariz, Calif, Chicago, NY, Texas
    US Econ Ser - Veg Sit - Q - Chicago, NY

dl-LEUCINE
    Chem Mktg Rptr - W

LEVAFORM K
    Rubber World - SA

LEVAPREN: 400, 450, 452
    Rubber World - SA

LGB CLAY
    Rubber World - SA

LICORICE ROOT
    Chem Mktg Rptr - W - NY
    J of Commerce - W - NY

LIGHT BULBS
    US Stat Rptg Ser - Agri Prices - Annual Summary - A - US and by states

LIMA BEANS
    See BEANS: LIMA

LIME
    Chem Mktg Rptr - W - NY
    US Labor Stat Bur - Wholesale Prices & Price Indexes - M

LIME: CHEMICAL PEBBLE
    Chem Mktg Rptr - W - East

LIME: HIGH CALCIUM
    Can Chem Processing - M - Can

LIME: HYDRATED
    Rubber World - SA
    US Labor Stat Bur - Wholesale Prices & Price Indexes - M

LIME JUICE
    Alaska Bev Analyst - M - Alaska
    Ariz Bev J - M - Ariz

LIME OIL
    Chem Mktg Rptr - W - NY
    J of Commerce - W - NY

LIMES
    US Agri Mktg Ser - Fruit & Veg Prices - A - Chicago, NY

LIMESTONE: GROUND
    US Stat Rptg Ser - Agri Prices - Annual Summary - A - US and by states

d-LIMONENE
    Chem Mktg Rptr - W - NY

LINALOE WOOD OIL
    J of Commerce - W - NY

LINALOOL
    J of Commerce - W - NY

LINALOOL: EX BOIS DE ROSE OIL
    Chem Mktg Rptr - W - NY

LINALOOL OXIDE
    Chem Mktg Rptr - W - NY

LINALYL ACETATE
    J of Commerce - W - NY

LINALYL ACETATE: EX BOIS DE ROSE OIL
    Chem Mktg Rptr - W - NY

LINALYL BENZOATE
    Chem Mktg Rptr - W - NY

COMMODITY PRICES

LINALYL CINNAMATE
   Chem Mktg Rptr - W - NY

LINALYL FORMATE
   Chem Mktg Rptr - W - NY

LINALYL ISOBUTYRATE
   Chem Mktg Rptr - W - NY

LINALYL PROPIONATE
   Chem Mktg Rptr - W - NY

LINDANE
   Chem Mktg Rptr - W - NY
   J of Commerce - W - NY

LINDE CHEMICAL-LOADED MOLECULAR SIEVE CU-2015
   Rubber World - SA

LINDEN FLOWERS
   Chem Mktg Rptr - W - NY

LINDOL
   Rubber World - SA

LINEN EFFECT RAYONS
   J of Commerce - W
   US Labor Stat Bur - Wholesale Prices & Price Indexes - M

LINEREX
   Rubber World - SA

LINOLEATE: LEAD FUSED
   Am Paint J - W

LINOLEIC ACID
   Rubber World - SA

LINOLEUM: FELT-BASE, INLAID
   US Stat Rptg Ser - Agri Prices - Annual Summary - A - US and by states

LINOTYPE-MONOTYPE
   Comm Bul - W

LINSEED MEAL
   Dly Mkt Rec - D - Minneapolis
   Feed Bul - D - Minneapolis
   Feedstuffs - W - Buffalo, Chicago, Ft. Worth, Kansas City
   J of Commerce - D - Minneapolis
   US Agri Mktg Ser - Feed Mkt News - W - Chicago, Minneapolis
   US Agri Mktg Ser - Peanut Mkt News - W - US
   US Econ Ser - Fats & Oils Sit - 5/yr - Minneapolis, NY
   US Econ Ser - Feed Sit - Q - Minneapolis
   Wall Street J - D - Minneapolis

LINSEED OIL
   Am Paint J - W - Minneapolis
   Chem Mktg Rptr - W - Minneapolis, NY
   Chicago Hide - D - Minneapolis
   Dly Mkt Rec - D - Minneapolis
   Fats & Oils - D - Minneapolis
   J of Commerce - D
   Purch World - M - NY
   US Econ Ser - Fats & Oils Sit - 5/yr - Minneapolis, NY
   US Labor Stat Bur - Wholesale Prices & Price Indexes - M
   Wall Street J - D - NY

LINSEED OIL FATTY ACID
   Chem Mktg Rptr - W - NY

LINSEED OILMEAL
   Chem Mktg Rptr - W - Minneapolis
   Comm Rev - W - US
   Dairynews - S - Buffalo, Boston, NY, Philadelphia

LIQUEURS
   Alaska Bev Analyst - M - Alaska
   Ariz Bev J - M - Ariz
   Bev Media - M - NY
   Bev News - M
   Buck Bev J - M - Ohio
   Ill Bev J - M - Ill
   Ky Bev J - M - Ky
   Md-Wash-Del Bev J - M - Md-DC-Del
   Mich Bev News - IR - Mich
   NJ Bev J - M - NJ
   Patterson's - M - Calif
   RI Bev J - M - RI

COMMODITY PRICES

LITHARGE
   Chem Mktg Rptr - W
   J of Commerce - W - NY
   Rubber World - SA

LITHARGE: COMMERCIAL POWDERED
   Am Paint J - W

LITHIUM
   Chem Mktg Rptr - W - NY
   Met Wk - W

LITHIUM BROMIDE
   Chem Mktg Rptr - W - NY

LITHIUM CARBONATE
   Chem Mktg Rptr - W - NY
   J of Commerce - W - NY

LITHIUM CHLORIDE
   Chem Mktg Rptr - W - NY
   J of Commerce - W - NY

LITHIUM FLUORIDE
   Chem Mktg Rptr - W - NY

LITHIUM HYDRIDE
   Chem Mktg Rptr - W - NY

LITHIUM HYDROXIDE
   Chem Mktg Rptr - W - NY

LITHIUM HYPOCHLORITE
   Chem Mktg Rptr - W

LITHIUM INGOT
   Eng Min J - M
   Min Rec - W

LITHIUM NITRATE
   Chem Mktg Rptr - W - NY

LITHIUM STEARATE
   Chem Mktg Rptr - W - NY

LITHIUM SULFATE
   Chem Mktg Rptr - W - NY

LITHOL MAROON TONER
   Am Paint J - W

LITHOL RED TONER
   Am Paint J - W
   Chem Mktg Rptr - W - NY

LITHOL RUBINE RED TONER
   Chem Mktg Rptr - W - NY

LITHOL RUBINE TONER
   Am Paint J - W

LITHOPANE
   Am Paint J - W
   Rubber World - SA

LIVESTOCK
   <u>See</u> specific types

LIVING ROOM SETS: 2 PIECE, UPHOLSTERED
   US Stat Rptg Ser - Agri Prices - Annual Summary - A - US and by states

LOBELIA HERB
   J of Commerce - W - NY

LOCKS: DOOR
   US Labor Stat Bur - Wholesale Prices & Price Indexes - M

LOCUST BEAN
   J of Commerce - W - NY

LOCUST BEAN GUM
   Chem Mktg Rptr - W - NY

LOOMITE
   Rubber World - SA

LUBREX
   Rubber World - SA

LUBRICATING OIL MATERIALS
   US Labor Stat Bur - Wholesale Prices & Price Indexes - M

LUBRI-FLO
   Rubber World - SA

COMMODITY PRICES

LUGGAGE: ATTACHE CASE, NONLEATHER
   US Labor Stat Bur - Wholesale Prices & Price Indexes - M

LUGGAGE: WEEKEND CASE, WOMEN'S, NONLEATHER
   US Labor Stat Bur - Wholesale Prices & Price Indexes - M

LUMBER
   J of Commerce - D - Chicago
   UN Bul Stat - M - Canada, US
   Wall Street J - D - Chicago

LUPAR
   Rubber World - SA

LUPULIN
   J of Commerce - W - NY

2,4-LUTIDINE
   Chem Mktg Rptr - W - NY

LYCOPODIUM
   Chem Mktg Rptr - W - NY
   J of Commerce - W - NY

LYKAPON
   Rubber World - SA

l-LYSINE
   J of Commerce - W - NY

l-LYSINE MONOHYDROCHLORIDE
   Chem Mktg Rptr - W
   US Labor Stat Bur - Wholesale Prices & Price Indexes - M

M

MACARONI
   US Labor Stat Bur - Wholesale Prices & Price Indexes - M

MACE
   Chem Mktg Rptr - W - NY
   J of Commerce - W - NY

MACE NO. 1
   Natl Provision - W - Chicago

MACKEREL: JACK, CANNED
   US Labor Stat Bur - Wholesale Prices & Price Indexes - M

MAGCARB L
   Rubber World - SA

MAGNESIA
   Chem Mktg Rptr - W - Nev

MAGNESIA: CALCINED
   Rubber World - SA

MAGNESITE
   Eng Min J - M - Luning Nev, Port Joe Fla

MAGNESIUM
   Chem Mktg Rptr - W - Freeport Tex
   Indus Wk - W
   Iron Age - W
   Met Wk - W

MAGNESIUM: PIG
   Am Met Mkt/Met News - D - Freeport Tex
   Eng Min J - M
   Iron Age - W
   Min Rec - W
   North Miner - W - Freeport Tex
   Purch World - M

MAGNESIUM: PIG INGOT
   US Labor Stat Bur - Wholesale Prices & Price Indexes - M

MAGNESIUM: TURNINGS
   Am Met Mkt/Met News - D - US

MAGNESIUM ALLOY INGOT
   Foundry - M

MAGNESIUM ALLOYS
   Am Met Mkt/Met News - D - Freeport Tex

MAGNESIUM BROMIDE
   Chem Mktg Rptr - W - US

COMMODITY PRICES

MAGNESIUM CARBONATE
  Chem Mktg Rptr - W - US
  J of Commerce - W - NY
  Rubber World - SA

MAGNESIUM CHLORIDE
  Chem Mktg Rptr - W - US

MAGNESIUM EXTRUSION
  US Labor Stat Bur - Wholesale Prices
    & Price Indexes - M

MAGNESIUM GLUCONATE
  Chem Mktg Rptr - W - East

MAGNESIUM HYDROXIDE
  Chem Mktg Rptr - W - US
  Rubber World - SA

MAGNESIUM INGOT
  Am Met Mkt/Met News - D - US
  Eng Min J - M
  Iron Age - W
  North Miner - W - Freeport Tex

MAGNESIUM LAURYL SULFATE
  Chem Mktg Rptr - W - US

MAGNESIUM NITRATE
  Chem Mktg Rptr - W - US

MAGNESIUM OXIDE
  Chem Mktg Rptr - W - US
  J of Commerce - W - NY
  Rubber World - SA

MAGNESIUM OXIDE DISPERSION
  Rubber World - SA

MAGNESIUM PHOSPHATE
  Chem Mktg Rptr - W - NY

MAGNESIUM SILICOFLUORIDE
  Chem Mktg Rptr - W - US

MAGNESIUM STEARATE
  Am Paint J - W
  Chem Mktg Rptr - W - NY
  Rubber World - SA

MAGNESIUM STICKS
  Iron Age - W

MAGNESIUM SULFATE
  Chem Mktg Rptr - W - US
  J of Commerce - W - NY
  US Labor Stat Bur - Wholesale Prices
    & Price Indexes - M

MAGNESIUM TRISILICATE
  Chem Mktg Rptr - W - NY

MAGOX: OP, 40
  Rubber World - SA

MAHOGANY: PHILIPPINE, AFRICAN, HONDURAN
  Comm Bul - W - Boston

MAIZE
  UN Bul Stat - M - US

MALATHION
  Chem Mktg Rptr - W - US
  J of Commerce - W - NY
  US Stat Rptg Ser - Agri Prices -
    Annual Summary - A - US and
    by states

MALEIC ACID
  Chem Mktg Rptr - W - NY
  Rubber World - SA

MALEIC ANHYDRIDE
  Am Paint J - W
  Chem Mktg Rptr - W - US
  J of Commerce - W - NY

MALIC ACID
  Chem Mktg Rptr - W - NY
  J of Commerce - W - NY
  Rubber World - SA

MALT
  J of Commerce - W - NY
  US Labor Stat Bur - Wholesale Prices
    & Price Indexes - M

MALT BEVERAGES
  RI Bev J - M - RI

MALT LIQUOR
  Ariz Bev J - M - Ariz

COMMODITY PRICES

MANDARIN OIL
J of Commerce - W - NY

MANDELIC ACID
Chem Mktg Rptr - W - NY

MANDRAKE
J of Commerce - W - NY

MANGANESE
Chem Mktg Rptr - W - US
Eng Min J - M
J of Commerce - D - NY
Met Wk - W

MANGANESE ACETATE
Chem Mktg Rptr - W - NY

MANGANESE BORATE
Chem Mktg Rptr - W - NY

MANGANESE BRONZE
Iron Age - W

MANGANESE BRONZE INGOT
Foundry - M

MANGANESE CARBONATE
Chem Mktg Rptr - W - US

MANGANESE CHLORIDE
Chem Mktg Rptr - W - NY

MANGANESE DIOXIDE
Chem Mktg Rptr - W - NY
US Labor Stat Bur - Wholesale Prices
& Price Indexes - M

MANGANESE ELECTRO POWDER
Am Met Mkt/Met News - D - US

MANGANESE GLUCONATE
Chem Mktg Rptr - W - NY

MANGANESE HYDRATE
Chem Mktg Rptr - W - NY

MANGANESE HYPOPHOSPHITE
Chem Mktg Rptr - W - NY

MANGANESE NAPHTHENATE
Chem Mktg Rptr - W - NY

MANGANESE NAPHTHENATE: LIQUID
Am Paint J - W

MANGANESE OCTOATE
Am Paint J - W

MANGANESE ORE
Eng Min J - M

MANGANESE RESINATE
Chem Mktg Rptr - W - NY

MANGANESE SULFATE
Chem Mktg Rptr - W - NY

MANGANESE TALLATE
Am Paint J - W
Chem Mktg Rptr - W - NY

MANGROVE BARK
J of Commerce - W - NY

MANILA GUM: DBB, C
J of Commerce - W - NY

MANILA GUM: LOBA C, DBB, LAS, MA, PHILIPPINE PALE BAND, PHILIPPINE PALE CHIPS, PHILIPPINE SORTS
Am Paint J - W - NY

MANILA HEMP
J of Commerce - W - NY

MANILA ROPE
US Stat Rptg Ser - Agri Prices - Annual Summary - A - US and by states

MAN-MADE FIBER GRAY GOODS: ACETATE TAFFETA
Dly News Rec - D

MAN-MADE FIBER GRAY GOODS: FILAMENT FABRICS
J of Commerce - W

MAN-MADE FIBER GRAY GOODS: PLAIN LINING TWILL (ALL RAYON)
Am Textile Rptr/Bul - M
Dly News Rec - D

COMMODITY PRICES

MAN-MADE FOBER GRAY GOODS:
POLYESTER-COTTON BLENDS
   J of Commerce - W

MAN-MADE FIBER GRAY GOODS:
POLYESTER-COTTON BLENDS
(BATISTE, POPLIN)
   Am Textile Rptr/Bul - M
   Dly News Rec - D

MAN-MADE FIBER GRAY GOODS:
RAYON TAFFETA
   Am Textile Rptr/Bul - M
   Dly News Rec - D

MANNA
   J of Commerce - W - NY

MANNITOL
   Chem Mktg Rptr - W - US

MAPLE
   Comm Bul - W

MAPLE: FLOORING
   Comm Bul - W

MAPLE: FLOORING; NO.1
COMMON
   US Labor Stat Bur - Wholesale Prices
   & Price Indexes - M

MAPLE: SOFT
   Comm Bul - W

MARBON 8000A-E
   Rubber World - SA

MARGARINE
   See OLEOMARGARINE

MARINE DIESEL FUEL
   Platt's - D - Houston, Los Angeles,
   New Orleans, NY, Miami

MARINE OILS
   Am Paint J - W - NY

MARJORAM
   J of Commerce - W - NY
   Natl Provision - W - Chicago

MARJORAM OIL
   J of Commerce - W - NY

MARKET WOODPULP
   See WOODPULP

MASTIC GUM
   J of Commerce - W - NY

MATICO LEAVES
   J of Commerce - W - NY

MATTRESS AND BOX SPRING SETS:
INNERSPRING
   US Stat Rptg Ser - Agri Prices -
   Annual Summary - A - US and
   by states

MAYONNAISE
   US Labor Stat Bur - Wholesale Prices
   & Price Indexes - M

MBT
   Rubber World - SA

MBTS
   Rubber World - SA

MCNAMEE CLAY
   Rubber World - SA

MEAT AND BONE MEAL
   Calif Farm - S - Los Angeles, San
   Francisco
   Chicago Hide - D - Chicago and Ill
   area
   Fats & Oils - D - Chicago and Ill
   area
   Feed Bul - D - Denver, Ft. Worth,
   Ill, Omaha
   Feedstuffs - W - Atlanta, Boston,
   Chicago, Ft. Worth, Los Angeles

MEAT MEAL
   Comm Bul - W - US
   Feedstuffs - W
   Mo Rural - S - Kansas City Mo
   US Agri Mktg Ser - Feed Mkt News - W
   US Econ Ser - Feed Sit - Q - Chicago
   US Labor Stat Bur - Wholesale Prices
   & Price Indexes - M

COMMODITY PRICES

MELAMINE
    Chem Mktg Rptr - W - US
    J of Commerce - W - NY
    Mod Pckg-Encyclo & Plan Guide -
      A - US

MELONS: HONEYDEW
    US Econ Ser - Veg Sit - Q

MENHADEN OIL
    Am Paint J - W - NY
    Chem Mktg Rptr - W - Atlantic
      Coast, Gulf ports
    US Labor Stat Bur - Wholesale Prices
      & Price Indexes - M

MENHADEN OIL: CRUDE
    US Econ Ser - Fats & Oils Sit -
      5/yr - Baltimore

MENHADEN OIL: LIGHT PRESSED
    US Econ Ser - Fats & Oils Sit -
      5/yr - NY

MENTHOL
    Chem Mktg Rptr - W - NY
    J of Commerce - W - NY
    US Labor Stat Bur - Wholesale Prices
      & Price Indexes - M

MERAC
    Rubber World - SA

MERCAPTAN: 3B, 4P, DDM 80 & 100, PTM
    Rubber World - SA

MERCAPTAN NORMAL OCTYL 1
    Rubber World - SA

MERCAPTAN TERTIARY OCTYL 1
    Rubber World - SA

2-MERCAPTOBENZOTHIAZOLE
    Chem Mktg Rptr - W - US

MERCAPTOBENZOTHIAZYL
    Chem Mktg Rptr - W - US

MERCURIC CHLORIDE
    Chem Mktg Rptr - W - US
    J of Commerce - W - NY

MERCURIC OXIDE
    Chem Mktg Rptr - W - US
    J of Commerce - W - NY

MERCUROUS CHLORIDE
    Chem Mktg Rptr - W
    J of Commerce - W - NY

MERCURY
    Am Met Mkt/Met News - D - US
    Barron's - W - NY
    Chem Mktg Rptr - W - NY
    Eng Min J - M - NY
    Iron Age - W - NY
    J of Commerce - D - NY
    Met Wk - W
    Min Rec - W
    NY Times - D
    Purch World - M - NY
    US Labor Stat Bur - Wholesale Prices
      & Price Indexes - M
    Wall Street J - D - NY
    West Miner - M - US

MESITYL OXIDE
    Am Paint J - W
    Chem Mktg Rptr - W - US

METALLIC BROWN
    Am Paint J - W

METAL PRODUCTS
    US Labor Stat Bur - Wholesale Prices
      & Price Indexes - M

METALS: SCRAP
    J of Commerce - W

METHACRYLATE STYRENES
    Mod Pckg-Encyclo & Plan Guide -
      A - US

METHACRYLIC ACID
    Chem Mktg Rptr - W - NY

METHANOL
    Am Paint J - W
    Chem Mktg Rptr - W - Gulf coast,
      Los Angeles
    J of Commerce - W - NY
    Purch World - M - Gulf coast
    US Labor Stat Bur - Wholesale Prices
      & Price Indexes - M

COMMODITY PRICES

METHAPYRILENE FUMARATE
Chem Mktg Rptr - W - NY

METHAPYRILENE
HYDROXYANALOGUE
Chem Mktg Rptr - W - NY

METHASAN
Rubber World - SA

METHAZATE
Rubber World - SA

dl-METHIONINE
Chem Mktg Rptr - W - NY

METHOX
Rubber World - SA

METHOXYCHLOR
Chem Mktg Rptr - W - NY

METHYL ABIETATE
Chem Mktg Rptr - W - East

METHYL ACETONE
Chem Mktg Rptr - W - East
J of Commerce - W - NY

METHYL ACRYLATE
Chem Mktg Rptr - W - NY

METHYL ALCOHOL
US Labor Stat Bur - Wholesale Prices
& Price Indexes - M

METHYL AMYL ACETATE
Am Paint J - W
Chem Mktg Rptr - W - East

METHYL AMYL ALCOHOL
Am Paint J - W
Chem Mktg Rptr - W - NY

n-METHYLANILINE
Chem Mktg Rptr - W - NY

METHYL ANTHRANILATE
Chem Mktg Rptr - W - NY
J of Commerce - W - NY

METHYL BENZOATE
Chem Mktg Rptr - W - NY

METHYL BROMIDE
Chem Mktg Rptr - W - NY

METHYL BUTYL KETONE
Am Paint J - W

METHYL n-BUTYL KETONE
Chem Mktg Rptr - W - NY

METHYLCELLULOSE
Am Paint J - W
Chem Mktg Rptr - W - NY

METHYL CHLORIDE
Chem Mktg Rptr - W - US
US Labor Stat Bur - Wholesale Prices
& Price Indexes - M

METHYL CINNAMATE
Chem Mktg Rptr - W - NY

METHYL p-CRESOL
Chem Mktg Rptr - W - NY

METHYLENE BLUE
Chem Mktg Rptr - W - NY

METHYLENE CHLORIDE
Am Paint J - W
Chem Mktg Rptr - W - NY
J of Commerce - W - NY
Rubber World - SA

METHYL ETHYL KETONE
Am Paint J - W
Chem Mktg Rptr - W - East
Rubber World - SA
US Labor Stat Bur - Wholesale Prices
& Price Indexes - M

2-METHYL-5-ETHYL PYRIDINE
Chem Mktg Rptr - W - US

METHYL ETHYL TUADS
Rubber World - SA

METHYL EUGENOL
Chem Mktg Rptr - W - NY

COMMODITY PRICES

METHYL FORMATE
  Chem Mktg Rptr - W - US

METHYL GLUCOSIDE
  Am Paint J - W - Argo Illinois

METHYL HEPTENOL
  Chem Mktg Rtrp - W - NY

METHYL HEPTENONE
  Chem Mktg Rptr - W - NY

METHYL HEPTIN CARBONATE
  Chem Mktg Rptr - W - NY

METHYL P-HYDROXYBENZOATE
  Chem Mktg Rptr - W - NY

METHYL IONONE
  Chem Mktg Rptr - W - NY
  J of Commerce - W - NY

METHYL ISOAMYL KETONE
  Am Paint J - W
  Chem Mktg Rptr - W - NY
  Rubber World - SA

METHYL ISOBUTYL ACETATE
  J of Commerce - W - NY

METHYLISOBUTYL CARBINOL
  Am Paint J - W
  Chem Mktg Rptr - W - NY

METHYL ISOBUTYL KETONE
  Am Paint J - W
  Chem Mktg Rptr - W - NY
  Rubber World - SA

METHYL ISOEUGENOL
  Chem Mktg Rptr - W - NY

METHYL METHACRYLATE
  Chem Mktg Rptr - W - NY

b-METHYLNAPHTHALENE
  Chem Mktg Rptr - W - US

METHYL NAPHTHYL KETONE
  Chem Mktg Rptr - W - NY

METHYL PARATHION
  Chem Mktg Rptr - W - US
  J of Commerce - W - NY
  US Labor Stat Bur - Wholesale Prices
    & Price Indexes - M

METHYL PHENYLACETATE
  Chem Mktg Rptr - W - NY

METHYL ROSEANILINE CHLORIDE
  Chem Mktg Rptr - W - NY

METHYL SALICYLATE
  Chem Mktg Rptr - W - NY
  Rubber World - SA

METHYL THIRAM
  Rubber World - SA

METHYL TUADS
  Rubber World - SA

2-METHYL-5-VINYL PYRIDINE
  Chem Mktg Rptr - W - US

METHYL VIOLET TONER
  Chem Mktg Rptr - W - US

METHYL ZIMATE
  Rubber World - SA

METHYL ZIMATE SLURRY
  Rubber World - SA

METHYL ZIRAM: 0571, 0579, 0577
  Rubber World - SA

MICA
  Chem Mktg Rptr - W - East

MICA: DRY GROUND, WET GROUND
  Am Paint J - W

MICA: 160-MESH WATER GROUND, AAA, WET GROUND 160 MESH & 325 MESH
  Rubber World - SA

MICA: TRIPLE A, AA, WO, WESTERN 325
  Rubber World - SA

COMMODITY PRICES

MICROCRYSTALLINE WAX
   Chem Mktg Rptr - W - US

MICROFLAKE WAX: 115, 123
   Rubber World - SA

MICRO-MICA
   Rubber World - SA

MICRO VELVA: A, B
   Rubber World - SA

MICRO WAX: #12, #15
   Rubber World - SA

MIDDLINGS
   US Labor Stat Bur - Wholesale Prices & Price Indexes - M
   US Stat Rptg Ser - Agri Prices - M - US and by states
   US Stat Rptg Ser - Agri Prices - Annual Summary - A - US and by states

MIDDLINGS: WHEAT
   US Econ Ser - Feed Sit - Q - Buffalo, Minneapolis

MILK
   Agri Let - W - US
   Neb Farm - S
   Ont Milk Prod - M - Ont
   Penmarva - M - Pa
   Producer's Guide - M - US
   US Econ Ser - Demand Sit - Q - US
   US Econ Ser - Mktg & Trans Sit - Q - US
   US Labor Stat Bur - Retail Food Prices - M - US and 23 cities
   US Labor Stat Bur - Wholesale Prices & Price Indexes - M
   US Stat Rptg Ser - Agri Prices - M - US and by states
   US Stat Rptg Ser - Agri Prices - Annual Summary - A - US and by states
   US Stat Rptg Ser Wis - Prices Received - M - Wis

MILK: CANNED
   J of Commerce - W - NY
   US Econ Ser - Dairy Sit - 5/yr - US

MILK: DRY SKIM
   Dairy Rec - M - East, Midwest
   Feedstuffs - W - Buffalo, Chicago, Kansas City, Minneapolis
   US Stat Rptg Ser - Dairy Prod - M - US

MILK: DRY WHOLE
   Dairy Rec - M - East, NY
   US Cons & Mktg Ser - Dairy Mkt Stat - A - NY
   US Econ Ser - Dairy Sit - 5/yr - US
   US Stat Rptg Ser - Dairy Prod - M - US

MILK: EVAPORATED
   Dairy Rec - M - NY
   US Cons & Mktg Ser - Dairy Mkt Stat - A - Chicago, East, Los Angeles, Seattle
   US Econ Ser - Dairy Sit - 5/yr - US
   US Labor Stat Bur - Retail Food Prices - M - US and 23 cities
   US Labor Stat Bur - Wholesale Prices & Price Indexes - M
   US Stat Rptg Ser - Agri Prices - Annual Summary - A - US and by states
   US Stat Rptg Ser - Dairy Prod - M - US

MILK: FLUID
   US Cons & Mktg Ser - Dairy Mkt Stat - A - Wis

MILK: FRESH
   US Econ Ser - Dairy Sit - 5/yr - US

MILK: MANUFACTURING GRADE
   Calif Farm - S - San Joaquin
   Dairy Rec - M - US
   US Stat Rptg Ser - Dairy Prod - M - US
   US Stat Rptg Ser Wis - Average Price Milk - M - Minnesota, Wisconsin

MILK: NONFAT DRY
   Dairy Rec - M - Atlanta, Chicago, NY, West coast
   J of Commerce - W - NY
   US Cons & Mktg Ser - Dairy Mkt Stat - A - Atlanta, Chicago, Los Angeles, NY, Seattle
   US Econ Ser - Dairy Sit - 5/yr - US
   US Labor Stat Bur - Wholesale Prices & Price Indexes - M
   US Stat Rptg Ser - Dairy Prod - M - US

COMMODITY PRICES

MILK: SWEETENED CONDENSED SKIM
   Dairy Rec – M – US

MILK: WHOLE POWDER
   J of Commerce – W – NY

MILLFEEDS
   Comm Rev – W – US
   Feed Bul – D

MILLFEEDS: SHORTS, MILLRUN, BRAN, MIDDLINGS
   Feedstuffs – W – Los Angeles

MILLICAL
   Rubber World – SA

MILLREX
   Rubber World – SA

MILLWORK: DOORS – DOUGLAS FIR EXTERIOR, PONDEROSA PINE EXTERIOR, FLUSH TYPE
   US Labor Stat Bur – Wholesale Prices & Price Indexes – M

MILLWORK: KITCHEN CABINET
   US Labor Stat Bur – Wholesale Prices & Price Indexes – M

MILLWORK: MOULDING, PONDEROSA PINE
   US Labor Stat Bur – Wholesale Prices & Price Indexes – M

MILLWORK: WINDOW SASH, PONDEROSA PINE
   US Labor Stat Bur – Wholesale Prices & Price Indexes – M

MILO
   Dairyman – M – Los Angeles
   J of Commerce – D – Chicago

MINERAL OIL
   Chem Mktg Rptr – W – US

MINERAL RUBBER: GRANULAR, HMR SOLID
   Rubber World – SA

MINERAL SPIRITS
   Am Paint J – W – NY
   Chem Mktg Rptr – W – Houston, NJ, NY
   US Labor Stat Bur – Wholesale Prices & Price Indexes – M

MINERAL SPIRITS: ODORLESS
   Am Paint J – W – NY

MISTRON VAPOR
   Rubber World – SA

MOCA
   Rubber World – SA

MODACRYLIC: STAPLE & TOW
   Mod Textiles Mag – M

MODICOL: N, OG, S, VD, VE
   Rubber World – SA

MODIFIED COPOLYMER
   Mod Pckg-Encyclo & Plan Guide – A – US

MODIFIED STYRENE
   Mod Pckg-Encyclo & Plan Guide – A – US

MOHAIR
   US Stat Rptg Ser – Agri Prices – M – Tex

MOLASSES
   Dairyman – M – Los Angeles
   Dairynews – S – Buffalo, Boston, NY, Philadelphia

MOLASSES: BLACKSTRAP
   US Agri Mktg Ser – Feed Mkt News – W – Chicago, Los Angeles, New Orleans, NY
   US Econ Ser – Feed Sit – Q – NY

MOLASSES: CANE
   Feedstuffs – W – Atlanta, Boston, Chicago, San Francisco

MOLASSES: CITRUS
   Feedstuffs – W – Atlanta

COMMODITY PRICES

MOLASSES: CORN
   Feedstuffs - W - Kansas City

MOLASSES: FEEDING
   Feedstuffs - W

MOLD WIZ: 249, U-5-6, 1-C
   Rubber World - SA

MOLYBDATED ORANGE
   Am Paint J - W
   Chem Mktg Rptr - W - NY
   J of Commerce - W - NY

MOLYBDENUM
   Chem Mktg Rptr - W - US
   Eng Min J - M
   Iron Age - W
   Met Wk - W
   West Miner - M - US

MOLYBDENUM CLIMAX OXIDE
   Purch World - M

MOLYBDENUM CONCENTRATES
   Eng Min J - M

MOLYBDENUM ORE
   North Miner - W

MOLYBDENUM POWDER
   Am Met Mkt/Met News - D - US

MOLYBDENUM TRIOXIDE
   Chem Mktg Rptr - W - NY

MOLYBDIC ACID
   Chem Mktg Rptr - W - US

MOLYBDIC TRIOXIDE
   West Miner - M - US

MONEL: CLIPPINGS, TURNINGS, CASTINGS, OLD SHEET, RODS
   Comm Bul - W

MONEL SCRAP
   Second Raw Materials - M - Boston, Houston, NY, Pittsburgh

MONEX
   Rubber World - SA

MONOAMMONIUM PHOSPHATE
   Chem Mktg Rptr - W - Fla

MONOBUTYLAMINE
   Am Paint J - W
   Chem Mktg Rptr - W - East

MONO-TERT-BUTYL-M-CRESOL
   Chem Mktg Rptr - W - US

MONOCHLOROBENZENE
   Chem Mktg Rptr - W - US
   J of Commerce - W - NY

MONOETHANOLAMINE
   Chem Mktg Rptr - W - East
   Rubber World - SA

MONOETHYLAMINE
   Am Paint J - W
   Chem Mktg Rptr - W - East

MONOISOPROPANOLAMINE
   Chem Mktg Rptr - W - NY

MONOMETHYLAMINE
   Chem Mktg Rptr - W - NY

MONOPOTASSIUM GLUTAMATE
   Chem Mktg Rptr - W - NY

MONOSODIUM GLUTAMATE
   Chem Mktg Rptr - W - NY
   US Labor Stat Bur - Wholesale Prices & Price Indexes - M

MONO THIURAD
   Rubber World - SA

MONTAN WAX
   Chem Mktg Rptr - W - US
   Rubber World - SA

MORFAX
   Rubber World - SA

MORFLEX
   Rubber World - SA

MORPHINE
   Chem Mktg Rptr - W - US

COMMODITY PRICES

MORPHINE HYDROCHLORIDE
Chem Mktg Rptr - W - US

MORPHINE SULFATE
Chem Mktg Rptr - W - US
J of Commerce - W - NY

MORPHOLINE
Chem Mktg Rptr - W - East

MORTHANE: 670, 680, 700
Rubber World - SA

MOSHER-AA OOLITIC
Rubber World - SA

MOTOR OIL
US Stat Rptg Ser - Agri Prices -
    Annual Summary - A - US and
    by states

MOTS #1
Rubber World - SA

MOWERS: LAWN, POWER
US Stat Rptg Ser - Agri Prices -
    Annual Summary - A - US and
    by states

MOWERS: TRACTOR
US Stat Rptg Ser - Agri Prices -
    Annual Summary - A - US and
    by states

MULCH
Lancaster Farm - W - Lancaster Pa

MULLEIN FLOWERS
J of Commerce - W - NY

MULLRUN
Dairyman - M - Los Angeles

MULTIFLEX: MM, 1DX
Rubber World - SA

MUNTZ NETAL
Iron Age - W

MURIATIC ACID
See HYDROCHLORIC ACID

MUSHROOMS
US Agri Mktg Ser - Fruit & Veg
    Prices - A - Chicago, NY

MUSHROOMS: CANNED
US Labor Stat Bur - Wholesale Prices
    & Price Indexes - M

MUSK
Chem Mktg Rptr - W - NY
J of Commerce - W - NY

MUSTARD FLOUR
Natl Provision - W - Chicago

MUSTARD SEED
Chem Mktg Rptr - W - NY
J of Commerce - W - NY
Natl Provision - W - Chicago

MYRISTIC ACID
Chem Mktg Rptr - W - NY

MYRISTIC ACID 95%
Rubber World - SA

MYRRH GUM
Chem Mktg Rptr - W - NY
J of Commerce - W - NY

N

NA: 22, 225, 101
Rubber World - SA

NACCONOL: 40F, 90F
Rubber World - SA

NACCOTAN A
Rubber World - SA

NAILS
US Stat Rptg Ser - Agri Prices -
    Annual Summary - A - US and
    by states

NAPHTHA: AROMATIC HIGH FLASH
Am Paint J - W - NY

COMMODITY PRICES

NAPHTHA: VM & P
   Am Paint J - W - NY
   Chem Mktg Rptr - W - Houston, NJ, NY
   Rubber World - SA

NAPHTHALENE
   Chem Mktg Rptr - W - US
   J of Commerce - W - NY
   Purch World - M
   US Labor Stat Bur - Wholesale Prices & Price Indexes - M

a-NAPHTHOL
   Chem Mktg Rptr - W - NY
   J of Commerce - W - NY

b-NAPHTHOL
   Chem Mktg Rptr - W - US
   J of Commerce - W - NY

NAPHTHOL ARYLID RED TONER
   Chem Mktg Rptr - W - NY

NAPHTHOL RED: DRY, LIGHT, MEDIUM, DARK
   Am Paint J - W

a-NAPHTHYLAMINE
   Chem Mktg Rptr - W - NY
   J of Commerce - W - NY

b-NAPHTHYLAMINE
   Chem Mktg Rptr - W - US
   J of Commerce - W - NY

NATKA 1200 HARD CLAY
   Rubber World - SA

NAUGAWHITE
   Rubber World - SA

NBC
   Rubber World - SA

NEATSFOOT OIL
   Chem Mktg Rptr - W - US

NEBONY
   Rubber World - SA

NECTARINES
   US Agri Mktg Ser - Friut & Veg Prices - A - Chicago, Calif, NY

NEOMYCIN SULFATE
   Chem Mktg Rptr - W - NY
   J of Commerce - W - NY
   US Labor Stat Bur - Wholesale Prices & Price Indexes - M

NEOPENTYL GLYCOL
   Chem Mktg Rptr - W - NY

NEOPHAX: A, D, AND K FACTICE
   Rubber World - SA

NEOPRENE CATALYZER NC-8
   Rubber World - SA

NEOPRENE PEPTIZER: P-12, W-9, WH-2
   Rubber World - SA

NEOZONE: A, D
   Rubber World - SA

NEPHELINE SYENITE
   Am Paint J - W - Ont
   Can Chem Processing - M - Can

NEROL
   Chem Mktg Rptr - W - NY

NEROLIDOL
   Chem Mktg Rptr - W - NY

NEROLIN
   Chem Mktg Rptr - W - NY

NEROLI OIL
   Chem Mktg Rptr - W - NY

NEUTROLEUM: DELTA, GAMMA
   Rubber World - SA

NEVASTAIN: A, B, 21
   Rubber World - SA

NEVCHEM 100
   Rubber World - SA

COMMODITY PRICES

NEVILE AND WINTHER'S ACID
   Chem Mktg Rptr - W - NY

NEVILLAC: 10, TS
   Rubber World - SA

NEVILLE
   Rubber World - SA

NEVILLE RESINS
   Rubber World - SA

NIACIN
   Chem Mktg Rptr - W - NY

NIACINAMIDE
   Chem Mktg Rptr - W - NY
   J of Commerce - W - NY

NICKEL
   Can Min J - IR - NY
   Chem Mktg Rptr - W - US
   Indus Wk - W
   Iron Age - W
   J of Commerce - D - NY
   Met Wk - W
   North Miner - W - Can, US
   UN Bul Stat - M - US
   West Miner - M - US

NICKEL: ANODE
   Comm Bul - W
   Finishers' Mgt - M

NICKEL: CARBONYL POWDER
   Am Met Mkt/ Met News - D - US

NICKEL: CATHODE
   Eng Min J - M
   Min Rec - W

NICKEL: CATHODE SHEETS
   US Labor Stat Bur - Wholesale Prices & Price Indexes - M

NICKEL: ELECTROLYTIC
   Purch World - M

NICKEL: ELECTROLYTIC CATHODES
   Am Met Mkt/Met News - D - US

NICKEL: FALCONBRIDGE CATHODES
   Am Met Mkt/Met News - D - Thorold, Ont

NICKEL: FERRONICKEL FN4, FN3, FN1
   Am Met Mkt/Met News - D - Baltimore

NICKEL: "F" SHOT
   Am Met Mkt/Met News - D - US

NICKEL: GRADE F
   Am Met Mkt/Met News - D - NY

NICKEL: IN FERRONICKEL
   Am Met Mkt/Met News - D - Riddle Ore

NICKEL: MILL PRODUCTS
   Am Met Mkt/Met News - D - US

NICKEL: SHEETS, CLIPS, RODS, ENDS, TURNINGS
   Comm Bul - W

NICKEL: SINTER
   Eng Min J - M

NICKEL ACETATE
   Chem Mktg Rptr - W - East
   J of Commerce - W - NY

NICKEL ALLOYS
   Iron Age - W

NICKEL ALLOY SHAPES
   US Labor Stat Bur - Wholesale Prices & Price Indexes - M

NICKEL CARBONATE
   Chem Mktg Rptr - W - East
   Finishers' Mgt - M
   J of Commerce - W - NY

NICKEL CHLORIDE
   Chem Mktg Rptr - W - East
   Finishers' Mgt - M
   J of Commerce - W - NY

NICKEL FLUOBORATE
   Chem Mktg Rptr - W - East
   J of Commerce - W - NY

COMMODITY PRICES

NICKEL NITRATE
   Chem Mktg Rptr - W - East
   J of Commerce - W - NY

NICKEL OXIDE
   Chem Mktg Rptr - W - NY

NICKEL OXIDE SINTER
   Am Met Mkt/Met News - D - US
   Iron Age - W - Buffalo

NICKEL POWDERS
   Am Met Mkt/Met News - D - US

NICKEL SCRAP
   Iron Age - W
   Second Raw Materials - M - Chicago, NY, Philadelphia

NICKEL SHOT
   Am Met Mkt/Met News - D - NY

NICKEL SULFATE
   Chem Mktg Rptr - W - East
   Finishers' Mgt - M
   J of Commerce - W - NY

NICOTINAMIDE
   Chem Mktg Rptr - W - NY

NICOTINIC ACID
   Chem Mktg Rptr - W - NY

NIGHTGOWNS: MISSES' & JUNIORS'
   US Labor Stat Bur - Wholesale Prices & Price Indexes - M

NIGHTGOWNS: WOMEN'S
   US Labor Stat Bur - Wholesale Prices & Price Indexes - M
   US Stat Rptg Ser - Agri Prices - Annual Summary - A - US and by states

NIKETHAMIDE
   Chem Mktg Rptr - W - NY

NIOBIUM
   Eng Min J - M
   Met Wk - W

NITER CAKE
   See SODIUM SULFATE

NITRIC ACID
   Chem Mktg Rptr - W - US
   J of Commerce - W - NY
   US Labor Stat Bur - Wholesale Prices & Price Indexes - M

m-NITROANILINE
   J of Commerce - W - NY

o-NITROANILINE
   Chem Mktg Rptr - W - NY
   J of Commerce - W - NY

p-NITROANILINE
   Chem Mktg Rptr - W - NY
   J of Commerce - W - NY

o-NITROANISOLE
   Chem Mktg Rptr - W - NY

p-NITROANISOLE
   Chem Mktg Rptr - W - NY

NITROBENZENE
   Chem Mktg Rptr - W - NY
   J of Commerce - W - NY

p-NITROBENZOIC ACID
   Chem Mktg Rptr - W - US

NITROCELLULOSE
   Am Paint J - W
   Chem Mktg Rptr - W - US
   US Labor Stat Bur - Wholesale Prices & Price Indexes - M

o-NITROCHLOROBENZENE
   Chem Mktg Rptr - W - NY

p-NITROCHLOROBENZENE
   Chem Mktg Rptr - W - US

2-NITRO-P-CRESOL
   Chem Mktg Rptr - W - NY

NITROETHANE
   Am Paint J - W
   Chem Mktg Rptr - W - US

COMMODITY PRICES

NITROGEN FERTILIZER MATERIALS
US Stat Rptg Ser - Agri Prices -
Annual Summary - A - US and
by states

NITROGENOUS SEWAGE SLUDGE
Chem Mktg Rptr - W - Chicago

NITROGENOUS TANKAGE
Chem Mktg Rptr - W - Carrollville
Wis, Forbes Me, Slatersville RI
US Labor Stat Bur - Wholesale Prices
& Price Indexes - M

NITROGEN SOLUTIONS
Chem Mktg Rptr - W - US
US Labor Stat Bur - Wholesale Prices
& Price Indexes - M
US Stat Rptg Ser - Agri Prices -
Annual Summary - A - US and
by states

NITROL
Rubber World - SA

NITROMETHANE
Am Paint J - W
Chem Mktg Rptr - W - East

o-NITROPHENOL
Chem Mktg Rptr - W - US
J of Commerce - W - NY

p-NITROPHENOL
J of Commerce - W - NY

NITROPORE: OBSH, SD
Rubber World - SA

2-NITROPROPANE
Am Paint J - W
Chem Mktg Rptr - W - East

NITROSAN (R)
Rubber World - SA

NITROTOLUENE
J of Commerce - W - NY

m-NITROTOLUENE
Chem Mktg Rptr - W - NY

o-NITROTOLUENE
Chem Mktg Rptr - W - NY
J of Commerce - W - NY

p-NITROTOLUENE
Chem Mktg Rptr - W - US
J of Commerce - W - NY

2-NITRO-P-TOLUIDINE
Chem Mktg Rptr - W - NY

m-NITRO-P-TOLUIDINE
J of Commerce - W - NY

NOBS: NO. 1
Rubber World - SA

NON-FER-AL
Rubber World - SA

NONISOL 100
Rubber World - SA

NONOX
Rubber World - SA

NONIX: WSP
Rubber World - SA

NONYLPHENOL
Chem Mktg Rptr - W - East

NOPCO: 1097-M, 2271(EB), EB-1,
JMK, KOY, NXZ
Rubber World - SA

NOPCOSANT
Rubber World - SA

NOPCOSANT-L
Rubber World - SA

NOPCOWAX 22-DS
Rubber World - SA

NOSCAPINE
Chem Mktg Rptr - W - NY

NPI: 201-C, 202-F
Rubber World - SA

COMMODITY PRICES

NUCAP: 200, 200L
  Rubber World - SA

NULOK: 321L, 321SP
  Rubber World - SA

NO. 1 COMPOSITION: SCRAP
  Second Raw Materials - M - Chicago, Houston, NY, Pittsburgh, St. Louis

NUTMEG
  Chem Mktg Rptr - W - NY
  J of Commerce - W - NY

NUTMEG OIL
  Chem Mktg Rptr - W - NY
  J of Commerce - W - NY

NUTS
  See specific entries

NUTS (METAL)
  US Labor Stat Bur - Wholesale Prices & Price Indexes - M

NUX VOMICA
  J of Commerce - W - NY

NYLON
  J of Commerce - W - NY
  Mod Pckg-Encyclo & Plan Guide - A - US

NYLON: FILAMENT YARNS
  US Labor Stat Bur - Wholesale Prices & Price Indexes - M

NYLON: MONOFILAMENT
  Mod Textiles Mag - M

NYLON: STAPLE & TOW
  Mod Textiles Mag - M

NYLON: TIRE YARN
  US Labor Stat Bur - Wholesale Prices & Price Indexes - M

NYLON: TRICOT KNIT, FINISHED
  US Labor Stat Bur - Wholesale Prices & Price Indexes - M

NYLON GRAY GOODS
  Dly News Rec - D
  J of Commerce - W

NYLON GRAY GOODS: TAFFETA
  US Labor Stat Bur - Wholesale Prices & Price Indexes - M

NYLON HOSIERY: WOMEN'S
  US Labor Stat Bur - Wholesale Prices & Price Indexes - M
  US Stat Rptg Ser - Agri Prices - Annual Summary - A - US and by states

NYLON N-16
  Rubber World - SA

NYLON TRICOT
  Dly News Rec - D
  J of Commerce - W

NYLON YARNS
  Mod Textiles Mag - M

NYTAL: 200, 300
  Rubber World - SA

O

OAK: FLOORING
  US Stat Rptg Ser - Agri Prices - Annual Summary - A - US and by states

OAK: FLOORING, RED OR WHITE
  Comm Bul - W - Boston

OAK: RED
  Comm Bul - W

OAK: RED, NO. 1 COMMON
  US Labor Stat Bur - Wholesale Prices & Price Indexes - M

COMMODITY PRICES

OAK: WHITE
   Comm Bul - W
   US Labor Stat Bur - Wholesale Prices & Price Indexes - M

OAT FEED: REGROUND
   Feedstuffs - W - Chicago

OATS
   Agri Let - W - US
   Barron's - W - Chicago
   Comm Rev - W - US
   Dly Mkt Rec - D - Chicago, Winnipeg
   Fin Post - W - Chicago, Winnipeg
   Free Press Farm - W - Chicago, Winnipeg
   J of Commerce - D - Chicago, NY, Winnipeg
   Lancaster Farm - W - Lancaster Pa
   NY Times - D - Chicago
   US Stat Rptg Ser - Agri Prices - M - US and by states
   US Stat Rptg Ser - Agri Prices - Annual Summary - A - US and by states
   US Stat Rptg Ser Wis - Prices Received - M - Wis
   Wall Street J - D - Chicago, Winnipeg
   West Producer - W - Chicago, Winnipeg

OATS: CRIMPED
   Feedstuffs - W - Atlanta, Boston, Chicago, Kansas City

OATS: FEED
   Feedstuffs - W

OATS: GROUND
   Dairynews - S - Buffalo, Boston, NY, Philadelphia

OATS: NO. 1 WHITE
   US Econ Ser - Feed Sit - Q - Chicago

OATS: NO. 2
   US Labor Stat Bur - Wholesale Prices & Price Indexes - M

OATS: NO. 2, EXTRA HEAVY
   US Agri Mktg Ser - Feed Mkt News - W - Chicago, Minneapolis

OATS: NO. 2 EXTRA HEAVY WHITE
   US Agri Mktg Ser - Grain Mkt News - W - Chicago, Minneapolis

OATS: NO. 2 HEAVY WHITE
   US Agri Mktg Ser - Grain Mkt News - W - Toledo

OATS: NO. 2 WHITE
   NY Times - D - Chicago
   US Agri Mktg Ser - Grain Mkt News - W - Kansas City
   US Econ Ser - Feed Sit - Q - Minneapolis

OATS: PULVERIZED
   Feedstuffs - W - Chicago

OATS: ROLLED
   Dairyman - M - Los Angeles
   Feedstuffs - W - Atlanta, Boston, Chicago, Kansas City
   US Stat Rptg Ser - Agri Prices - Annual Summary - A - US and by states

OATS: SEED
   US Stat Rptg Ser - Agri Prices - Annual Summary - A - US and by states

OATS: WHITE
   Dly Mkt Rec - D - Minneapolis

OBTS
   Rubber World - SA

OCEAN PERCH FILLET: FROZEN
   US Labor Stat Bur - Wholesale Prices & Price Indexes - M

OCHER: DOMESTIC, FRENCH TYPE
   Am Paint J - W

OCHRE
   Eng Min J - M - Ga

COMMODITY PRICES

OCOTEA CYMBARUM OIL
  Chem Mktg Rptr - W - NY

1-OCTADECANOL
  Chem Mktg Rptr - W - East

OCTAMINE
  Rubber World - SA

n-OCTANE
  Chem Mktg Rptr - W - Houston

1-OCTANOL
  Chem Mktg Rptr - W - East

OCTYL ALCOHOL
  Chem Mktg Rptr - W - NY

tert-OCTYLAMINE
  Chem Mktg Rptr - W - US

n-OCTYL N-DECYL PHTHALATE
  Chem Mktg Rptr - W - NY

OCTYLPHENOL
  Chem Mktg Rptr - W - US

OFFICE SUPPLIES
  US Bur Dom Comm - Pulp Q - Q

OFFICE SUPPLIES AND ACCESSORIES: INDEX CARDS
  US Labor Stat Bur - Wholesale Prices & Price Indexes - M

OIL: CRUDE
  NY Times - D - Mid-continent

OIL BURNER: CONVERSION TYPE
  US Labor Stat Bur - Wholesale Prices & Price Indexes - M

OIL FILTERS (MOTOR SUPPLIES)
  US Stat Rptg Ser - Agri Prices - Annual Summary - A - US and by states

OILS: ESSENTIAL
  J of Commerce - W

OILS: VEGETABLE
  See also specific types

OILS: VEGETABLE, VULCANIZED BROWN, SPECIAL #219
  Rubber World - SA

OITICICA OIL
  Am Paint J - W - NY
  Chem Mktg Rptr - W - NY
  J of Commerce - D
  US Econ Ser - Fats & Oils Sit - 5/yr - NY

OLATE: FLAKES
  Rubber World - SA

OLEFIN: MONOFILAMENT AND YARN
  Mod Textiles Mag - M

OLEFIN: STAPLE & TOW
  Mod Textiles Mag - M

OLEIC ACID
  Chem Mktg Rptr - W - NY
  Rubber World - SA
  US Labor Stat Bur - Wholesale Prices & Price Indexes - M

OLEOMARGARINE
  Natl Provision - W
  US Econ Ser - Dairy Sit - 5/yr - US
  US Econ Ser - Fats & Oils Sit - 5/yr - Chicago, Eastern US
  US Econ Ser - Mktg & Trans Sit - Q - US
  US Labor Stat Bur - Retail Food Prices - M - US and 23 cities
  US Labor Stat Bur - Wholesale Prices & Price Indexes - M
  US Stat Rptg Ser - Agri Prices - Annual Summary - A - US and by states

OLIBANUM GUM
  Chem Mktg Rptr - W - NY
  J of Commerce - W - NY

OLIVE OIL
  Chem Mktg Rptr - W - NY
  J of Commerce - W
  US Econ Ser - Fats & Oils Sit - 5/yr - NY

OLIVES: STUFFED COCKTAIL
  Alaska Bev Analyst - M - Alaska

OLIVINE
  Chem Mktg Rptr - W - US

COMMODITY PRICES

OMYA: BLK 3, BSH
   Rubber World - SA

ONIONS
   Nation's Restaurant - S - Boston, Chicago, NY
   US Econ Ser - Veg Sit - Q - US
   US Labor Stat Bur - Wholesale Prices & Price Indexes - M
   US Stat Rptg Ser - Agri Prices - M - US

ONIONS: DRY
   US Agri Mktg Ser - Fruit & Veg Prices - A - Calif, Chicago, Colo, NY, Tex

ONIONS: YELLOW
   US Labor Stat Bur - Retail Food Prices - M - US and 23 cities

OPD: 101, 400
   Rubber World - SA

OPEX: 40, 42, 93, 100
   Rubber World - SA

OPIUM
   Chem Mktg Rptr - W - US

OPIUM GUM
   J of Commerce - W - NY

ORANGE JUICE: CANNED
   J of Commerce - W
   US Labor Stat Bur - Wholesale Prices & Price Indexes - M
   US Stat Rptg Ser - Agri Prices - Annual Summary - A - US and by states

ORANGE JUICE: FRESH
   US Labor Stat Bur - Retail Food Prices - M - US and 23 cities

ORANGE JUICE: FRESH CHILLED
   US Labor Stat Bur - Wholesale Prices & Price Indexes - M

ORANGE JUICE: FROZEN
   J of Commerce - W - Fla
   US Econ Ser - Mktg & Trans Sit - Q - US

ORANGE JUICE: FROZEN CONCENTRATE
   J of Commerce - D - NY
   NY Times - D
   US Labor Stat Bur - Retail Food Prices - M - US and 23 cities
   US Labor Stat Bur - Wholesale Prices & Price Indexes - M
   US Stat Rptg Ser - Agri Prices - Annual Summary - A - US and by states
   Wall Street J - D - NY

ORANGE OIL
   Chem Mktg Rptr - W - US
   J of Commerce - W - NY
   US Labor Stat Bur - Wholesale Prices & Price Indexes - M

ORANGE PEEL
   Chem Mktg Rptr - W - NY

ORANGE PEEL: SWEET, BITTER
   J of Commerce - W - NY

ORANGES
   Calif Farm - S - central Calif
   Fla Field Rpt - W - Fla
   US Agri Mktg Ser - Fruit & Veg Prices - A - Calif, Chicago, NY, Tex
   US Econ Ser - Mktg & Trans Sit - Q - US
   US Labor Stat Bur - Retail Food Prices - M - US and 23 cities
   US Labor Stat Bur - Wholesale Prices & Price Indexes - M
   US Stat Rptg Ser - Agri Prices - M - Ariz, Calif, Fla, Tex, US
   US Stat Rptg Ser - Agri Prices - Annual Summary - A - US and by states

COMMODITY PRICES

ORCHARDGRASS SEED
  Seed World - A - US and by states
  US Stat Rptg Ser - Agri Prices -
    Annual Summary - A - US and
    by states

OREGANO
  J of Commerce - W - NY

ORGANO-SILICONE FLUID: UNION CARBIDE L-522
  Rubber World - SA

ORIGANUM OIL
  Chem Mktg Rptr - W - NY
  J of Commerce - W - NY

ORRIS ROOT
  Chem Mktg Rptr - W - NY
  J of Commerce - W - NY

ORVUS: AB GRANULES, ES PASTE, WA PASTE
  Rubber World - SA

OSAGE ORANGE EXTRACT
  J of Commerce - W - NY

OSMIUM
  Am Met Mkt/Met News - D - US
  Eng Min J - M
  Met Wk - W

OURICURY WAX
  Chem Mktg Rptr - W - NY
  J of Commerce - W - NY

OVERALLS: MEN'S, BOYS'
  US Stat Rptg Ser - Agri Prices -
    Annual Summary - A - US and
    by states

OW 3910 WHITE
  Rubber World - SA

O-X-A-F
  Rubber World - SA

OXALIC ACID
  Chem Mktg Rptr - W - NY
  J of Commerce - W - NY

OXIDE: PURE BROWN SYNTHETIC
  Am Paint J - W

b-OXYNAPHTHOLIC ACID
  Chem Mktg Rptr - W - NY

OXYSTOP: 320, 330, 999
  Rubber World - SA

OYSTERS: FRESH
  US Labor Stat Bur - Wholesale Prices
    & Price Indexes - M

OYSTER SHELLS
  Am Paint J - W
  US Stat Rptg Ser - Agri Prices -
    Annual Summary - A - US and
    by states

OZOKERITE: 3 STAR NATURAL YELLOW, SNOW-WHITE, WHITE 145 & 177
  Rubber World - SA

OZONE PROTECTOR: 80, 49-461
  Rubber World - SA

OZONITE: GL, T
  Rubber World - SA

OZONO
  Rubber World - SA

OZOSTOP 6000-P
  Rubber World - SA

P

P-10 RICINOLEIC ACID
  Rubber World - SA

PACKAGING ACCESSORIES: GUMMED TAPE
  J of Commerce - W
  US Bur Dom Comm - Pulp Q - Q
  US Labor Stat Bur - Wholesale Prices
    & Price Indexes - M

COMMODITY PRICES

PACKINGHOUSE FEEDS
    Natl Provision - W - Chicago, Midwest

PADLOCK: PIN TUMBLER
    US Labor Stat Bur - Wholesale Prices & Price Indexes - M

PAILS: STEEL
    US Labor Stat Bur - Wholesale Prices & Price Indexes - M

PAINT: INTERIOR WALL, EXTERIOR HOUSE
    US Stat Rptg Ser - Agri Prices - Annual Summary - A - US and by states

PAINT MATERIALS
    J of Commerce - W

PAINTS
    US Labor Stat Bur - Wholesale Prices & Price Indexes - M

PALLADIUM
    Am Met Mkt/Met News - D - US
    Can Min J - IR - NY
    Chem Mktg Rptr - W - US
    Eng Min J - M
    Finishers' Mgt - M
    Iron Age - W
    J of Commerce - D - NY
    Met Wk - W
    Min Rec - W
    NY Times - D

PALMAROSA OIL
    Chem Mktg Rptr - W - NY
    J of Commerce - W - NY

PALMITIC ACID
    Chem Mktg Rptr - W - NY
    Rubber World - SA

PALM OIL
    Chem Mktg Rptr - W - NY
    J of Commerce - D
    US Econ Ser - Fats & Oils Sit - 5/yr - NY

PALM OIL ACID
    Chem Mktg Rptr - W - NY

PAMAK: 4A, 25A
    Rubber World - SA

PANAREZ: 3-210, 6-210, 7-210
    Rubber World - SA

PAPAIN
    J of Commerce - W - NY

PAPAVERINE HYDROCHLORIDE
    Chem Mktg Rptr - W - NY

PAPER: BAGS AND SHIPPING SACKS
    US Bur Dom Comm - Pulp Q - Q

PAPER: BAGS AND SHIPPING SACKS, CEMENT SHIPPING SACKS
    US Labor Stat Bur - Wholesale Prices & Price Indexes - M

PAPER: BAGS AND SHIPPING SACKS, GROCERY BAGS
    US Labor Stat Bur - Wholesale Prices & Price Indexes - M

PAPER: BAGS, PROCESSED
    J of Commerce - W

PAPER: BOND, NO. 1, SULFITE, WATER-MARKED
    J of Commerce - W
    Purch World - M

PAPER: BOOK, A GRADE
    US Bur Dom Comm - Pulp Q - Q
    US Labor Stat Bur - Wholesale Prices & Price Indexes - M

PAPER: BOOK, NO. 2 PLAIN OFFSET
    US Bur Com Comm - Pulp Q - Q
    US Labor Stat Bur - Wholesale Prices & Price Indexes - M

PAPER: BUTCHER'S
    US Bur Dom Comm - Pulp Q - Q

COMMODITY PRICES

PAPER: GUMMED TAPE
   J of Commerce - W
   US Bur Dom Comm - Pulp Q - Q
   US Labor Stat Bur - Wholesale Prices
     & Price Indexes - M

PAPER: MULTIWALL KRAFT
   Purch World - M

PAPER: NEWSPRINT
   J of Commerce - W - NY
   UN Bul Stat - M - Can, US
   US Bur Dom Comm - Pulp Q - Q
   US Labor Stat Bur - Wholesale Prices
     & Price Indexes - M

PAPER: OFFSET, NO. 1 GRADE
   J of Commerce - W
   Purch World - M

PAPER: POUCH
   Mod Pckg-Encyclo & Plan Guide -
     A - US

PAPER: RAGBOUND, 25%
   J of Commerce - W

PAPER: REINFORCED TAPE
   Purch World - M

PAPER: SANITARY AND HEALTH
PRODUCTS
   US Bur Dom Comm - Pulp Q - Q

PAPER: SANITARY AND HEALTH
PRODUCTS, NAPKINS, INDUSTRIAL
   US Labor Stat Bur - Wholesale Prices
     & Price Indexes - M

PAPER: SANITARY AND HEALTH
PRODUCTS, PAPER TOWELS
   US Labor Stat Bur - Wholesale Prices
     & Price Indexes - M

PAPER: SANITARY AND HEALTH
PRODUCTS, TOILET TISSUE
   US Labor Stat Bur - Wholesale Prices
     & Price Indexes - M
   US Stat Rptg Ser - Agri Prices -
     Annual Summary - A - US and
     by states

PAPER: TOP GRADE MACHINE-
COATED OFFSET
   J of Commerce - W

PAPER: WAXED
   Mod Pckg-Encyclo & Plan Guide -
     A - US

PAPER: WAXING
   US Bur Dom Comm - Pulp Q - Q
   US Labor Stat Bur - Wholesale Prices
     & Price Indexes - M

PAPER: WOOD BOND
   US Bur Dom Comm - Pulp Q - Q
   US Labor Stat Bur - Wholesale Prices
     & Price Indexes - M

PAPER: WRAPPING
   J of Commerce - W
   US Bur Dom Comm - Pulp Q - Q
   US Labor Stat Bur - Wholesale Prices
     & Price Indexes - M

PAPER: WRAPPING, STANDARD
KRAFT
   Purch World - M

PAPER: WRITING, RAG CONTENT
   US Bur Dom Comm - Pulp Q - Q
   US Labor Stat Bur - Wholesale Prices
     & Price Indexes - M

PAPERBOARD
   Paperbd Pckg - A
   See also CONTAINERBOARD,
     BOXBOARD

PAPERBOARD: CHIP ROLLS, .009
   Official Bd Mkts - W - US

PAPERBOARD: CLAY-COATED
   Official Bd Mkts - W - US

PAPERBOARD: FILLED NEWS
   Official Bd Mkts - W - US

PAPERBOARD: FOURDRINIER KRAFT
TEST LINER
   Official Bd Mkts - W - US

COMMODITY PRICES

PAPERBOARD: PLAIN CHIP
   Official Bd Mkts – W – US

PAPERBOARD: SEMICHEMICAL
   Official Bd Mkts – W – US

PAPERBOARD: WHITE LINED, .020
   Official Bd Mkts – W – US

PAPER: WHITE WRAPPING NEWS
   J of Commerce – W

PAPER MILL SUPPLIES
   See WASTE PAPER

PAPI
   Rubber World – SA

PAPRIKA
   Chem Mktg Rptr – W – NY
   J of Commerce – W – NY
   Natl Provision – W – Chicago

PAPRIKA OLEORESIN
   J of Commerce – W – NY

PARACHLOR RED
   Am Paint J – W

PARADENE: 1, 33, 35, 2
   Rubber World – SA

PARAFFIN
   Chem Mktg Rptr – W – NY
   J of Commerce – W

PARA-FLUX: REGULAR, 2016, 4156
   Rubber World – SA

PARAFORMALDEHYDE
   Chem Mktg Rptr – W – NY
   J of Commerce – W – NY

PARAGON CLAY
   Rubber World – SA

PARALDEHYDE
   Chem Mktg Rptr – W – East

PARA LUBE
   Rubber World – SA

PARAPLEX: G-25, G-40, G-54, G-56, G-59, G-62
   Rubber World – SA

PARATHION
   US Stat Rptg Ser – Agri Prices –
     Annual Summary – A – US and
     by states

PARATHION: ETHYL
   Chem Mktg Rptr – W – US

PARA TONER RED
   Am Paint J – W
   Chem Mktg Rptr – W – NY
   J of Commerce – W – NY

PARA TONER RED: CHLORINATED
   Am Paint J – W

PAR CLAY
   Rubber World – SA

PARICIN 1
   Rubber World – SA

PARSLEY OIL
   J of Commerce – W – NY

PASSION FLOWER HERB
   J of Commerce – W – NY

PATCHOULI LEAVES
   J of Commerce – W – NY

PATCHOULI OIL
   Chem Mktg Rptr – W – NY
   J of Commerce – W – NY

PEACHES
   US Agri Mktg Ser – Fruit & Veg Prices –
     A – Calif, Chicago, Colo, Ga, NY,
     Wash
   US Labor Stat Bur – Wholesale Prices &
     Price Indexes – M
   US Stat Rptg Ser – Agri Prices – M – US
   US Stat Rptg Ser – Agri Prices –
     Annual Summary – A – US and
     by states

COMMODITY PRICES

PEACHES: CANNED
    J of Commerce - W
    US Labor Stat Bur - Wholesale Prices
        & Price Indexes - M

PEACHES: DRIED
    J of Commerce - W

PEACHES: PROCESSED
    US Stat Rptg Ser - Agri Prices -
        Annual Summary - A - US and
        by states

PEANUT BUTTER
    US Econ Ser - Fats & Oils Sit -
        5/yr - US

PEANUT MEAL
    Feedstuffs - W - Atlanta, Ft. Worth,
        Memphis
    US Agri Mktg Ser - Feed Mkt News -
        W - Southeast mills
    US Agri Mktg Ser - Peanut Mkt
        News - W - Southeast, Southwest
    US Econ Ser - Fats & Oils Sit - 5/yr -
        Southeast mills
    US Econ Ser - Feed Sit - Q -
        Southeast mills

PEANUT OIL
    Chem Mktg Rptr - W - Southeast
    Chicago Hide - D - South
    Fats & Oils - D - South
    J of Commerce - D
    Natl Provision - W
    US Agri Mktg Ser - Peanut Mkt
        News - W - Southeast, Southwest
    Wall Street J - D - Southeast

PEANUT OIL: CRUDE
    US Econ Ser - Fats & Oils Sit -
        5/yr - Southeast mills
    US Labor Stat Bur - Wholesale Prices
        & Price Indexes - M

PEANUT OIL: REFINED
    US Econ Ser - Fats & Oils Sit -
        5/yr - NY
    US Labor Stat Bur - Wholesale Prices
        & Price Indexes - M

PEANUT OILMEAL
    Chem Mktg Rptr - W - Southeast

PEANUTS
    US Agri Mktg Ser - Peanut Mkt News -
        W - US
    US Econ Ser - Fats & Oils Sit - 5/yr -
        US
    US Labor Stat Bur - Wholesale Prices
        & Price Indexes - M
    US Stat Rptg Ser - Agri Prices - M -
        US and by states
    US Stat Rptg Ser - Agri Prices -
        Annual Summary - A - US and
        by states

PEANUTS: SEED
    US Stat Rptg Ser - Agri Prices -
        Annual Summary - A - US and
        by states

PEARS
    US Agri Mktg Ser - Fruit & Veg
        Prices - A - Chicago, NY,
        Wash
    US Labor Stat Bur - Wholesale Prices
        & Price Indexes - M
    US Stat Rptg Ser - Agri Prices -
        M - US

PEARS: CANNED
    J of Commerce - W
    US Labor Stat Bur - Retail Food
        Prices - M - US and 23 cities
    US Labor Stat Bur - Wholesale Prices
        & Price Indexes - M

PEAS: CANNED
    J of Commerce - W
    US Labor Stat Bur - Retail Food
        Prices - M - US and 23 cities
    US Labor Stat Bur - Wholesale Prices
        & Price Indexes - M
    US Stat Rptg Ser - Agri Prices -
        Annual Summary - A - US and
        by states

PEAS: DRIED
    J of Commerce - W - NY

COMMODITY PRICES

PEAS: DRY FIELD
US Stat Rptg Ser - Agri Prices - M - US

PEAS: DRY, GREENS, YELLOWS, BLACKS, LENTILS
Ida Farm - S - Palouse County
Wash Farm - S - Spokane

PEAS: FROZEN
J of Commerce - W
US Econ Ser - Mktg & Trans Sit - Q - US
US Labor Stat Bur - Wholesale Prices & Price Indexes - M
US Stat Rptg Ser - Agri Prices - Annual Summary - A - US and by states

PEAS: GREEN
US Agri Mktg Ser - Fruit & Veg Prices - A - Chicago, NY

PEAS: SEED
Seed World - A - US and by states

PECANS
J of Commerce - W - NY
US Labor Stat Bur - Wholesale Prices & Price Indexes - M

PECAN (WOOD)
Comm Bul - W

PECTIN
Chem Mktg Rptr - W - NY

PEERLESS RUBBER LUBE: NO. 744
Rubber World - SA

PELARGONIC ACID
Chem Mktg Rptr - W - East

PENACOLITE RESIN: B 1A, R-2170
Rubber World - SA

PENBRO
Rubber World - SA

PENICILLIN
US Labor Stat Bur - Wholesale Prices & Price Indexes - M

PENICILLIN: POTASSIUM
Chem Mktg Rptr - W - NY
J of Commerce - W - NY

PENICILLIN: PROCAINE
Chem Mktg Rptr - W - NY
J of Commerce - W - NY

PENNAC
Rubber World - SA

PENNOX: A, A-S, HR, ODP
Rubber World - SA

PENNSTOP
Rubber World - SA

PENNYROYAL HERB
J of Commerce - W - NY

PENNYROYAL OIL
Chem Mktg Rptr - W - NY
J of Commerce - W - NY

PENNZONE: B, E, L
Rubber World - SA

PENTACHLOROPHENOL
Chem Mktg Rptr - W - NY
US Labor Stat Bur - Wholesale Prices & Price Indexes - M

PENTAERYTHRITOL
Am Paint J - W
Chem Mktg Rptr - W - NY
J of Commerce - W - NY
US Labor Stat Bur - Wholesale Prices & Price Indexes - M

PENTALYN: A, H
Rubber World - SA

PENTANE
Chem Mktg Rptr - W - Borger Tex

tert-PENTANOIC ACID
Chem Mktg Rptr - W - NY

PENTOBARBITAL
Chem Mktg Rptr - W - NY
US Labor Stat Bur - Wholesale Prices & Price Indexes - M

COMMODITY PRICES

PENTOBARBITAL-SODIUM
   Chem Mktg Rptr - W - NY

PENTYLENE TETRAZOL
   Chem Mktg Rptr - W - NY

PEPPER
   J of Commerce - W - NY

PEPPER: BLACK
   Chem Mktg Rptr - W - NY
   J of Commerce - W - NY
   Natl Provision - W - Chicago
   Wall Street J - D - NY

PEPPER: BLACK, WHOLE
   US Labor Stat Bur - Wholesale Prices
     & Price Indexes - M

PEPPER: RED
   Chem Mktg Rptr - W - NY
   J of Commerce - W - NY

PEPPER: RED CAYENNE
   Natl Provision - W - Chicago

PEPPER: WHITE
   Chem Mktg Rptr - W - NY
   J of Commerce - W - NY
   Natl Provision - W - Chicago

PEPPERMINT LEAVES
   Chem Mktg Rptr - W - NY
   J of Commerce - W - NY

PEPPERMINT OIL
   Chem Mktg Rptr - W - NY
   J of Commerce - W - NY
   US Labor Stat Bur - Wholesale Prices
     & Price Indexes - M

PEPPERS: FROZEN
   J of Commerce - W

PEPPERS: GREEN
   US Agri Mktg Ser - Fruit & Veg
     Prices - A - Calif, Chicago,
     Fla, NY, Tex
   US Labor Stat Bur - Retail Food
     Prices - M - US and 23 cities
   US Stat Rptg Ser - Agri Prices - M - US

PEPTON: 22, 65B, 65
   Rubber World - SA

PERCH FILLET: FROZEN
   US Labor Stat Bur - Retail Food
     Prices - M - US and 23 cities

PERCHLOROETHYLENE
   Chem Mktg Rptr - W - NY
   J of Commerce - W - NY
   Rubber World - SA

PERI ACID
   Chem Mktg Rptr - W - NY

PERMALUX
   Rubber World - SA

PERMANENT RED
   Chem Mktg Rptr - W - NY

PERMANENT RED 2B
   Am Paint J - W

PERU BALSAM
   Chem Mktg Rptr - W - NY

PET FOOD: DOG
   US Labor Stat Bur - Wholesale Prices
     & Price Indexes - M

PETITGRAIN OIL
   Chem Mktg Rptr - W - NY
   J of Commerce - W - NY

PETROFLUX MV
   Rubber World - SA

PETROLATUM
   Chem Mktg Rptr - W - US

PETROLEUM: CRUDE
   UN Bul Stat - M - US
   US Labor Stat Bur - Wholesale Prices
     & Price Indexes - M

PETROLEUM E
   J of Commerce - W - NY

PETROLEUM ETHER
   Rubber World - SA

COMMODITY PRICES

PETROLEUM PITCH
  Chem Mktg Rptr - W - East Coast

PETROLEUM PRODUCTS
  UN Bul Stat - M - US

PETROLEUM SULFONATE
  Chem Mktg Rptr - W - US

PETROLEUM TOLUENE
  J of Commerce - W - NY

PEWTER: NO. 1
  Comm Bul - W

PEWTER SCRAP
  Second Raw Materials - M - Boston,
  NY, Philadelphia, Toronto

PHENACETIN
  Chem Mktg Rptr - W - NY
  J of Commerce - W - NY
  US Labor Stat Bur - Wholesale Prices
  & Price Indexes - M

o-PHENETIDINE
  Chem Mktg Rptr - W - East

p-PHENETIDINE
  Chem Mktg Rptr - W - NY

PHENOBARBITAL
  Chem Mktg Rptr - W - NY
  J of Commerce - W - NY
  US Labor Stat Bur - Wholesale Prices
  & Price Indexes - M

PHENOBARBITAL-SODIUM
  Chem Mktg Rptr - W - NY

PHENOL
  Chem Mktg Rtpr - W - East
  J of Commerce - W - NY
  US Labor Stat Bur - Wholesale Prices
  & Price Indexes - M

PHENOLICS
  J of Commerce - W - NY
  Mod Pckg-Encyclo & Plan Guide -
  A - US

PHENOLPHTHALEIN
  Chem Mktg Rptr - W - US
  J of Commerce - W - NY

p-PHENOLSULFONIC ACID
  Chem Mktg Rptr - W - NY

PHENOTHIAZINE
  Chem Mktg Rptr - W - US

PHENOXY
  Mod Pckg-Encyclo & Plan Guide - A - US

PHENYLACETALDEHYDE
  Chem Mktg Rptr - W - NY
  J of Commerce - W - NY

PHENYL ACETATE
  Chem Mktg Rptr - W - US

PHENYLACETIC ACID
  Chem Mktg Rptr - W - NY

dl-PHENYLALANINE
  Chem Mktg Rptr - W - NY

1-PHENYL-3-CARBETHOXY
PYRAZALONE-5
  Chem Mktg Rptr - W - East

m-PHENYLENEDIAMINE
  Chem Mktg Rptr - W - NY
  J of Commerce - W - NY

o-PHENYLENEDIAMINE
  Chem Mktg Rptr - W - NY

p-PHENYLENEDIAMINE
  Chem Mktg Rptr - W - NY

PHENYLEPHRINE HYDROCHLORIDE
  Chem Mktg Rptr - W - NY

PHENYLETHYL ACETATE
  Chem Mktg Rptr - W - NY

2-PHENYLETHYL ALCOHOL
  Chem Mktg Rptr - W - NY

b-PHENYLETHYLAMINE
  Chem Mktg Rptr - W - NY

COMMODITY PRICES

PHENYLETHYLPHENYL ACETATE
   Chem Mktg Rptr - W - NY

PHENYLHYDRAZINE
   Chem Mktg Rptr - W - NY

PHENYL MERCURY ACETATE:
LIQUID, POWDER
   Am Paint J - W - NY

PHENYL MERCURY OLEATE
   Am Paint J - W

1-PHENYL-3-METHYL-5-PYRAZOLONE
   Chem Mktg Rptr - W - East

o-PHENYLPHENOL
   Chem Mktg Rptr - W - US

p-PHENYLPHENOL
   Chem Mktg Rptr - W - US

PHENYLPROPANOLAMINE
HYDROCHLORIDE
   Chem Mktg Rptr - W - NY
   US Labor Stat Bur - Wholesale Prices
     & Price Indexes - M

PHENYLSALICYLATE
   Chem Mktg Rptr - W - East

PHLOXINE TONER (RED)
   Chem Mktg Rptr - W - NY

PHOSFLEX: 112, 179A, 179C, 179EG
   Rubber World - SA

PHOSGENE
   Chem Mktg Rptr - W - US

PHOSPHATE ROCK
   Chem Mktg Rptr - W - US
   Eng Min J - M - Fla
   US Labor Stat Bur - Wholesale Prices
     & Price Indexes - M

PHOSPHORIC ACID
   Can Chem Processing - M - Can
   Chem Mktg Rptr - W - US
   J of Commerce - W - NY
   US Labor Stat Bur - Wholesale Prices
     & Price Indexes - M

PHOSPHORUS
   Chem Mktg Rptr - W - US
   US Labor Stat Bur - Wholesale Prices
     & Price Indexes - M

PHOSPHORUS BRONZE
   Iron Age - W

PHOSPHORUS OXYCHLORIDE
   Chem Mktg Rptr - W - US

PHOSPHORUS PENTASULFIDE
   Chem Mktg Rptr - W - US

PHOSPHORUS PENTOXIDE
   Chem Mktg Rptr - W - US

PHOSPHORUS SESQUISULFIDE
   Chem Mktg Rptr - W - US

PHOSPHORUS TRICHLORIDE
   Chem Mktg Rptr - W - US

PHTHALIC ANHYDRIDE
   Am Paint J - W
   Chem Mktg Rptr - W - NY
   J of Commerce - W - NY
   Purch World - M
   US Labor Stat Bur - Wholesale Prices
     & Price Indexes - M

PHTHALIMIDE
   Chem Mktg Rptr - W - NY

PHTHALOCYANINE BLUE B TONER
   Am Paint J - W

PHTHALOCYANINE BLUE TONER
   Chem Mktg Rptr - W - US
   J of Commerce - W - NY
   US Labor Stat Bur - Wholesale Prices
     & Price Indexes - M

PHTHALOCYANINE GREEN B TONER
   Am Paint J - W

PHTHALOCYANINE GREEN TONER
   Chem Mktg Rptr - W - US
   J of Commerce - W - NY

PHTHALYLSULFACETAMIDE
   Chem Mktg Rptr - W - NY

COMMODITY PRICES

PICCO: A-12 PLASTICIZER, A15, A60, AND A700 EMULSIONS, AP RESINS, AROMATIC PLASTICIZERS, D-12 RECLAIMING AGENT, PHENOLIC RESINS
  Rubber World - SA

PICCOCIZER: 30, R
  Rubber World - SA

PICCOFLEX RESINS
  Rubber World - SA

PICCOLASTIC RESINS
  Rubber World - SA

PICCOLYTE RESINS
  Rubber World - SA

PICCOPALE EMULSION: A-1, A-20, A-22, A-41, A-55, C-1, N-3
  Rubber World - SA

PICCOUMARON RESINS
  Rubber World - SA

PICCOVAR RESINS
  Rubber World - SA

PICKLES: FRESH CUCUMBER
  US Labor Stat Bur - Wholesale Prices & Price Indexes - M

a-PICOLINE
  Chem Mktg Rptr - W - US

g-PICOLINE
  Chem Mktg Rptr - W - US

PICRIC ACID
  Chem Mktg Rptr - W - Charlotte NC

PIGEONS
  Lancaster Farm - W - Fogelsville Pa

PIGMENT GREEN
  Chem Mktg Rptr - W - NY

PIGMENT GREEN B
  Am Paint J - W

PIGMENT 33
  Rubber World - SA

PIGS: FEEDER
  Farm & Dairy - W - Ohio
  Free Press Farm - W - Edmonton
  US Agri Mktg Ser - Livestock Mkt News - W - St. Joseph, Sioux Falls, South Mo, Tenn
  US Stat Rptr Ser - Agri Prices Annual Summary - A - US and by states

PIKE: YELLOW, UNPROCESSED
  US Labor Stat Bur - Wholesale Prices & Price Indexes - M

PILOCARPINE HYDROCHLORIDE
  Chem Mktg Rptr - W - NY

PIMENTA OIL
  Chem Mktg Rptr - W

PIMENTO
  Chem Mktg Rptr - W - NY

PIMENTO BERRY OIL
  J of Commerce - W - NY

PIMENTO LEAF OIL
  Chem Mktg Rptr - W - NY
  J of Commerce - W - NY

PINE
  See also PONDEROSA PINE

PINE: FRAMING LUMBER, DROP SIDING
  US Stat Rptg Ser - Agri Prices - Annual Summary - A - US and by states

PINE: YELLOW, FLOORING
  US Stat Rptr Ser - Agri Prices - Annual Summary - A - US and by states

PINEAPPLE: CANNED
  J of Commerce - W
  US Labor Stat Bur - Wholesale Prices & Price Indexes - M

COMMODITY PRICES

PINEAPPLE: PROCESSED
    US Stat Rptg Ser - Agri Prices -
    Annual Summary - A - US and
    by states

PINEAPPLE-GRAPEFRUIT JUICE:
CANNED
    US Labor Stat Bur - Retail Food
    Prices - M - US and 23 cities

PINEAPPLE JUICE: CANNED
    US Labor Stat Bur - Wholesale Prices
    & Price Indexes - M

PINEAPPLES
    US Agri Mktg Ser - Fruit & Veg
    Prices - A - south Tex

p-PINENE
    Chem Mktg Rptr - W - Fla

PINE NEEDLE OIL
    J of Commerce - W - NY

PINE OIL
    Am Paint J - W - NY
    Chem Mktg Rptr - W - NY

PINK ROOT
    J of Commerce - W - NY

PIPERAZINE
    Chem Mktg Rptr - W - East
    J of Commerce - W - NY

PIPERAZINE CITRATE
    Chem Mktg Rptr - W - NY

PIPERAZINE DIHYDROCHLORIDE
    Chem Mktg Rptr - W - NY

PIPERAZINE HEXAHYDRATE
    Chem Mktg Rptr - W - NY

PIPERAZINE PHOSPHATE
    Chem Mktg Rptr - W - NY

PIPERIDINE
    Chem Mktg Rptr - W - US

PIPERONAL
    Chem Mktg Rptr - W - NY
    J of Commerce - W - NY

PIPERONYL BUTOXIDE
    Chem Mktg Rptr - W - East

PITCH: BURGUNDY, HARDWOOD,
STEARIN
    Rubber World - SA

PITCHFORKS
    US Stat Rptg Ser - Agri Prices -
    Annual Summary - A - US and
    by states

PITT-CONSOL: 500, 500NS, 555
ANTIOXIDANT (LIQUID, POWDER)
    Rubber World - SA

PLASTICIZER: LP, MP, MT-511,
OLN, SC
    Rubber World - SA

PLASTIC MOULDING COMPOUNDS
    J of Commerce - W

PLASTICS
    Chem Pur - 13/yr

PLASTIC TUBING
    US Stat Rptg Ser - Agri Prices -
    Annual Summary - A - US and
    by states

PLASTIKATOR: 85, 88, FH, OT
    Rubber World - SA

PLASTOGEN
    Rubber World - SA

PLASTOLEIN
    Rubber World - SA

PLASTOMAG
    Rubber World - SA

PLASTONE
    Rubber World - SA

PLATES: PAPER, EARTHENWARE
    US Stat Rptg Ser - Agri Prices -
    Annual Summary - A - US and
    by states

COMMODITY PRICES

PLATINUM
    Am Met Mkt/Met News – D – US
    Chem Mktg Rptr – W – US
    Eng Min J – M
    Finishers' Mgt – M
    Iron Age – W
    J of Commerce – D – NY
    Met Wk – W
    Min Rec – W
    North Miner – W – US
    NY Times – D – NY
    Oil Dly – D – US
    Purch World – M
    US Labor Stat Bur – Wholesale Prices
        & Price Indexes – M
    Wall Street J – D – NY
    West Miner – M – US

PLIERS
    US Labor Stat Bur – Wholesale Prices
        & Price Indexes – M

PLIOFILM
    Mod Pckg-Encyclo & Plan Guide – A – US

PLOWS: MOLDBOARD
    US Stat Rptg Ser – Agri Prices –
        Annual Summary – A – US and
        by states

PLUMBING FIXTURES
    US Labor Stat Bur – Wholesale Prices
        & Price Indexes – M

PLUMS
    US Agri Mktg Ser – Fruit & Veg
        Prices – A – Calif, Chicago, NY

PLYWOOD
    J of Commerce – D – Chicago
    NY Times – D – Chicago
    Wall Street J – D – Chicago

PLYWOOD: BIRCH
    Comm Bul – W – Boston

PLYWOOD: FIR
    Comm Bul – W – Northeast

PLYWOOD: INTERIOR
    US Stat Rptg Ser – Agri Prices –
        Annual Summary – A – US and
        by states

PLYWOOD: LAUAN
    Comm Bul – W – Boston

PODOPHYLLIN
    J of Commerce – W – NY

POKE ROOT
    J of Commerce – W – NY

POLYAC
    Rubber World – SA

POLY-BD LIQUID RESIN: CS 15, R-45 HT, M
    Rubber World – SA

POLYBUTADIENE PEPTIZER B-17
    Rubber World – SA

POLYCARBONATE
    Mod Pckg-Encyclo & Plan Guide – A – US

POLYCARBONATE RESIN
    J of Commerce – W – NY

POLYCIN
    Rubber World – SA

POLYCIZER: 162, 662-BPA, 332, 532, 632, DBS, 962-DOS
    Rubber World – SA

POLY-CONE: 100X, 125X, 150X, 1000
    Rubber World – SA

POLY-DISPERSIONS
    Rubber World – SA

POLYESTER: FILAMENT YARN
    US Labor Stat Bur – Wholesale Prices
        & Price Indexes – M

POLYESTER: MONOFILAMENT & YARN
    Mod Textiles Mag – M

COMMODITY PRICES

POLYESTER: NONHEAT-SEALING,
HEAT-SEALING, SARAN-COATED
   Mod Pckg-Encyclo & Plan Guide -
     A - US

POLYESTER: STAPLE
   US Labor Stat Bur - Wholesale Prices
    & Price Indexes - M

POLYESTER: STAPLE & TOW
   Mod Textiles Mag - M

POLYESTER BATISTE
   Dly News Rec - D

POLYESTER/COTTON BATISTE
   US Labor Stat Bur - Wholesale Prices
    & Price Indexes - M

POLYESTER/COTTON BROADCLOTH,
GRAY
   US Labor Stat Bur - Wholesale Prices
    & Price Indexes - M

POLYESTER/COTTON POPLIN
   US Labor Stat Bur - Wholesale Prices
    & Price Indexes - M

POLYESTER/COTTON PRINT CLOTH,
GRAY
   US Labor Stat Bur - Wholesale Prices
    & Price Indexes - M

POLYESTER-COTTON YARN
   Dly News Rec - D - NY

POLYESTER DOUBLE KNIT FABRIC
   US Labor Stat Bur - Wholesale Prices
    & Price Indexes - M

POLYESTER FIBER: BATISTE
   J of Commerce - W

POLYESTER MODULUS RAYON
   NY Times - D - NY

POLYESTER NINON
   Dly News Rec - D

POLYESTERS
   J of Commerce - W - NY

POLYETHYLENE
   J of Commerce - W - NY
   Mod Pckg-Encyclo & Plan Guide -
    A - US

POLYETHYLENE-CELLOPHANE
   Mod Pckg-Encyclo & Plan Guide -
    A - US

POLYETHYLENE-POLYESTER
   Mod Pckg-Encyclo & Plan Guide -
    A - US

POLYETHYLENE RESIN
   Purch World - M

POLYETHYLENE SCRAP
   Purch World - M - NY

POLYFAX: #1, 2, 5, 12
   Rubber World - SA

POLYFIL CLAY: 40, 70, 80, DL, FB,
HG90, RB, XB
   Rubber World - SA

POLYGARD
   Rubber World - SA

POLYISOPRENE PEPTIZER IR-3
   Rubber World - SA

POLYLITE
   Rubber World - SA

POLYLUBE
   Rubber World - SA

POLYMEL: ACTISIL C-2, D, DX;
PLASTICIL NS; SUBLAC PX-5
   Rubber World - SA

POLYMERIC PLASTICIZER NP-10
   Rubber World - SA

POLYMYXIN SULFATE
   Chem Mktg Rptr - W - NY

POLYOXYETHYLENE SORBITAN
MONOSTEARATE
   Chem Mktg Rptr - W - US

COMMODITY PRICES

POLYOXYETHYLENE SORBITAN
TRISTEARATE
   Chem Mktg Rptr - W - US

POLYPALE ESTER 10
   Rubber World - SA

POLYPROPYLENE
   J of Commerce - W - NY
   Mod Pckg-Encyclo & Plan Guide -
      A - US
   Purch World - M

POLYSTYRENE
   J of Commerce - W - NY
   Mod Pckg-Encyclo & Plan Guide -
      A - US
   Purch World - M

POLYSTYRENE SCRAP
   Purch World - M - NY

POLYSULFONE
   J of Commerce - W - NY

POLYVINYL ACETATE
   J of Commerce - W - NY
   US Labor Stat Bur - Wholesale Prices
      & Price Indexes - M

POLYVINYL ACETATE: HOMO-
POLYMER EMULSION, COPOLYMER
   Am Paint J - W

POLYVINYL ACETATE FIBER
   See trade-mark: VINYON

POLYVINYL CHLORIDE
   J of Commerce - W - NY

POLY-ZOLE: ADV, AZDN
   Rubber World - SA

PONDEROSA PINE: SELECTS AND
SHOP
   Comm Bul - W

PONDEROSA PINE BOARDS
   Comm Bul - W

PONDEROSA PINE LUMBER: BOARDS
NO. 3, NO. 4
   US Labor Stat Bur - Wholesale Prices
      & Price Indexes - M

PONDEROSA PINE LUMBER: SHOP,
NO. 2
   US Labor Stat Bur - Wholesale Prices
      & Price Indexes - M

PONTIANAK GUM: NUBS, CHIPS
   Am Paint J - W - NY

POPLAR
   Comm Bul - W

POPLAR: NO. 1 COMMON, NO. 2B
COMMON
   US Labor Stat Bur - Wholesale Prices
      & Price Indexes - M

POPPY SEED
   Chem Mktg Rptr - W - NY
   J of Commerce - W - NY

PORK
   US Econ Ser - Mktg & Trans Sit -
      Q - US

PORK: FAT BACKS, CURED
   Natl Provision - W - Chicago

PORK: FRESH
   Natl Provision - W - Chicago

PORK: FROZEN
   Natl Provision - W - Chicago

PORK: FROZEN VARIETY MEATS
   Natl Provision - W - Chicago

PORK AND BEANS: CANNED
   US Labor Stat Bur - Wholesale Prices
      & Price Indexes - M

PORK BELLIES
   Natl Provision - W - Chicago

PORK BELLIES: FRESH
   J of Commerce - D - Chicago

COMMODITY PRICES

PORK BELLIES: FROZEN
   Barron's - W
   Dly Mkt Rec - D - Chicago
   Free Press Farm - W - Chicago
   J of Commerce - D - Chicago
   NY Times - D
   Wall Street J - D - Chicago

PORK CUTS
   Lancaster Farm - W - NY
   US Econ Ser - Livestock Sit - BM - US
   US Labor Stat Bur - Retail Food Prices - M - US and 23 cities
   US Stat Rptg Ser - Agri Prices - Annual Summary - A - US and by states

PORK CUTS: FRESH
   US Agri Mktg Ser - Livestock Mkt News - W - Chicago, East coast, Los Angeles, Midwest

PORK CUTS: SMOKED, BACON
   Calif Farm - S - Los Angeles
   Natl Provision - W - Chicago
   US Labor Stat Bur - Retail Food Prices - M - US and 23 cities
   US Stat Rptr Ser - Agri Prices - Annual Summary - A - US and by states

PORK CUTS: SMOKED, HAM
   J of Commerce - D - NY
   Natl Provision - W - Chicago
   US Agri Mktg Ser - Livestock Mkt News - W - Chicago, East coast, Los Angeles, Midwest
   US Labor Stat Bur - Retail Food Prices - M - US and 23 cities
   US Labor Stat Bur - Wholesale Prices & Price Indexes - M
   US Stat Rptg Ser - Agri Prices - Annual Summary - A - US and by states

PORK LOINS
   Calif Farm - S - Los Angeles
   J of Commerce - D - NY
   Nation's Restaurant - S - East coast, Los Angeles, Midwest
   Neb Farm - S - Chicago

   US Agri Mktg Ser - Livestock Mkt News - W - Chicago, East coast, Los Angeles, Midwest
   US Labor Stat Bur - Wholesale Prices & Price Indexes - M

PORK SAUSAGE
   US Stat Rptg Ser - Agri Prices - Annual Summary - A - US and by states

PORK TRIMMINGS
   US Agri Mktg Ser - Livestock Mkt News - W - Chicago, Colo, East coast, Los Angeles, Midwest
   See also SAUSAGE MATERIALS

PORK VARIETY MEATS
   US Agri Mktg Ser - Livestock Mkt News - W - Chicago, Denver, East, Mo River points, West

POROFON: ADC/R, B 13/CP50, BSH
   Rubber World - SA

POST: WOOD, STEEL (LINE FENCE)
   US Stat Rptg Ser - Agri Prices - Annual Summary - A - US and by states

POTASH
   Eng Min J - M - Carlsbad, Saskatchewan, Trona Calif

POTASH: CAUSTIC
   Can Chem Processing - M - Can
   Chem Mktg Rptr - W - US
   J of Commerce - W - NY
   US Labor Stat Bur - Wholesale Prices & Price Indexes - M

POTASH: MURIATE
   Eng Min J - M
   J of Commerce - W - NY
   US Stat Rptg Ser - Agri Prices - Annual Summary - A - US and by states

POTASH: SULFATE
   Eng Min J - M
   J of Commerce - W - NY

COMMODITY PRICES

POTASSIUM ACETATE
  Chem Mktg Rptr - W - East

POTASSIUM ACID TARTRATE
  Chem Mktg Rptr - W - NY
  J of Commerce - W - NY

POTASSIUM BICARBONATE
  Chem Mktg Rptr - W - NY

POTASSIUM BICHROMATE
  Chem Mktg Rptr - W - US
  J of Commerce - W - NY

POTASSIUM BIFLUORIDE
  Chem Mktg Rptr - W - US

POTASSIUM BITARTRATE
  Chem Mktg Rptr - W - NY
  J of Commerce - W - NY

POTASSIUM BOROHYDRIDE
  Chem Mktg Rptr - W - US

POTASSIUM BROMATE
  Chem Mktg Rptr - W - NY

POTASSIUM BROMIDE
  Chem Mktg Rptr - W - NY
  J of Commerce - W - NY

POTASSIUM CARBONATE
  Chem Mktg Rptr - W - NY
  Finishers' Mgt - M
  J of Commerce - W - NY

POTASSIUM CHLORATE
  Chem Mktg Rptr - W - US
  J of Commerce - W - NY
  US Labor Stat Bur - Wholesale Prices
    & Price Indexes - M

POTASSIUM CHLORIDE
  Chem Mktg Rptr - W - US

POTASSIUM CHLORIDE MURIATE
  US Labor Stat Bur - Wholesale Prices
    & Price Indexes - M

POTASSIUM CHROMATE
  Chem Mktg Rptr - W - US

POTASSIUM CITRATE
  Chem Mktg Rptr - W - NY
  J of Commerce - W - NY

POTASSIUM CYANIDE
  Chem Mktg Rptr - W - East
  Finishers' Mgt - M - NY
  J of Commerce - W - NY

POTASSIUM FLUOBORATE
  Chem Mktg Rptr - W - US

POTASSIUM FLUORIDE
  Chem Mktg Rptr - W - NY

POTASSIUM GLUCONATE
  Chem Mktg Rptr - W - US
  J of Commerce - W - NY

POTASSIUM GUAIACOLSULFONATE
  Chem Mktg Rptr - W - US

POTASSIUM HYDROXIDE
  Can Chem Processing - M - Can
  Chem Mktg Rptr - W - US
  J of Commerce - W - NY
  US Labor Stat Bur - Wholesale Prices
    & Price Indexes - M

POTASSIUM IODIDE
  Chem Mktg Rptr - W - NY
  J of Commerce - W - NY
  US Labor Stat Bur - Wholesale Prices
    & Price Indexes - M

POTASSIUM-MAGNESIUM SULFATE
  Chem Mktg Rptr - W - US

POTASSIUM MANURE SALT
  Chem Mktg Rptr - W - US

POTASSIUM META-BISULFITE
  Chem Mktg Rptr - W - NY

POTASSIUM MURIATE
  Chem Mktg Rptr - W - Carlsbad,
    Trona Calif, Sask Can

POTASSIUM NITRATE
  Chem Mktg Rptr - W - US
  J of Commerce - W - NY

COMMODITY PRICES

POTASSIUM OLEATE
  Rubber World - SA

POTASSIUM OXALATE
  Chem Mktg Rptr - W - NY

POTASSIUM PENTABORATE
  Chem Mktg Rptr - W - US

POTASSIUM PERCHLORATE
  Chem Mktg Rptr - W - US

POTASSIUM PERMANGANATE
  Chem Mktg Rptr - W - US
  J of Commerce - W - NY

POTASSIUM PERSULFATE
  Chem Mktg Rptr - W - US
  J of Commerce - W - NY

POTASSIUM PRUSSIATE
  J of Commerce - W - NY

POTASSIUM PYROPHOSPHATE
  Chem Mktg Rptr - W - US

POTASSIUM SALICYLATE
  Chem Mktg Rptr - W - US

POTASSIUM SILICATE
  Chem Mktg Rptr - W - US

POTASSIUM SILICOFLUORIDE
  Chem Mktg Rptr - W - NY
  Rubber World - SA

POTASSIUM-SODIUM TARTRATE
  Chem Mktg Rptr - W - East

POTASSIUM STANNATE
  Chem Mktg Rptr - W - NY
  Finishers' Mgt - M
  J of Commerce - W - NY

POTASSIUM SULFATE
  Chem Mktg Rptr - W - Carlsbad,
    NY, Ogden Utah, Trona Calif
  US Labor Stat Bur - Wholesale Prices
    & Price Indexes - M

POTASSIUM THIOCYANATE
  Chem Mktg Rptr - W - NY

POTASSIUM TITANATE
  Chem Mktg Rptr - W - US

POTASSIUM-TITANIUM FLUORIDE
  Chem Mktg Rptr - W - US

POTASSIUM-ZIRCONIUM FLUORIDE
  Chem Mktg Rptr - W - US

POTATOES
  Fin Post - W
  Ida Farm - S - Idaho Falls
  Mont Farm - S - Idaho Falls
  Neb Farm - S - Omaha
  NY Times - D - NY
  Ore Farm - S - Klamath Falls
  US Agri Mktg Ser - Fruit & Veg
    Prices - A - Calif, Chicago, Colo,
    Fla, NY, Tex
  US Econ Ser - Mktg & Trans Sit -
    Q - US
  US Labor Stat Bur - Retail Food
    Prices - M - US and 23 cities
  US Stat Rptg Ser - Agri Prices - M -
    US and by states
  US Stat Rptg Ser - Agri Prices -
    Annual Summary - A - US and
    by states
  Utah Farm - S - Idaho Falls
  Wall Street J - D - NY
  Wash Farm - S - Idaho Falls

POTATOES: CALIFORNIA LONG WHITES
  J of Commerce - D - NY

POTATOES: FLORIDA RED BLISS
  J of Commerce - D - NY

POTATOES: FRENCH FRIED, FROZEN
  J of Commerce - W
  US Labor Stat Bur - Retail Food
    Prices - M - US and 23 cities

POTATOES: IDAHO
  Packer - W - Chicago

POTATOES: IDAHO RUSSET
  J of Commerce - D - NY
  Wall Street J - D - Chicago

COMMODITY PRICES

POTATOES: INSTANT MASHED
  US Labor Stat Bur - Retail Food
    Prices - M - US and 23 cities

POTATOES: IRISH
  US Stat Rptg Ser - Agri Prices -
    Annual Summary - A - US and
    by states

POTATOES: LONG WHITE
  US Econ Ser - Veg Sit - Q - Chicago,
    NY

POTATOES: MAINE
  Free Press Farm - W - NY
  Packer - W - NY

POTATOES: MAINE WHITE
  J of Commerce - D - NY

POTATOES: MINNESOTA RED BLISS
  J of Commerce - D - NY

POTATOES: MONTANA RUSSET
  J of Commerce - D - NY

POTATOES: NORTH DAKOTA RED BLISS
  J of Commerce - D - NY

POTATOES: ROUND RED, ROUND WHITE
  US Econ Ser - Veg Sit - Q -
    Chicago, NY

POTATOES: RUSSET
  Calif Farm - S - Klamath basin
  Nation's Restaurant - S - Boston,
    Chicago, NY

POTATOES: SEED
  US Stat Rptg Ser - Agri Prices -
    Annual Summary - A - US and
    by states

POTATOES: SWEET
  See SWEET POTATOES

POTATOES: WASHINGTON RUSSET
  J of Commerce - D - NY

POTATOES: WHITE
  US Labor Stat Bur - Wholesale Prices
    & Price Indexes - M - Chicago,
    Los Angeles, NY

POTATOES: WISCONSIN RUSSET
  J of Commerce - D - NY

POULTRY
  See CHICKENS, PULLETS,
    TURKEYS

POULTRY BY-PRODUCT MEAL
  Chicago Hide - D - Midsouth,
    Southeast
  Fats & Oils - D - Midsouth, Southeast
  Feed Bul - D - Delmarva, Midsouth
  Feedstuffs - W - Atlanta, Baltimore,
    Boston, Kansas City, Los Angeles

PRENOL A
  Rubber World - SA

PRESPERSIONS
  Rubber World - SA

PRETZELS
  US Labor Stat Bur - Retail Food
    Prices - M - US and 23 cities

PRICKLY ASH BARK
  J of Commerce - W - NY

PRINCE CLAY
  Rubber World - SA

PROCAINE HYDROCHLORIDE
  Chem Mktg Rptr - W - NY

PROCESS STIFFENER 710
  Rubber World - SA

PRODUCT GL1
  Rubber World - SA

PROPANE
  J of Commerce - D
  Oil Dly - D - NY

b-PROPIOLACTONE
  Chem Mktg Rptr - W - US

COMMODITY PRICES

PROPIONATE
    Mod Pckg-Encyclo & Plan Guide - A - US

PROPIONIC ACID
    Chem Mktg Rptr - W - East

PROPYL ACETATE
    Am Paint J - W

n-PROPYL ACETATE
    Chem Mktg Rptr - W - NY

PROPYL ALCOHOL
    Am Paint J - W
    J of Commerce - W - NY

n-PROPYL ALCOHOL
    Chem Mktg Rptr - W - NY

n-PROPYLAMINE
    Chem Mktg Rptr - W - NY

PROPYLENE
    Chem Mktg Rptr - W - Tex and La Gulf coast

PROPYLENE DICHLORIDE
    Rubber World - SA

n-PROPYLENE DICHLORIDE
    Chem Mktg Rptr - W - East

PROPYLENE GLYCOL
    Chem Mktg Rptr - W - East
    J of Commerce - W - NY
    US Labor Stat Bur - Wholesale Prices & Price Indexes - M

PROPYLENE GLYCOL MONOMETHYL ETHER
    Chem Mktg Rptr - W - East

PROPYLENE OXIDE
    Chem Mktg Rptr - W - US

n-PROPYL GALLATE
    Chem Mktg Rptr - W - US

n-PROPYL-p-HYDROXYBENZOATE
    Chem Mktg Rptr - W - NY

PROPYL THIOURACIL
    Chem Mktg Rptr - W - NY

PROPYL ZITHATE
    Rubber World - SA

PROTAMON S
    Rubber World - SA

PROTATEK A-155
    Rubber World - SA

PROTEKTOR: NORMAL, G-HAY 3108
    Rubber World - SA

PROTOL: 3888, 4328
    Rubber World - SA

PRUNE JUICE: CANNED
    US Labor Stat Bur - Wholesale Prices & Price Indexes - M

PRUNES
    US Agri Mktg Ser - Fruit & Veg Prices - A - Chicago, Ida, Mich, NY, Wash
    US Labor Stat Bur - Wholesale Prices & Price Indexes - M

PRUNES: DRIED
    J of Commerce - W

PSEUDOCUMENE
    Chem Mktg Rptr - W - NY

PSYLLIUM HUSKS
    J of Commerce - W - NY

PSYLLIUM SEED
    Chem Mktg Rptr - W - NY
    J of Commerce - W - NY

PULLETS
    Lancaster Farm - W - Fogelsville Pa

PULSATILLA LEAVES
    J of Commerce - W - NY

PULSES
    Comm Rev - W - US

COMMODITY PRICES

PUMICE
  Chem Mktg Rptr - W - NY
  Rubber World - SA

PUMICE STONE
  Am Paint J - W

PURECAL: O, SC, T, U
  Rubber World - SA

PYRAX: A, B, WA
  Rubber World - SA

PYRAZOLONE RED
  Chem Mktg Rptr - W - US

PYRETHRUM
  Chem Mktg Rptr - W - US
  J of Commerce - W - NY

PYRETHRUM FLOWERS
  Chem Mktg Rptr - W - NY
  US Labor Stat Bur - Wholesale Prices
    & Price Indexes - M

PYRIDINE
  Chem Mktg Rptr - W - NY
  J of Commerce - W - NY

PYRIDOXINE
  J of Commerce - W - NY

PYRIDOXINE HYDROCHLORIDE
  Chem Mktg Rptr - W - NY

PYRITES
  Chem Mktg Rptr - W - NY
  Eng Min J - M - Climax Colo

PYROGALLIC ACID
  J of Commerce - W - NY

PYROGALLOL
  Chem Mktg Rptr - W- NY

PYROPHYLLITE
  Rubber World - SA

Q

QDO
  Rubber World - SA

QUARTZ ROCK CRYSTALS
  Eng Min J - M

QUASSIA
  J of Commerce - W - NY

QUASSIA CHIPS
  Chem Mktg Rptr - W - NY

QUEBRACHO EXTRACT
  J of Commerce - W - NY

QUEEN CLAY
  Rubber World - SA

QUERCITRON EXTRACT
  J of Commerce - W - NY

QUICKLIME
  Can Chem Processing - M - Can
  Chem Mktg Rptr - W - East

QUICKSILVER
  See MERCURY

QUIKOTE
  Rubber World - SA

QUINACRIDONE: RED, SCARLET, MAROON, VIOLET
  Chem Mktg Rptr - W - NY

QUINACRIDONE PIGMENT: RED
  US Labor Stat Bur - Wholesale Prices
    & Price Indexes - M

QUINCE SEED
  Chem Mktg Rptr - W - NY
  J of Commerce - W - NY

QUINCY-1
  Rubber World - SA

COMMODITY PRICES

QUINIDINE SULFATE
Chem Mktg Rptr - W - NY
J of Commerce - W - NY

QUININE HYDROCHLORIDE
Chem Mktg Rptr - W - NY
J of Commerce - W - NY

QUININE SULFATE
Chem Mktg Rptr - W - NY
J of Commerce - W - NY

QUINOLINE
Chem Mktg Rptr - W - NY

p-QUINONEDIOXIME
Rubber World - SA

R

R: 95, 97, 97-S, 99-S
Rubber World - SA

RABBITS
Lancaster Farm - W - Fogelsville Pa

RABBITS: READY-TO-COOK
US Cons & Mktg Ser - Poultry Mkt Stat - A - Los Angeles, San Francisco

RADIATORS (SCRAP)
Second Raw Materials - M - Boston, Buffalo, Montreal

RADIOS: CLOCK, PORTABLE TRANSISTOR
US Stat Rptg Ser - Agri Prices - Annual Summary - A - US and by states

RADISHES
US Agri Mktg Ser - Fruit & Veg Prices - A - Chicago, NY

RAGS: OSNABURG CUTTINGS
Purch World - M - NY

RAGS: ROOFING
Purch World - M

RAGS: WHITE WIPERS
Purch World - M - NY

RAISINS: DRIED
J of Commerce - W
US Labor Stat Bur - Wholesale Prices & Price Indexes - M

RANGE OIL
Platt's - D - Chicago, St. Louis, Minneapolis/St. Paul

RANGES: GAS, ELECTRIC
US Stat Rptg Ser - Agri Prices - Annual Summary - A - US and by states

RAPESEED
Dly Mkt Rec - D - Winnipeg
Fin Post - W - Thunder Bay, Vancouver
Fin Times Can - W - Winnipeg
Free Press Farm - W - Thunder Bay, Vancouver
J of Commerce - D - Winnipeg
Wall Street J - D - Winnipeg
West Producer - W - Winnipeg

RAPESEED OIL
Chem Mktg Rptr - W - NY
J of Commerce - D
US Econ Ser - Fats & Oils Sit - 5/yr - NY

RASPBERRIES
US Agri Mktg Ser - Fruit & Veg Prices - A - Mich, NJ, NY

RAUWOLFIA SERPENTINA
J of Commerce - W - NY

RAUWOLFIA SERPENTINA ROOT
Chem Mktg Rptr - W - NY

RAYON: STAPLE & TOW
Mod Textiles Mag - M

COMMODITY PRICES

RAYON: TIRE FABRIC
   US Labor Stat Bur - Wholesale Prices
     & Price Indexes - M

RAYON ACETATE
   See ACETATE

RAYON CHALLIS GRAY GOODS
   Dly News Rec - D
   J of Commerce - W

RAYON FILAMENT YARN
   US Econ Ser - Stat Cotton - A - US

RAYON GRAY GOODS: LINEN EFFECT
   J of Commerce - W
   US Labor Stat Bur - Wholesale Prices
     & Price Indexes - M

RAYON GRAY GOODS: LINING TWILL
   US Labor Stat Bur - Wholesale Prices
     & Price Indexes - M

RAYON GRAY GOODS: TWILL
   Purch World - M - NY

RAYON STAPLE
   US Econ Ser - Stat Cotton - A - US

RAYON YARN
   Mod Textiles Mag - M
   UN Bul Stat - M - US

RAYON YARN: VISCOSE, WEAVING
   US Labor Stat Bur - Wholesale Prices
     & Price Indexes - M

RC: 17 CLAY, 32 CLAY
   Rubber World - SA

R-2 CRYSTALS
   Rubber World - SA

RECCO CLAY
   Rubber World - SA

REDAX
   Rubber World - SA

RED CLOVER SEED
   US Stat Rptg Ser - Agri Prices -
     Annual Summary - A - US and
     by states

RED DOG
   Dly Mkt Rec - D - Minneapolis

RED OIL
   J of Commerce - D
   Rubber World - SA

RED OXIDE
   J of Commerce - W - NY

REDWOOD
   Comm Bul - W

REDWOOD LUMBER: BOARDS, BEVEL SIDING
   US Labor Stat Bur - Wholesale Prices
     & Price Indexes - M

REFRIGERATORS
   US Stat Rptg Ser - Agri Prices -
     Annual Summary - A - US and
     by states

RELISH: SWEET PICKLE
   US Labor Stat Bur - Retail Food
     Prices - M - US and 23 cities

RENEX 600 SERIES
   Rubber World - SA

REOGEN
   Rubber World - SA

REOGEN HF
   Rubber World - SA

RESERPINE
   Chem Mktg Rptr - W - NY
   J of Commerce - W - NY
   US Labor Stat Bur - Wholesale Prices
     & Price Indexes - M

RESIN: 731D, 7000, EMULSION P-370
   Rubber World - SA

COMMODITY PRICES

RESINEX: L-4, 100, RESINS
    Rubber World - SA

RESORCINOL
    Chem Mktg Rptr - W - US
    J of Commerce - W - NY
    Rubber World - SA

RESORCINOL MONOACETATE
    Chem Mktg Rptr - W - NY

RETARDER: AK, BA, ESEN, J, PD, W, 2N
    Rubber World - SA

RETROCURE
    Rubber World - SA

REXANOL
    Rubber World - SA

RGB BLOWING AGENT
    Rubber World - SA

RHATANY ROOT
    J of Commerce - W - NY

RHC
    J of Commerce - W - NY

RHENIUM
    Eng Min J - M
    Met Wk - W

RHODAMINE RED TONER
    Chem Mktg Rptr - W - US

RHODINOL
    Chem Mktg Rptr - W - NY

RHODIUM
    Am Met Mkt/Met News - D - US
    Eng Min J - M
    Finishers' Mgt - M
    Iron Age - W
    Met Wk - W

RHOPLEX: AC-33, B-15, E-32
    Rubber World - SA

RHUBARB
    US Agri Mktg Ser - Fruit & Veg Prices - A - NY

RHUBARB ROOT
    Chem Mktg Rptr - W - NY
    J of Commerce - W - NY

RIA: CS, NC
    Rubber World - SA

RIBOFLAVIN
    Chem Mktg Rptr - W - NY
    J of Commerce - W - NY

RIBOFLAVIN 5-PHOSPHATE SODIUM
    Chem Mktg Rptr - W - NY

RICE
    J of Commerce - W
    US Econ Ser - Demand Sit - Q - US
    US Labor Stat Bur - Retail Food Prices - M - US and 23 cities
    US Labor Stat Bur - Wholesale Prices & Price Indexes - M
    US Stat Rptg Ser - Agri Prices - M - US and by states
    US Stat Rptg Ser - Agri Prices - Annual Summary - A - Ark, Calif, La, Miss, Mo, Tex, US

RICE: NO. 1 MILLED
    Calif Farm - S - Calif

RICE BRAN
    Calif Farm - S - northern Calif
    Feedstuffs - W - Atlanta, Memphis, San Francisco, Stuttgart Ark
    US Agri Mktg Ser - Feed Mkt News - W - Ark, Calif, La, Tex

RICE BRAN OIL
    Chem Mktg Rptr - W - NY

RICE MILLFEEDS
    Feedstuffs - W - Atlanta, Memphis, Stuttgart Ark

RICINOLEIC ACID
    Rubber World - SA

RIDACTO ACID
    Rubber World - SA

COMMODITY PRICES

RIFLE: REPEATING, CENTER FIRE AND RIM FIRE
   US Labor Stat Bur - Wholesale Prices & Price Indexes - M

RIO RESIN
   Rubber World - SA

ROASTERS
   Lancaster Farm - W - Fogelsville Pa
   US Cons & Mktg Ser - Poultry Mkt Stat - A - Boston, Chicago, Los Angeles, San Francisco

ROASTERS: READY-TO-COOK, ICED
   US Cons & Mktg Ser - Poultry Mkt Stat - A - NY

ROCKERS: SWIVEL, UPHOLSTERED
   US Stat Rptg Ser - Agri Prices - Annual Summary - A - US and by states

RODO: NO. 0, NO. 4, NO. 10
   Rubber World - SA

ROOFING: COMPOSITION MINERAL SURFACE, GALVANIZED STEEL
   US Stat Rptg Ser - Agri Prices - Annual Summary - A - US and by states

ROOT BEER
   Alaska Bev Analyst - M - Alaska

ROPE: MANILA
   US Stat Rptg Ser - Agri Prices - Annual Summary - A - US and by states

ROSE BUDS
   J of Commerce - W - NY

ROSEMARY LEAVES
   J of Commerce - W - NY

ROSEMARY OIL
   Chem Mktg Rptr - W - NY
   J of Commerce - W - NY

ROSE OIL
   Chem Mktg Rptr - W - NY
   J of Commerce - W - NY

ROSIN
   Purch World - M - NY

ROSIN: WOOD
   Rubber World - SA

ROTAX
   Rubber World - SA

ROTENONE RESIN
   Chem Mktg Rptr - W - NY

ROVALAC: 133, 134
   Rubber World - SA

RPA: 2, 3, 3 CONCENTRATED, 6
   Rubber World - SA

RR-10
   Rubber World - SA

R SALT
   Chem Mktg Rptr - W - US
   J of Commerce - W - NY

RT-3
   Rubber World - SA

RUBBER
   J of Commerce - D - NY
   UN Bul Stat - M - US

RUBBER: NATURAL
   US Labor Stat Bur - Wholesale Prices & Price Indexes - M

RUBBER: NO. 1 RIBBED SMOKED SHEETS
   Purch World - M - NY

RUBBER: NO. 1 STANDARD, RIB-SMOKED SHEETS
   NY Times - D - NY

RUBBER: PERFUMES
   Rubber World - SA

COMMODITY PRICES

RUBBER: RECLAIMED
   US Labor Stat Bur - Wholesale Prices
    & Price Indexes - M

RUBBER: SMOKED SHEETS
   Barron's - W - NY
   Wall Street J - D - NY

RUBBER: SYNTHETIC
   US Labor Stat Bur - Wholesale Prices
    & Price Indexes - M

RUBBER CEMENT
   US Labor Stat Bur - Wholesale Prices
    & Price Indexes - M

RUBBER COATING 24
   Rubber World - SA

RUBBEROL COMPOUND
   Rubber Wrold - SA

RUBBER SCRAP
   J of Commerce - W
   Purch World - M - East

RUBBER SOLVENT
   Chem Mktg Rptr - W - NJ, NY,
    Houston
   Rubber World - SA

RUE HERB
   J of Commerce - W - NY

RUE OIL
   J of Commerce - W - NY

RUM
   Alaska Bev Analyst - M - Alaska
   Ariz Bev J - M - Ariz
   Bev Media - M - NY
   Bev News - M
   Buck Bev J - M - Ohio
   Ill Bev J - M - Ill
   Ky Bev J - M - Ky
   Md-Wash-Del Bev J - M - Md, DC,
    Del
   Mich Bev News - IR - Mich
   Patterson's - M - Calif
   RI Bev J - M - RI
   Wis Bev J - M - Wis

RUM: IMPORTED
   NJ Bev J - M - NJ

RUM: FLAVORED
   Ariz Bev J - M - Ariz

RUTHENIUM
   Am Met Mkt/Met News - W - US
   Eng Min J - M
   Met Wk - W

RUTIN
   J of Commerce - W - NY

RYE
   Dly Mkt Rec - D - Minneapolis,
    Winnipeg
   Fin Post - W - Winnipeg
   Free Press Farm - W - Winnipeg
   J of Commerce - D - Minneapolis,
    Winnipeg
   US Econ Ser - Wheat Sit - Q -
    US markets
   US Stat Rptg Ser - Agri Prices - M -
    US and by states
   US Stat Rptg Ser - Agri Prices -
    Annual Summary - A - US and
    by states
   Wall Street J - D - Winnipeg
   West Producer - W - Winnipeg

RYE: NO. 2
   Barron's - W - Minneapolis
   NY Times - D - Minneapolis
   US Agri Mktg Ser - Grain Mkt News -
    W - Minneapolis
   US Labor Stat Bur - Wholesale Prices
    & Price Indexes - M
   Wall Street J - D - Minneapolis

RYE: SEED
   US Stat Rptg Ser - Agri Prices -
    Annual Summary - A - US and
    by states

RYEGRASS SEED
   Seed World - A - US and by states
   US Stat Rptg Ser - Agri Prices -
    Annual Summary - A - US and
    by states

COMMODITY PRICES

RYE WHISKEY
See WHISKEY: RYE

RZ-100
Rubber World - SA

S

SABADILLA POWDER
J of Commerce - W - NY

SACCHARIN
Chem Mktg Rptr - W - NY
J of Commerce - W - NY

S ACID
Chem Mktg Rptr - W - US

SAFFLOWER
US Agri Mktg Ser - Feed Mkt News - W - Los Angeles, San Francisco

SAFFLOWER MEAL
Feedstuffs - W - Los Angeles, San Francisco

SAFFLOWER OIL
Am Paint J - W - Chicago, East coast, San Francisco
Chem Mktg Rptr - W - NY
J of Commerce - D
US Econ Ser - Fats & Oils Sit - 5/yr - NY

SAFFRON FLOWERS
J of Commerce - W - NY

SAFROL
J of Commerce - W - NY

SAG: 470 SILICONE ANTIFOAM FLUID, 470 SILICONE ANTIFOAM EMULSION
Rubber World - SA

SAGE
J of Commerce - W - NY
Natl Provision - W - Chicago

SAGE LEAVES
Chem Mktg Rptr - W - NY

SAGE OIL
Chem Mktg Rptr - W - NY
J of Commerce - W - NY

ST. JOHN'S BREAD
Chem Mktg Rptr - W - NY

SAKE
Bev Media - M - NY
Ill Bev J - M - Ill
Md-Wash-Del Bev J - M - Md, DC, Del
Patterson's - M - Calif

SALAD DRESSING
US Stat Rptg Ser - Agri Prices - Annual Summary - A - US and by states

SALAD DRESSING: ITALIAN
US Econ Ser - Fats & Oils Sit - 5/yr - US
US Labor Stat Bur - Retail Food Prices - M - US and 23 cities

SALAD DRESSING: MAYONNAISE
US Labor Stat Bur - Wholesale Prices & Price Indexes - M

SALAD OIL
US Econ Ser - Fats & Oils Sit - 5/yr - US
US Labor Stat Bur - Retail Food Prices - M - US and 23 cities
US Labor Stat Bur - Wholesale Prices & Price Indexes - M

SAL AMMONIAC
J of Commerce - W - NY

SALICYLALDEHYDE
Chem Mktg Rptr - W - NY

SALICYLAMIDE
Chem Mktg Rptr - W - NY

SALICYLIC ACID
Chem Mktg Rptr - W - NY
J of Commerce - W - NY
US Labor Stat Bur - Wholesale Prices & Price Indexes - M

COMMODITY PRICES

SALMON
    US Stat Rptg Ser – Agri Prices –
    Annual Summary – A – US and
    by states

SALMON: CANNED
    J of Commerce – W
    US Labor Stat Bur – Wholesale Prices
    & Price Indexes – M

SALMON: UNPROCESSED
    US Labor Stat Bur – Wholesale Prices
    & Price Indexes – M

SALT
    Chem Mktg Rptr – W – US
    J of Commerce – W – NY
    Natl Provision – W – Chicago

SALT: ROCK
    US Labor Stat Bur – Wholesale Prices
    & Price Indexes – M

SALT: STOCK
    US Stat Rptg Ser – Agri Prices –
    Annual Summary – A – US and
    by states

SALTCAKE
    Chem Mktg Rptr – W – US

SALTPETER
    Chem Mktg Rptr – W – US
    J of Commerce – W – NY

SAND: CONSTRUCTION
    US Labor Stat Bur – Wholesale Prices
    & Price Indexes – M

SANDALWOOD OIL
    Chem Mktg Rptr – W – NY
    J of Commerce – W – NY

SANDARAC GUM
    J of Commerce – W – NY

SANTICIZER: 140, 141, 165, B-16,
E-15, M-17
    Rubber World – SA

SANTOCURE
    Rubber World – SA

SANTOCURE: 26, MOR, MOR-90,
NS, NS-50
    Rubber World – SA

SANTOFLEX
    Rubber World – SA

SANTOGARD PVI
    Rubber World – SA

SANTOVAR A
    Rubber World – SA

SANTOWHITE: 54, 54S
    Rubber World – SA

SARAN
    Mod Pckg-Encyclo & Plan Guide –
    A – US

SARAN: MONOFILAMENT
    Mod Textiles Mag – M

SARCOSINE
    Chem Mktg Rptr – W – US

SARDINES: CANNED
    J of Commerce – W
    US Labor Stat Bur – Retail Food
    Prices – M – US and 23 cities
    US Labor Stat Bur – Wholesale Prices
    & Price Indexes – M

SARKOSYL NL-30
    Rubber World – SA

SARSAPARILLA ROOT
    J of Commerce – W – NY

SARTOMER: SR-206, 297, 350,
SARET 500, 515
    Rubber World – SA

SASSAFRAS BARK
    J of Commerce – W – NY

SASSAFRAS OIL
    J of Commerce – W – NY

SATIN
    See ACETATE SATIN GRAY GOODS

COMMODITY PRICES

SATINTONE: 1, 2, SPECIAL
    Rubber World - SA

SAUERKRAUT: CANNED
    J of Commerce - W

SAUSAGE CASINGS
    Natl Provision - W

SAUSAGE MATERIALS: FRESH
    Natl Provision - W - Chicago

SAUSAGES
    US Labor Stat Bur - Retail Food
       Prices - M - US and 23 cities

SAUSAGES: DOMESTIC
    Natl Provision - W - Chicago

SAUSAGES: DRY
    Natl Provision - W - Chicago

SCAMMONY ROOT
    J of Commerce - W - NY

SC 25 CLAY
    Rubber World - SA

SCHAEFFER'S SALT
    Chem Mktg Rptr - W - NY
    J of Commerce - W - NY

SCHENECTADY
    Rubber World - SA

SCOPOLAMINE HYDROBROMIDE
    Chem Mktg Rptr - W - NY

SCORCHGUARD "O"
    Rubber World - SA

SCOTCH WHISKEY
    See WHISKEY: SCOTCH

SCOURING POWDER
    US Stat Rptg Ser - Agri Prices -
       Annual Summary - A - US and
       by states

SCRAP: NONFERROUS
    US Labor Stat Bur - Wholesale Prices
       & Price Indexes - M

SCREENINGS
    Feedstuffs - W - Buffalo, Chicago,
       Kansas City, Minneapolis, St. Paul

SCREW DRIVER
    US Labor Stat Bur - Wholesale Prices
       & Price Indexes - M

SEBACIC ACID
    Chem Mktg Rptr - W - US

SECCO CLAY
    Rubber World - SA

SEEDINE
    Rubber World - SA

SEEDS
    J of Commerce - W

SELDLITZ MIXTURE
    Chem Mktg Rptr - W - NY

SELENAC ETHYL
    Rubber World - SA

SELENAC METHYL
    Rubber World - SA

SELENIUM
    Chem Mktg Rptr - W - NY
    Eng Min J - M
    Met Wk - W

SELENIUM POWDER
    Am Met Mkt/Met News - D - US

SENEGA ROOT
    J of Commerce - W - NY

SENNA LEAVES
    Chem Mktg Rptr - W - NY
    J of Commerce - W - NY

SEPARATING AGENT
    Rubber World - SA

SEQUESTRENE: 30A, AA, NA3
    Rubber World - SA

SERPENTARIA
    J of Commerce - W - NY

COMMODITY PRICES

SESAME
    Natl Provision - W - Chicago

SESAME OIL
    Chem Mktg Rptr - W - NY
    US Econ Ser - Fats & Oils Sit - 5/yr - NY

SESAME SEED
    Chem Mktg Rptr - W - NY
    J of Commerce - W - NY

SETSIT: 5, 51, 9
    Rubber World - SA

SEWING MACHINES: PORTABLE, WITH CASE
    US Stat Rptg Ser - Agri Prices - Annual Summary - A - US and by states

SF-96
    Rubber World - SA

SHEEP
    US Econ Ser - Livestock Sit - BM - San Angelo

SHEEP AND LAMBS
    Farm & Dairy - W - Ohio
    Free Press Farm - W - Montreal, Saskatoon, Toronto, Winnipeg
    Ida Farm - S - Northwest
    Lancaster Farm - W - Lancaster, New Holland Pa
    Mont Farm - S - Northwest
    Ore Farm - S - Midwest, Northwest
    US Stat Rptg Ser - Agri Prices - M - US and by states
    US Stat Rptg Ser - Agri Prices - Annual Summary - A - US and by states
    US Stat Rptg Ser Wis - Prices Received - M - Wis
    Utah Farm - S - Northwest
    Wash Farm - S
    Wool Sack - M - St. Paul

SHEEPS AND LAMBS: LIVESTOCK
    Man Co-op - W
    Natl Provision - W - Chicago, Omaha, St. Paul, Sioux City

SHEEP PELTS
    US Agri Mktg Ser - Livestock Mkt News - W - US

SHEEPSKINS
    Am Shoe - W
    Leather & Shoes - W

SHEETS: COTTON
    US Labor Stat Bur - Wholesale Prices & Price Indexes - M

SHEETS: PERCALE
    US Stat Rptg Ser - Agri Prices - Annual Summary - A - US and by states

SHELLAC
    J of Commerce - W - NY
    Rubber World - SA
    US Labor Stat Bur - Wholesale Prices & Price Indexes - M

SHELLAC: BLEACHED, BONE-DRY
    Chem Mktg Rptr - W - NY

SHELLAC: BLEACHED, BONE-DRY REFINED
    Am Paint J - W - NY

SHELLAC: BONE-DRY
    Purch World - M - NY

SHELLAC: HIGH GRADE ORANGE, LEMON NOS. 1 & 2, SUPERFINE ORANGE
    Am Paint J - W - NY

SHELLAC: ORANGE
    J of Commerce - W - NY

SHELLAC: ORANGE LEMON
    Chem Mktg Rptr - W - NY

SHELLAC: WHITE, BONE-DRY, REFINED BLEACHED, BUTTON NO. 1, LEMON NO. 1, SUPERFINE
    J of Commerce - W - NY

COMMODITY PRICES

SHINGLES: ASPHALT 3 IN 1 MINERAL SURFACE; WOOD, CEDAR
US Stat Rptg Ser - Agri Prices - Annual Summary - A - US and by states

SHINGLE STAIN OIL
Chem Mktg Rptr - W - US

SHIPLAP: COMMON PINE
US Stat Rptg Ser - Agri Prices - Annual Summary - A - US and by states

SHIRTS: MEN'S, BOYS'
US Labor Stat Bur - Wholesale Prices & Price Indexes - M

SHIRTS: MEN'S, DRESS
US Stat Rptg Ser - Agri Prices - Annual Summary - A - US and by states

SHIRTS: MEN'S, SPORT
US Stat Rptg Ser - Agri Prices - Annual Summary - A - US and by states

SHIRTS: MEN'S, WORK
US Labor Stat Bur - Wholesale Prices & Price Indexes - M
US Stat Rptg Ser - Agri Prices - Annual Summary - A - US and by states

SHORTENING
US Econ Ser - Fats & Oils Sit - 5/yr - Eastern US, NY
US Labor Stat Bur - Wholesale Prices & Price Indexes - M
US Stat Rptg Ser - Agri Prices - Annual Summary - A - US and by states

SHORTENING: HYDROGENATED
Natl Provision - W

SHORTENING: STANDARD
Natl Provision - W

SHORTS: GRAY
US Stat Rptg Ser - Agri Prices - Annual Summary - A - US and by states

SHOT GUNS
US Labor Stat Bur - Wholesale Prices & Price Indexes - M

SHOVELS
US Labor Stat Bur - Wholesale Prices & Price Indexes - M

SHOVELS: STEEL SCOOP
US Stat Rptg Ser - Agri Prices - Annual Summary - A - US and by states

SHRIMP: FRESH, RAW BREADED FROZEN
US Labor Stat Bur - Wholesale Prices & Price Indexes - M

SHRIMP: FROZEN
US Labor Stat Bur - Retail Food Prices - M - US and 23 cities
US Labor Stat Bur - Wholesale Prices & Price Indexes - M

SIENNA: AMERICAN, BURNT POWDERED, RAW POWDERED
Am Paint J - W
J of Commerce - W - NY

SIENNA: ITALIAN, BURNT POWDERED
Am Paint J - W

SIENNA PIGMENT
Chem Mktg Rptr - W - US

SIERRA TALC
Rubber World - SA

SILACTO
Rubber World - SA

SILCRON
Rubber World - SA

COMMODITY PRICES

SILENE: D, EF, L
   Rubber World - SA

SILICA
   Rubber World - SA
   US Labor Stat Bur - Wholesale Prices
    & Price Indexes - M

SILICA: AMORPHOUS
   Am Paint J - W
   Chem Mktg Rptr - W - NY
   Eng Min J - M - Ark, III

SILICA: COLLOIDAL, CRYSTALLINE
   Am Paint J - W

SILICA: HARD-QUARTZ
   Chem Mktg Rptr - W - US

SILICOMANGANESE
   Eng Min J - M
   Met Wk - W

SILICON
   Met Wk - W

SILICON TETRACHLORIDE
   Chem Mktg Rptr - W - US

SILICONE GUM SOLUTIONS:
UNION CARBIDE W5-95 & -951
   Rubber World - SA

SILICONE OIL: UNION CARBIDE
L-45
   Rubber World - SA

SILICONE OIL EMULSIONS: UNION
CARBIDE LE-45, -45, & -450
   Rubber World - SA

SILICONE RUBBER BLEMSIL: SE 440,
SE 880
   Rubber World - SA

SILICONE RUBBER CURING
COMPOUND: UNION CARBIDE
K-1960
   Rubber World - SA

SILK: RAW
   J of Commerce - D - NY

SILREX: 15, S-1
   Rubber World - SA

SILVER
   Am Met Mkt/Met News - D - US
   Barron's - W - NY
   Can Min J - M - NY
   Eng Min J - M
   Fin Times Can - W
   Finishers' Mgt - M
   J of Commerce - D
   Met Wk - W
   Min Rec - W - NY
   North Miner - W - NY, Toronto
   NY Times - D - NY
   Purch World - M - NY
   Wall Street J - D - Chicago, NY
   West Miner - M - Can, US

SILVER: BARS
   US Labor Stat Bur - Wholesale Prices
    & Price Indexes - M

SILVER: BULLION
   Chem Mktg Rptr - W - NY

SILVER COIN
   J of Commerce - D
   Wall Street J - D - NY

SILVER CYANIDE
   Chem Mktg Rptr - W - NY
   J of Commerce - W - NY

SILVER INGOT
   Chem Mktg Rptr - W - NY
   Iron Age - W

SILVER NITRATE
   Chem Mktg Rptr - W - NY
   J of Commerce - W - NY
   US Labor Stat Bur - Wholesale Prices
    & Price Indexes - M

SIMARUBA BARK
   J of Commerce - W - NY

SISAL
   J of Commerce - W - NY

COMMODITY PRICES

SKINS: NYC TRIM
   Chicago Hide - D
   Hide & Leather Bul - D

SKIRTS: WOOL AND WOOL BLENDS, WOMEN'S
   US Stat Rptg Ser - Agri Prices -
     Annual Summary - A - US and
     by states

SLAB DIP #150
   Rubber World - SA

SLIPPERS
   See FOOTWEAR

SM: -55, -62, -2028, -2039, -2040, -2060, -2050
   Rubber World - SA

SNOBRITE CLAY
   Rubber World - SA

SNOWFLAKE WHITE
   Rubber World - SA

SNOW-WHITE OZAKERITE: 4, 160, 180
   Rubber World - SA

SNUFF
   US Labor Stat Bur - Wholesale Prices
     & Price Indexes - M

SOAP
   US Labor Stat Bur - Wholesale Prices
     & Price Indexes - M
   US Stat Rptg Ser - Agri Prices -
     Annual Summary - A - US and
     by states

SOAP BARK
   Chem Mktg Rptr - W - NY
   J of Commerce - W - NY

SOAP CHIPS NO. 538
   Rubber World - SA

SOCKS: MEN'S, WORK
   US Stat Rptg Ser - Agri Prices-
     Annual Summary - A - US and
     by states

SODA: ASH
   Can Chem Processing - M - Can
   Chem Mktg Rptr - W - US
   Finishers' Mgt - M
   J of Commerce - W - NY
   Purch World - M

SODA: CAUSTIC
   Can Chem Processing - M - Can
   Chem Mktg Rptr - W - US
   Finishers' Mgt - M - NY
   J of Commerce - W - NY
   Purch World - M
   Rubber World - SA
   US Labor Stat Bur - Wholesale Prices
     & Price Indexes - M

SODA: SAL
   Chem Mktg Rptr - W - US
   J of Commerce - W - NY

SODA BROMIDE
   J of Commerce - W - NY

SODIUM: METALLIC
   Chem Mktg Rptr - W - US

SODIUM ACETATE
   Chem Mktg Rptr - W - US
   J of Commerce - W - NY
   Rubber World - SA

SODIUM ALGINATE
   Chem Mktg Rptr - W - NY

SODIUM P-AMINOSALICYLATE
   Chem Mktg Rptr - W - NY

SODIUM-AMMONIUM PHOSPHATE
   Chem Mktg Rptr - W - NY

SODIUM ANTIMONIATE
   Chem Mktg Rptr - W - East

SODIUM ASCORBATE
   Chem Mktg Rptr - W - NY
   J of Commerce - W - NY

SODIUM BENZOATE
   Chem Mktg Rptr - W - NY
   J of Commerce - W - NY

COMMODITY PRICES

SODIUM BICARBONATE
   Chem Mktg Rptr - W - US
   J of Commerce - W - NY
   Rubber World - SA

SODIUM BICHROMATE
   Chem Mktg Rptr - W - US
   J of Commerce - W - NY
   US Labor Stat Bur - Wholesale Prices
     & Price Indexes - M

SODIUM BIFLUORIDE
   Chem Mktg Rptr - W - US

SODIUM BISULFATE
   Chem Mktg Rptr - W - US

SODIUM BISULFITE
   Chem Mktg Rptr - W - US
   J of Commerce - W - NY

SODIUM BORATE
   Chem Mktg Rptr - W - US

SODIUM BOROHYDRIDE
   Chem Mktg Rptr - W - US

SODIUM BROMIDE
   Chem Mktg Rptr - W - NY

SODIUM CARBONATE
   Chem Mktg Rptr - W - US
   Rubber World - SA
   US Labor Stat Bur - Wholesale Prices
     & Price Indexes - M

SODIUM CARBOXYMETHYL
CELLULOSE
   US Labor Stat Bur - Wholesale Prices
     & Price Indexes - M

SODIUM CHLORATE
   Can Chem Processing - M - Can
   Chem Mktg Rptr - W - South
   J of Commerce - W - NY
   US Labor Stat Bur - Wholesale Prices
     & Price Indexes - M

SODIUM CHLORIDE
   Chem Mktg Rptr - W - NY

SODIUM CHLORITE
   Chem Mktg Rptr - W - US

SODIUM CHROMATE
   Chem Mktg Rptr - W - US
   J of Commerce - W - NY

SODIUM CHROMATE TETRAHYDRATE
   Chem Mktg Rptr - W - US

SODIUM CITRATE
   Chem Mktg Rptr - W - NY
   J of Commerce - W - NY

SODIUM CYANATE
   Chem Mktg Rptr - W - US

SODIUM CYANIDE
   Chem Mktg Rptr - W - NY
   Finishers' Mgt - M
   J of Commerce - W - NY

SODIUM CYCLAMATE
   J of Commerce - W - NY

SODIUM DIACETATE
   Chem Mktg Rptr - W - US
   Rubber World - SA

SODIUM ERYTHORBATE
   Chem Mktg Rptr - W - NY
   J of Commerce - W - NY

SODIUM FERROCYANIDE
   Chem Mktg Rptr - W - NY

SODIUM FLUOBORATE
   Chem Mktg Rptr - W - US

SODIUM FLUORIDE
   Chem Mktg Rptr - W - US
   J of Commerce - W - NY

SODIUM-FORMALDEHYDE
SULFOXYLATE
   Chem Mktg Rptr - W - US

SODIUM FORMATE
   Chem Mktg Rptr - W - US

COMMODITY PRICES

SODIUM GLUCONATE
  Chem Mktg Rptr - W - NY
  J of Commerce - W - NY

SODIUM HEXAMETAPHOSPHATE
  Can Chem Processing - M - Can

SODIUM HYDRIDE
  Chem Mktg Rptr - W - US

SODIUM HYDRIDE OIL DISPERSION
  Chem Mktg Rptr - W - US

SODIUM HYDROSULFITE
  Chem Mktg Rptr - W - East
  J of Commerce - W - NY
  US Labor Stat Bur - Wholesale Prices
    & Price Indexes - M

SODIUM HYDROXIDE
  Can Chem Processing - M - Can
  Chem Mktg Rptr - W - US
  Finishers' Mgt - M - NY
  J of Commerce - W - NY
  Purch World - M
  Rubber World - SA
  US Labor Stat Bur - Wholesale Prices
    & Price Indexes - M

SODIUM HYPOCHLORITE
  Can Chem Processing - M - Can

SODIUM HYPOPHOSPHATE
  Finishers' Mgt - M

SODIUM HYPOPHOSPHITE
  Chem Mktg Rptr - W - US
  J of Commerce - W - NY

SODIUM HYPOSULFITE
  Chem Mktg Rptr - W - US

SODIUM IODIDE
  Chem Mktg Rptr - W - NY
  J of Commerce - W - NY

SODIUM LAURYL SULFATE
  Chem Mktg Rptr - W - US

SODIUM LIGNIN SULFONATE
  Chem Mktg Rptr - W - US

SODIUM METABORATE
  Chem Mktg Rptr - W - US

SODIUM METANILATE
  Chem Mktg Rptr - W - NY

SODIUM METAPHOSPHATE
  Chem Mktg Rptr - W - US

SODIUM METASILICATE
  Chem Mktg Rptr - W - US

SODIUM MOLYBDATE
  Chem Mktg Rptr - W - US

SODIUM MONOGLUTAMATE
  J of Commerce - W - NY

SODIUM NAPHTHIONATE
  Chem Mktg Rptr - W - NY
  J of Commerce - W - NY

SODIUM NITRATE
  Chem Mktg Rptr - W - US
  J of Commerce - W - NY

SODIUM NITRITE
  Chem Mktg Rptr - W - US

SODIUM ORTHOSILICATE
  Chem Mktg Rptr - W - US

SODIUM OXALATE
  Chem Mktg Rptr - W - US

SODIUM PENTACHLOROPHENATE
  Chem Mktg Rptr - W - US
  Rubber World - SA

SODIUM PERBORATE
  Chem Mktg Rptr - W - US
  J of Commerce - W - NY

SODIUM PEROXIDE
  Chem Mktg Rptr - W - East

SODIUM PHENOLSULFONATE
  Chem Mktg Rptr - W - NY

COMMODITY PRICES

SODIUM PHOSPHATE
 Can Chem Processing - M - Can
 Chem Mktg Rptr - W - US
 J of Commerce - W - NY

SODIUM PICRAMATE
 Chem Mktg Rptr - W - NY

SODIUM PROPIONATE
 Chem Mktg Rptr - W - US
 J of Commerce - W - NY

SODIUM PRUSSIATE
 J of Commerce - W - NY

SODIUM PYROPHOSPHATE: ACIDIC
 Can Chem Processing - M - Can
 Chem Mktg Rptr - W - US

SODIUM PYROPHOSPHATE: FERRIC, TETRABASIC
 Chem Mktg Rptr - W - US

SODIUM SALICYLATE
 Chem Mktg Rptr - W - US
 J of Commerce - W - NY

SODIUM SESQUICARBONATE
 Chem Mktg Rptr - W - US

SODIUM SESQUISILICATE
 Can Chem Processing - M - Toronto
 Chem Mktg Rptr - W - US

SODIUM SILICATE
 Can Chem Processing - M - Toronto
 Chem Mktg Rptr - W - US
 J of Commerce - W - NY
 US Labor Stat Bur - Wholesale Prices
  & Price Indexes - M

SODIUM SILICOFLUORIDE
 Chem Mktg Rptr - W - US
 Rubber World - SA

SODIUM SILICO-STANNATE
 J of Commerce - W - NY

SODIUM STANNATE
 Chem Mktg Rptr - W - East
 Finishers' Mgt - M

SODIUM STEARATE
 Rubber World - SA

SODIUM SULFANILATE
 Chem Mktg Rptr - W - US

SODIUM SULFATE
 Can Chem Processing - M - Can
 Chem Mktg Rptr - W - East
 J of Commerce - W - NY
 US Labor Stat Bur - Wholesale Prices
  & Price Indexes - M

SODIUM SULFHYDRATE
 Chem Mktg Rptr - W - US

SODIUM SULFIDE
 Chem Mktg Rptr - W - East
 US Labor Stat Bur - Wholesale Prices
  & Price Indexes - M

SODIUM SULFITE
 Chem Mktg Rptr - W - US

SODIUM TETRABORATE
 US Labor Stat Bur - Wholesale Prices
  & Price Indexes - M

SODIUM TETRASULFIDE
 Chem Mktg Rptr - W - US

SODIUM THIOCYANATE
 Chem Mktg Rptr - W - US

SODIUM THIOSULFATE
 Chem Mktg Rptr - W - US

SODIUM TITANATE
 Chem Mktg Rptr - W - US

SODIUM TRICHLOROACETATE
 Chem Mktg Rptr - W - East

SODIUM TRIPOLYPHOSPHATE
 Can Chem Processing - M - Can
 Chem Mktg Rptr - W - US
 US Labor Stat Bur - Wholesale Prices
  & Price Indexes - M

SODIUM TUNGSTATE
 Chem Mktg Rptr - W - NY

COMMODITY PRICES

SODIUM-ZIRCONYL SULFATE
  Chem Mktg Rptr - W - US

SOFA BEDS
  US Stat Rptg Ser - Agri Prices - Annual Summary - A - US and by states

SOFTWOOD PLYWOOD VENEERS
  US Labor Stat Bur - Wholesale Prices & Price Indexes - M

SOFTWOOD, WESTERN: INTERIOR PANEL AND SHEATHING, EXTERIOR PANEL
  US Labor Stat Bur - Wholesale Prices & Price Indexes - M

SOLAR 40
  Rubber World - SA

SOLDER JOINTS (SCRAP)
  Second Raw Materials - M - Buffalo

SOLDER POWDER
  Am Met Mkt/Met News - D - US

SOLES: RUBBER
  US Labor Stat Bur - Wholesale Prices & Price Indexes - M

SOLRICIN 135
  Rubber World - SA

SOLROS
  Rubber World - SA

SOLVENOL: 1, 2
  Rubber World - SA

SOLVENT NAPHTHA: PETROLEUM
  Chem Mktg Rptr - W - Houston, NJ, NY

SORBIC ACID
  J of Commerce - W - NY

SORBITAN MONOSTEARATE
  Chem Mktg Rptr - W - NY

SORBITAN TRISTEARATE
  Chem Mktg Rptr - W - NY

SORBITOL
  Am Paint J - W
  Chem Mktg Rptr - W - US
  J of Commerce - W - NY
  Rubber World - SA

SORGHUM: FORAGE
  US Stat Rptg Ser - Agri Prices - Annual Summary - A - US and by states

SORGHUM: NO. 1 YELLOW
  J of Commerce - D - Kansas City

SORGHUM: NO. 2 YELLOW
  US Agri Mktg Ser - Feed Mkt News - W - Fort Worth, Kansas City

SOUP: BEAN, CHICKEN
  US Labor Stat Bur - Retail Food Prices - M - US and 23 cities

SOUP: CONDENSED CANNED
  US Labor Stat Bur - Wholesale Prices & Price Indexes - M

SOUTHERN PINE LUMBER: FLOORING (C & BETTER), FINISH (C & BETTER), DROP SIDING (C & BETTER), DIMENSION NO. 1, DIMENSION NO. 2, BOARDS NOS. 2 & 3, TIMBERS NO. 1, STUDS
  US Labor Stat Bur - Wholesale Prices & Price Indexes - M

SOUTHERN PINE LUMBER: FRAMING
  Comm Bul - W

SOUTHERN PINE LUMBER: NO. 2
  J of Commerce - W

SOUTHERN YELLOW PINE BOARDS
  Comm Bul - W

SOWS
  Free Press Farm - W - Calgary, Montreal, Saskatoon, Toronto, Winnipeg
  Lancaster Farm - W - New Holland Pa
  Natl Provision - W - Chicago
  US Agri Mktg Ser - Livestock Mkt News - W - Baltimore, Kansas City, Omaha, Peoria

COMMODITY PRICES

US Econ Ser - Livestock Sit - BM
US Labor Stat Bur - Wholesale Prices & Price Indexes - M

SOWS: LIVESTOCK
Farm & Dairy - W - Ohio

SOYA FATTY ACID
Rubber World - SA

SOYA FATTY ACID: ALKYD GRADES
Rubber World - SA

SOYA OIL
J of Commerce - D

SOYA PROTEIN
Am Paint J - W

SOYBEAN MEAL
Calif Farm - S - Los Angeles, San Francisco
Dly Mkt Rec - D - Chicago, Minneapolis
Feed Bul - D
Feedstuffs - W - Atlanta, Boston, Chicago, Fort Worth, Los Angeles
Fin Post - W - Chicago
J of Commerce - D - Chicago, Decatur
Mich Farm - S - Decatur
Mo Rural - S - Kansas City
Neb Farm - S
NY Times - D - Chicago
Poultry Times - W - Chicago
Soybean Dig - A - US
US Agri Mktg Ser - Feed Mkt News - W
US Agri Mktg Ser - Grain Mkt News - W - Decatur
US Agri Mktg Ser - Peanut Mkt News - W - US
US Econ Ser - Fats & Oils Sit - 5/yr - Atlanta, Chicago, Decatur, Memphis
US Econ Ser - Feed Sit - Q - Decatur
US Labor Stat Bur - Wholesale Prices & Price Indexes - M
US Stat Rptg Ser - Agri Prices - M - US and by states
US Stat Rptg Ser - Agri Prices - Annual Summary - A - US and by states
Wall Street J - D - Chicago, Decatur

SOYBEAN OIL
Am Paint J - W - Decatur, NY
Chem Mktg Rptr - W - Decatur
Chicago Hide - D - Decatur
Dly Mkt Rec - D - Chicago, Minneapolis
Fats & Oils - D - Decatur
Feed Bul - D - Decatur
Fin Post - W - Chicago
Natl Provision - W - Decatur
NY Times - D - Chicago
Soybean Dig - A - US
US Agri Mktg Ser - Grain Mkt News - W - Decatur
Wall Street J - D - Chicago, Decatur

SOYBEAN OIL: CRUDE
J of Commerce - D - Chicago, Decatur
US Econ Ser - Fats & Oils Sit - 5/yr - Decatur
US Labor Stat Bur - Wholesale Prices & Price Indexes - M

SOYBEAN OIL: REFINED
US Econ Ser - Fats & Oils Sit - 5/yr - NY
US Labor Stat Bur - Wholesale Prices & Price Indexes - M

SOYBEAN OIL ACID
Chem Mktg Rptr - W - NY

SOYBEAN OIL FOOTS, SOAPSTOCK, 95% ACID
Chem Mktg Rptr - W - NY

SOYBEAN OILMEAL
Chem Mktg Rptr - W - Decatur
Comm Rev - W - US
Dairynews - S - Boston, Buffalo, NY, Philadelphia

SOYBEANS
Agri Let - W - US
Barron's - W - Chicago
Dly Mkt Rec - D - Chicago
Fin Post - W - Chicago
Fin Times Can - W - Chicago
Free Press Farm - W - Chicago
Mich Farm - S - central Mich
NY Times - D - Chicago, NY

COMMODITY PRICES

Soybean Dig – A – US
US Econ Ser – Demand Sit – Q – US
US Econ Ser – Fats & Oils Sit – 5/yr – US
US Labor Stat Bur – Wholesale Prices & Price Indexes – M
US Stat Rptg Ser – Agri Prices – M – US and by states
US Stat Rptg Ser – Agri Prices – Annual Summary – A – US and by states
US Stat Rptg Ser Wis – Prices Received – M – Wis
Wall Street J – D – Chicago

SOYBEANS: FOR SEED
US Stat Rptg Ser – Agri Prices – Annual Summary – A – US and by states

SOYBEANS: NO. 1
Mo Rural – S – Kansas City, St. Joseph, St. Louis

SOYBEANS: NO. 1 YELLOW
Barron's – W – Chicago
J of Commerce – D – Chicago, Minneapolis
NY Times – D – Chicago
Soybean Dig – M
US Agri Mktg Ser – Grain Mkt News – W – central Ill, Chicago, Minneapolis
US Econ Ser – Fats & Oils Sit – 5/yr – Ill

SOYBEANS: NO. 2 YELLOW
Neb Farm – S – Omaha

SPAGHETTI: CANNED
US Labor Stat Bur – Retail Food Prices – M – US and 23 cities
US Labor Stat Bur – Wholesale Prices & Price Indexes – M

SPANDEX: STAPLE & TOW
Mod Textiles Mag – M

SPARERIBS
Nation's Restaurant – S – East coast, Los Angeles, Midwest

SPARK PLUGS
US Stat Rptg Ser – Agri Prices – Annual Summary – A – US and by states

SPARMITE
Rubber World – SA

SPDX-GH
Rubber World – SA

SPEARMINT LEAVES
Chem Mktg Rptr – W – NY
J of Commerce – W – NY

SPEARMINT OIL
Chem Mktg Rptr – W – NY
J of Commerce – W – NY

SPERMACETI WAX
Chem Mktg Rptr – W – NY
J of Commerce – W – NY

SPERM OIL
Chem Mktg Rptr – W – NY
J of Commerce – D
US Econ Ser – Fats & Oils Sit – 5/yr – NY

SPICES
J of Commerce – W

SPIEGELEISEN
Eng Min J – M
See also FERROALLOYS

SPINACH
US Agri Mktg Ser – Fruit & Veg Prices – A – Chicago, NJ, NY, Tex
US Econ Ser – Veg Sit – Q – Chicago, NY
US Labor Stat Bur – Retail Food Prices – M – US and 23 cities
US Stat Rptg Ser – Agri Prices – M – US

SPINACH: CANNED
J of Commerce – W

SPINACH: FROZEN
J of Commerce – W

COMMODITY PRICES

SPRAYERS: HAND
    US Stat Rptg Ser - Agri Prices - Annual Summary - A - US and by states

SPRUCE: 2 X 4
    Purch World - M - Toronto

SPRUCE OIL
    Chem Mktg Rptr - W - NY
    J of Commerce - W - NY

SQUABS: READY-TO-COOK, FROZEN
    US Cons & Mktg Ser - Poultry Mkt Stat - A - Los Angeles, NY

SQUILL ROOT WHITE
    J of Commerce - W - NY

SS: 4048, 4130
    Rubber World - SA

STABELITE: ESTER 10, RESIN
    Rubber World - SA

STABLEX: A, B, G
    Rubber World - SA

STAINLESS STEEL
    Am Paint J - W
    Comm Bul - W

STAINLESS STEEL POWDER
    Am Met Mkt/Met News - D - US

STAN-MAGNESIUM CARBONATE
    Rubber World - SA

STANNIC CHLORIDE
    Chem Mktg Rptr - W - US
    J of Commerce - W - NY

STANNOUS CHLORIDE
    Chem Mktg Rptr - W - US
    J of Commerce - W - NY

STANNOUS FLUOBORATE
    Chem Mktg Rptr - W - US

STANNOUS OXIDE
    Chem Mktg Rptr - W - US
    J of Commerce - W - NY

STANNOUS SULFATE
    Chem Mktg Rptr - W - US
    J of Commerce - W - NY

STAN-WHITE: 325, 400, 500, UF
    Rubber World - SA

STAPLE & TOW
    US Labor Stat Bur - Wholesale Prices & Price Indexes - M

STAPLES: FENCE
    US Stat Rptg Ser - Agri Prices - Annual Summary - A - US and by states

STARCH: LAUNDRY
    US Stat Rptg Ser - Agri Prices - Annual Summary - A - US and by states

STAY B
    Rubber World - SA

STAYBELITE: ESTER 10 RESIN
    Rubber World - SA

STEAM HOSE: RUBBER
    US Labor Stat Bur - Wholesale Prices & Price Indexes - M

STEARIC ACID
    Chem Mktg Rptr - W - NY
    J of Commerce - D
    Rubber World - SA
    US Labor Stat Bur - Wholesale Prices & Price Indexes - M

STEEL
    Comm Bul - W
    UN Bul Stat - M - US

STEEL: BARS
    Am Met Mkt/Met News - D - Midwest
    Indus Wk - W
    Purch World - M - Philadelphia, Pittsburgh

COMMODITY PRICES

STEEL: BASIC WIRE
   Purch World - M - Pittsburgh

STEEL: BILLETS
   Am Met Mkt/Met News - D - Midwest
   NY Times - D - Pittsburgh
   Purch World - M - Pittsburgh

STEEL: FINISHED
   Indus Wk - W

STEEL: PLATES
   Am Met Mkt/Met News - D - Midwest
   Indus Wk - W
   Oil Dly - D - US
   Purch World - M - Chicago, Pittsburgh

STEEL: SHEETS
   Am Met Mkt/Met News - D - Midwest
   Indus Wk - W
   Purch World - M - Detroit, Pittsburgh

STEEL: STAINLESS
   Am Paint J - W
   Comm Bul - W

STEEL: STAINLESS, POWDER
   Am Met Mkt/Met News - D - US

STEEL: STRIP
   Am Met Mkt/Met News - D - Midwest
   Indus Wk - W
   Purch World - M - Chicago

STEEL: STRUCTURAL SHAPES
   Am Met Mkt/Met News - D - Midwest
   Indus Wk - W
   Purch World - M - Chicago, Los Angeles, Pittsburgh

STEEL: TIN PLATE
   Am Met Mkt/Met News - D - Midwest
   Indus Wk - W

STEEL: TUBULAR GOODS
   Indus Wk - W

STEEL PIPE
   Indus Wk - W
   Oil Dly - D - US

STEEL PRODUCTS
   Indus Wk - W
   J of Commerce - W

STEEL PRODUCTS: FINISHED
   US Labor Stat Bur - Wholesale Prices & Price Indexes - M

STEEL PRODUCTS: SEMIFINISHED
   US Labor Stat Bur - Wholesale Prices & Price Indexes - M

STEEL RAILS
   Comm Bul - W
   Indus Wk - W

STEEL SCRAP
   Barron's - W - Chicago
   Foundry - M
   J of Commerce - W - Chicago, Pittsburgh
   NY Times - D - Pittsburgh
   Purch World - M - Chicago, Cleveland, Pittsburgh
   US Labor Stat Bur - Wholesale Prices & Price Indexes - M - Birmingham, Chicago, Pittsburgh, San Francisco
   Wall Street J - D - Chicago

STEEL WIRE
   Am Met Mkt/Met News - D - Midwest
   Indus Wk - W

STEERS
   Agri Let - W - US
   Fin Times Can - W - Chicago
   US Stat Rptg Ser - Agri Prices - M - US and by states
   US Stat Rptg Ser - Agri Prices - Annual Summary - A - US and by states
   US Stat Rptg Ser Wis - Prices Received - M - Wis

COMMODITY PRICES

STEERS: CHOICE
  Barron's - W - Omaha
  Fin Post - W
  Ida Farm - S - Intermountain
  J of Commerce - D - Chicago
  Mont Farm - S
  Natl Livestock - M - Omaha
  NY Times - D - NY
  Ore Farm - S
  Pa Farm - S
  US Agri Mktg Ser - Broiler Mktg
    Guide - Q - Omaha
  US Agri Mktg Ser - Turkey Mktg
    Guide - A - Omaha
  US Econ Ser - Livestock Sit -
    BM - Omaha
  Utah Farm - S - Intermountain
  Wall Street J - D - Omaha
  Wash Farm - S

STEERS: CHOICE BEEF
  J of Commerce - D - NY

STEERS: FEEDER
  Calif Farm - S - Stockton
  Dairyman - M - Pacific Northwest
  High Plains J - W - Kan
  Ida Farm - S
  Lancaster Farm - W - Oklahoma City
  Man Co-op - W
  Mo Rural - S - Kansas City
  Mont Farm - S
  Ore Farm - S
  US Agri Mktg Ser - Livestock Mkt
    News - W - Amarillo, Kansas
    City, Omaha, Sioux City
  Utah Farm - S
  Wash Farm - S

STEERS: LIVESTOCK
  Farm & Dairy - W - Ohio
  Man Co-op - W
  Mo Rural - S - Kansas City
  Natl Provision - W - Chicago,
    Kansas City, Louisville, Omaha
    St. Paul
  US Labor Stat Bur - Wholesale Prices
    & Price Indexes - M

STEERS: PRIME
  NY Times - D - NY

STEERS: SLAUGHTER
  Calif Farm - S - Calif
  Dairyman - M - Pacific Northwest
  Free Press Farm - W - Montreal,
    Saskatoon, Toronto, Winnipeg
  High Plains J - W - Kan
  Lancaster Farm - W - Lancaster Pa,
    Omaha, Peoria
  Neb Farm - S - Omaha
  US Agri Mktg Ser - Livestock Mkt
    News - W - Ga, Ill, Omaha,
    St. Paul, Sioux City
  US Econ Ser - Livestock Sit - BM -
    Omaha

STEERS: STOCKERS & FEEDERS
  Free Press Farm - W - Edmonton,
    Saskatoon, Winnipeg
  Neb Farm - S - Omaha
  US Econ Ser - Livestock Sit - BM -
    Kansas City

STILLINGIA ROOT
  J of Commerce - W - NY

STONE: CRUSHED, FOR CONCRETE
  US Labor Stat Bur - Wholesale Prices
    & Price Indexes - M

STONELITE
  Rubber World - SA

STRAMONIUM
  J of Commerce - W - NY

STRAMONIUM LEAVES
  Chem Mktg Rptr - W - NY

STRAW
  Lancaster Farm - W - Lancaster Pa

STRAWBERRIES
  US Agri Mktg Ser - Fruit & Veg
    Prices - A - Calif, Chicago, Fla,
    NY, Tex, Va
  US Labor Stat Bur - Retail Food
    Prices - M - US and 23 cities
  US Labor Stat Bur - Wholesale Prices
    & Price Indexes - M
  US Stat Rptg Ser - Agri Prices - M -
    US

COMMODITY PRICES

STRAWBERRIES: FROZEN
   J of Commerce - W
   US Labor Stat Bur - Wholesale Prices
     & Price Indexes - M
   US Stat Rptg Ser - Agri Prices -
     Annual Summary - A - US and
     by states

STREPTOMYCIN SULFATE
   Chem Mktg Rptr - W - NY
   US Labor Stat Bur - Wholesale Prices
     & Price Indexes - M

STRONTIUM CARBONATE
   Chem Mktg Rptr - W - US
   J of Commerce - W - NY

STRONTIUM NITRATE
   Chem Mktg Rptr - W - US

STRONTIUM SALICYLATE
   J of Commerce - W - NY

STROPHANTHUS
   J of Commerce - W - NY

STRUCTURAL CLAY PRODUCTS
   US Labor Stat Bur - Wholesale Prices
     & Price Indexes - M

STRUCTURAL METAL PRODUCTS: FABRICATED
   US Labor Stat Bur - Wholesale Prices
     & Price Indexes - M

STRYCHNINE: ALKALOID, POWDERED
   J of Commerce - W - NY

STRYCHNINE: SULFATE POWDER
   J of Commerce - W - NY

STYORYL, ACETATE
   Chem Mktg Rptr - W - NY

STYRAX: ASIATIC
   J of Commerce - W - NY

STYRENE ACRYLONITRILE
   Mod Pckg-Encyclo & Plan Guide -
     A - US

STYRENE ACRYLONITRILE COPOLYMER
   J of Commerce - W - NY

STYRENE BUTADIENE
   US Labor Stat Bur - Wholesale Prices
     & Price Indexes - M

STYRENE BUTADIENE: COPOLYMER RESINS
   Am Paint J - W - Akron Ohio, Gary Ind

STYRENE MONOMER
   Chem Mktg Rptr - W - NY
   Purch World - M
   Rubber World - SA
   US Labor Stat Bur - Wholesale Prices
     & Price Indexes - M

SUCCINIC ACID
   Chem Mktg Rptr - W - NY

SUCCINIC ANHYDRIDE
   Chem Mktg Rptr - W - NY

SUCROSE
   Chem Mktg Rptr - W - East

SUCROSE ACETATE ISOBUTYRATE
   Am Paint J - W
   Chem Mktg Rptr - W - NY

SUCROSE BENZOATE
   Am Paint J - W

SUCROSE OCTA-ACETATE
   Chem Mktg Rptr - W - NY

SUDANGRASS SEED
   US Stat Rptg Ser - Agri Prices -
     Annual Summary - A - US and
     by states

SUGAR
   Barron's - W
   Fin Post - W
   J of Commerce - D - NY, West Coast
   UN Bul Stat - M - US
   US Stat Rptg Ser - Agri Prices -
     Annual Summary - A - US and
     by states

COMMODITY PRICES

SUGAR: PACKERS' CURING
  Natl Provision - W - Chicago

SUGAR: RAW
  Natl Provision - W - NY
  NY Times - D - NY
  Stat Sugar Trade J - W - Chicago,
    East Coast, Pacific Coast
  Wall Street J - D - NY

SUGAR: REFINED
  Barron's - W - NY
  Natl Provision - W - Chicago
  NY Times - D - NY
  Stat Sugar Trade J - W - Chicago,
    East Coast, Pacific Coast
  US Labor Stat Bur - Retail Food
    Prices - M - US and 23 cities
  Wall Street J - D - NY

SUGAR BEET: GRANULATED
  US Labor Stat Bur - Wholesale Prices
    & Price Indexes - M

SUGAR BEET: REFINED
  US Agri Stabil - Sugar Rpt - M -
    Chicago, East, Pacific Coast,
    West

SUGAR CANE: RAW, GRANULATED
  US Labor Stat Bur - Wholesale Prices
    & Price Indexes - M

SUGAR CANE: REFINED
  US Agri Stabil - Sugar Rpt - M - US

SUGAR PINE: SELECTS AND SHOP
  Comm Bul - W

SUGAR PINE BOARDS
  Comm Bul - W

SUITS: MEN'S
  US Labor Stat Bur - Wholesale Prices
    & Price Indexes - M

SUITS: MEN'S, BOYS'
  US Stat Rptg Ser - Agri Prices -
    Annual Summary - A - US and
    by states

SUITS: MEN'S, WORK
  US Stat Rptg Ser - Agri Prices -
    Annual Summary - A - US and
    by states

SUITS: WOMEN'S, WOOL & WOOL BLENDS
  US Stat Rptg Ser - Agri Prices -
    Annual Summary - A - US and
    by states

SULFABENZAMIDE
  Chem Mktg Rptr - W - NY

SULFABENZAMIDE-SODIUM
  Chem Mktg Rptr - W - NY

SULFACETAMIDE
  Chem Mktg Rptr - W - NY

SULFADIAZINE
  Chem Mktg Rptr - W - NY
  US Labor Stat Bur - Wholesale Prices
    & Price Indexes - M

SULFADIAZINE-SODIUM
  Chem Mktg Rptr - W - NY

SULFADS
  Rubber World - SA

SULFAGUANIDINE
  Chem Mktg Rptr - W - NY

SULFAMERAZINE
  Chem Mktg Rptr - W - NY
  J of Commerce - W - NY

SULFAMERAZINE-SODIUM
  Chem Mktg Rptr - W - NY
  J of Commerce - W - NY

SULFAMETHAZINE
  Chem Mktg Rptr - W - NY

SULFAMIC ACID
  Chem Mktg Rptr - W - US

COMMODITY PRICES

SULFANILAMIDE
    Chem Mktg Rptr - W - NY
    J of Commerce - W - NY
    US Labor Stat Bur - Wholesale Prices
        & Price Indexes - M

SULFANILIC ACID
    Chem Mktg Rptr - W - US

SULFAPYRIDINE
    Chem Mktg Rptr - W - NY
    J of Commerce - W - NY
    US Labor Stat Bur - Wholesale Prices
        & Price Indexes - M

SULFAPYRIDINE-SODIUM
    Chem Mktg Rptr - W - NY

SULFAQUINOXALINE: VETERINARY
    Chem Mktg Rptr - W - US

SULFASAN R
    Rubber World - SA

SULFATHIAZOLE
    Chem Mktg Rptr - W - NY
    J of Commerce - W - NY
    US Labor Stat Bur - Wholesale Prices
        & Price Indexes - M

SULFATHIAZOLE-SODIUM
    Chem Mktg Rptr - W - NY
    J of Commerce - W - NY

SULFUR
    Can Chem Processing - M - Can
    Chem Mktg Rptr - W - US
    Eng Min J - M - Gulf ports
    US Labor Stat Bur - Wholesale Prices
        & Price Indexes - M

SULFUR: CRUDE
    J of Commerce - W - NY
    Purch World - M - Tampa Fla

SULFUR: DISPERSED, MC, RM90
    Rubber World - SA

SULFUR 60: INSOLUBLE
    Rubber World - SA

SULFUR: MIST BRAND
    Rubber World - SA

SULFUR: SPIDER BRAND
    Rubber World - SA

SULFUR DICHLORIDE
    Chem Mktg Rptr - W - US
    J of Commerce - W - NY
    Rubber World - SA

SULFUR DIOXIDE
    Can Chem Processing - M - Can
    Chem Mktg Rptr - W - US
    J of Commerce - W - NY
    US Labor Stat Bur - Wholesale Prices
        & Price Indexes - M

SULFUR FLOWERS
    Rubber World - SA

SULFURIC ACID
    Can Chem Processing - M - East Can
    Chem Mktg Rptr - W - US
    J of Commerce - W - NY
    Purch World - M
    US Labor Stat Bur - Wholesale Prices
        & Price Indexes - M

SULFUR MONOCHLORIDE
    Chem Mktg Rptr - W - US
    J of Commerce - W - NY
    Rubber World - SA
    US Labor Stat Bur - Wholesale Prices
        & Price Indexes - M

SUNFLOWER OIL
    Am Paint J - W - Minneapolis

SUNFLOWERS
    Free Press Farm - W - Alta, Man, Sask

SUNOLITE: 100, 127, 154, 160, 240, 666, SC
    Rubber World - SA

SUNPROOF 713
    Rubber World - SA

SUPERLOID
    Rubber World - SA

COMMODITY PRICES

SUPERPHOSPHATE
   Chem Mktg Rptr - W - US
   J of Commerce - W - NY
   US Labor Stat Bur - Wholesale Prices
     & Price Indexes - M
   US Stat Rptg Ser - Agri Prices -
     Annual Summary - A - US and
     by states

SUPHAX
   Rubber World - SA

SUPREX CLAY
   Rubber World - SA

SURFEX MM
   Rubber World - SA

SUSPENSO
   Rubber World - SA

SWANEE CLAY
   Rubber World - SA

SWEATERS: BOYS' PULLOVER
   US Stat Rptg Ser - Agri Prices -
     Annual Summary - A - US and
     by states

SWEATERS: WOMEN'S
   US Stat Rptg Ser - Agri Prices -
     Annual Summary - A - US and
     by states

SWEETCLOVER SEED
   US Stat Rptg Ser - Agri Prices -
     Annual Summary - A - US and
     by states

SWEET POTATOES
   Calif Farm - S - Atwater-Livingston
   US Agri Mktg Ser - Fruit & Veg
     Prices - A - Calif, Chicago,
     La, NY, Va
   US Econ Ser - Veg Sit - Q -
     Chicago, NY
   US Labor Stat Bur - Wholesale Prices
     & Price Indexes - M - Chicago,
     NY
   US Stat Rptg Ser - Agri Prices - M -
     US and by states

US Stat Rptg Ser - Agri Prices -
   Annual Summary - A - US and
   by states

SWEET POTATOES: CANNED
   J of Commerce - W
   US Labor Stat Bur - Wholesale Prices
     & Price Indexes - M

SYRUP: CANE AND CORN BLENDS,
MAPLE AND CORN BLENDS
   US Stat Rptg Ser - Agri Prices -
     Annual Summary - A - US and
     by states

SYRUP: CHOCOLATE
   US Labor Stat Bur - Retail Food
     Prices - M - US and 23 cities

SYNTHETIC GRAY GOODS
   See MAN-MADE FIBER GRAY
     GOODS

SYNTHOL
   Rubber World - SA

T

2, 4, 5-T
   US Labor Stat Bur - Wholesale Prices
     & Price Indexes - M
   US Stat Rptg Ser - Agri Prices -
     Annual Summary - A - US and
     by states

10 T
   Rubber World - SA

TA-11
   Rubber World - SA

TABLECLOTHS: COTTON
   US Stat Rptg Ser - Agri Prices -
     Annual Summary - A - US and
     by states

TAC
   Rubber World - SA

COMMODITY PRICES

2, 4, 5-T ACID
   Chem Mktg Rptr - W - US

TAFFETA
   See ACETATE TAFFETA GRAY
      GOODS

TALC
   Chem Mktg Rptr - W - US
   Eng Min J - M - Calif, Ga, NY, Vt
   Rubber World - SA
   US Labor Stat Bur - Wholesale Prices
     & Price Indexes - M

TALC: CALIFORNIA FIBROUS
WHITE, CALIFORNIA SEMIFIBROUS,
NY STATE FIBROUS & SEMIFIBROUS,
MONTANA ULTRA-FINE GRIND.
   Am Paint J - W

TALC: FIBROUS
   Chem Mktg Rptr - W - NY

TALLENE
   Rubber World - SA

TALLENE 58D
   Rubber World - SA

TALL OIL
   Chem Mktg Rptr - W - NY
   J of Commerce - D
   US Econ Ser - Fats & Oils Sit -
     5/yr - US
   US Labor Stat Bur - Wholesale Prices
     & Price Indexes - M

TALL OIL ACIDS
   Am Paint J - W
   Chem Mktg Rptr - W - NY

TALL OIL FATTY ACID
   Am Paint J - W
   Rubber World - SA

TALL OIL ROSIN
   Am Paint J - W - NY
   J of Commerce - D - NY

TALLOW
   Chem Mktg Rptr - W - NY
   J of Commerce - D - NY
   UN Bul Stat - M - US
   Wall Street J - D - NY

TALLOW: BLEACHABLE
   Barron's - W - NY

TALLOW: EDIBLE
   Chicago Hide - D - Chicago, Denver,
     Tex
   Fats & Oils - D - Chicago, Denver,
     Tex
   Natl Provision - W - Chicago,
     Denver
   US Agri Mktg Ser - Livestock Mkt
     News - W - Chicago, Denver,
     East, Mo River points, West
   US Econ Ser - Fats & Oils Sit -
     5/yr - Chicago
   US Labor Stat Bur - Wholesale Prices
     & Price Indexes - M

TALLOW: INEDIBLE
   Chicago Hide - D - Chicago
   Fats & Oils - D
   Feedstuffs - W - Boston, Buffalo,
     Fort Worth, Kansas City,
     Minneapolis, St. Paul
   Natl Provision - W - Chicago, NY,
     New Orleans
   US Agri Mktg Ser - Livestock Mkt
     News - W - Chicago, Denver,
     East, Mo River points, West
   US Econ Ser - Fats & Oils Sit -
     5/yr - Chicago, NY
   US Econ Ser - Feed Sit - Q - Chicago
   US Labor Stat Bur - Wholesale Prices
     & Price Indexes - M

TALLOW FATTY ACID
   Chem Mktg Rptr - W - NY
   Rubber World - SA

TAMARIND SEED
   J of Commerce - W - NY

TAMAL: 731, N, SN
   Rubber World - SA

COMMODITY PRICES

TANGELOS
    Calif Farm - S - Coachella
    US Agri Mktg Ser - Fruit & Veg
      Prices - A - Chicago, NY
    US Stat Rptg Ser - Agri Prices - M -
      Fla, US

TANGERINE OIL
    Chem Mktg Rptr - W - Fla

TANGERINES
    Calif Farm - S - Coachella
    US Agri Mktg Ser - Fruit & Veg
      Prices - A - Chicago, NY, Tex
    US Stat Rptg Ser - Agri Prices - M -
      US, Ariz, Calif, Fla

TANKAGE
    Chem Mktg Rptr - W - NY
    Feedstuffs - W - Baltimore, Boston,
      Chicago, Atlanta
    US Agri Mktg Ser - Feed Mkt News -
      W - Chicago, Kansas City,
      Minneapolis
    US Stat Rptg Ser - Agri Prices -
      Annual Summary - A - US and
      by states

TANKAGE: DIGESTER
    Chicago Hide - D - Chicago & Ill
    Fats & Oils - D - Chicago & Ill
    US Agri Mktg Ser - Livestock Mkt
      News - W - Chicago, Denver,
      East, Mo River points, West
    US Econ Ser - Feed Sit - Q - Chicago

TANKAGE: DRY
    US Labor Stat Bur - Wholesale Prices
      & Price Indexes - M

TANKAGE: DRY RENDERED
    Chicago Hide - D - Chicago &
      Northwest
    Fats & Oils - D - Chicago &
      Northwest
    Feed Bul - D - East, Midwest,
      Northeast
    Natl Provision - W - Chicago &
      Midwest

TANKAGE: NITROGENOUS
    Chem Mktg Rptr - W - Carrollville
      Wis, Forbes Me, Slatersville RI
    US Labor Stat Bur - Wholesale Prices
      & Price Indexes - M

TANKAGE: WET RENDERED
    Chicago Hide - D - Midwest
    Fats & Oils - D - Midwest
    Feed Bul - D - Midwest

TANKS: METAL
    US Labor Stat Bur - Wholesale Prices
      & Price Indexes - M

TANNIC ACID
    Chem Mktg Rptr - W - NY
    J of Commerce - W - NY

TANSY OIL
    J of Commerce - W - NY

TANTALUM
    Eng Min J - M
    J of Commerce - D - NY
    Met Wk - W

TANTALUM CARBIDE POWDER
    Am Met Mkt/Met News - D - US

TANTALUM OXIDE
    North Miner - W - US

TANTALUM POWDER
    Am Met Mkt/Met News - D - US

TAR ACID OIL
    Chem Mktg Rptr - W - NY

TARENE: 14, 20, 40
    Rubber World - SA

TARPINE
    Rubber World - SA

TAR TAC: NOS. 20, 30, 40
    Rubber World - SA

TARTAR EMETIC
    Chem Mktg Rptr - W - US
    J of Commerce - W - NY

COMMODITY PRICES

TARTARIC ACID
    Chem Mktg Rptr - W - US
    J of Commerce - W - NY

TBBS
    Rubber World - SA

TEA
    J of Commerce - W
    US Labor Stat Bur - Wholesale Prices
      & Price Indexes - M

TEA: ORANGE PEKOE
    US Stat Rptg Ser - Agri Prices -
      Annual Summary - A - US and
      by states

TEA BAGS
    Tea & Coffee Trade J - M - NY
    US Labor Stat Bur - Retail Food
      Prices - M - US and 23 cities

TEAK
    Comm Bul - W - Boston

TELEVISION SETS: BLACK AND
WHITE, COLOR
    US Stat Rptg Ser - Agri Prices -
      Annual Summary - A - US and
      by states

TELLOY
    Rubber World - SA

TELLURAC: ETHYL, RODFORM
    Rubber World - SA

TELLURIUM
    Am Met Mkt/Met News - D - US
    Eng Min J - M
    Met Wk - W

TEMPLES
    Fla Field Rpt - W - Fla
    US Stat Rptg Ser - Agri Prices - M -
      US, Fla

TENAMENE 3
    Rubber World - SA

TENOX: BHA, BHT, PG
    Rubber World - SA

TEPIDONE
    Rubber World - SA

TEQUILA
    Alaska Bev Analyst - M - Alaska
    Ariz Bev J - M - Ariz
    Bev Media - M - NY
    Bev News - M
    Buck Bev J - M - Ohio
    Ill Bev J - M - Ill
    Ky Bev J - M - Ky
    Md-Wash-Del Bev J - M - DC,
      Del, Md
    Mich Bev News - IR - Mich
    Patterson's - M - Calif
    RI Bev J - M - RI
    Wis Bev J - M - Wis

TERGITOL NONIONIC: NP-35, NPX
    Rubber World - SA

TERPINEOL
    Chem Mktg Rptr - W - NY
    J of Commerce - W - NY

TERPIN HYDRATE
    Chem Mktg Rptr - W - NY
    J of Commerce - W - NY

TERPINYL ACETATE
    Chem Mktg Rptr - W - NY

TERPINYL PROPIONATE
    Chem Mktg Rptr - W - NY

TETRACHLOROETHANE
    Chem Mktg Rptr - W - US

TETRACHLOROETHYLENE
    Chem Mktg Rptr - W - US

1-TETRADECANOL
    Chem Mktg Rptr - W - East

TETRAETHYLENE GLYCOL
    Chem Mktg Rptr - W - NY

TETRAETHYLENEPENTAMINE
    Chem Mktg Rptr - W - US

TETRAETHYL ORTHOSILICATE
    Chem Mktg Rptr - W - US

COMMODITY PRICES

TETRAETHYLTHIURAM DISULFIDE
Chem Mktg Rptr - W - NY

TETRAFLUOROETHYLENE
J of Commerce - W - NY

TETRAHYDROFURAN
Chem Mktg Rptr - W - East
Rubber World - SA

TETRAHYDROFURFURYL ALCOHOL
Chem Mktg Rptr - W - Memphis

TETRAHYDROLINALOOL
Chem Mktg Rptr - W - NY

TETRAHYDROPHTHALIC ANHYDRIDE
Chem Mktg Rptr - W - US

TETRONE A
Rubber World - SA

TEXTILES
See specific kinds

THALLIUM
Chem Mktg Rptr - W - NY
Eng Min J - M
Met Wk - W

THALLIUM SULFATE
Chem Mktg Rptr - W - NY

THEOBROMINE
J of Commerce - W - NY

THEOPHYLLINE
Chem Mktg Rptr - W - NY
J of Commerce - W - NY

THERMOFLEX A
Rubber World - SA

THIAMINE HYDROCHLORIDE
Chem Mktg Rptr - W - NY
J of Commerce - W - NY

THIAMINE MONONITRATE
Chem Mktg Rptr - W - NY

THIATE: B, BA, E, H, N, V
Rubber World - SA

THIOCARBANILIDE
Chem Mktg Rptr - W - NY
Rubber World - SA

THIOFIDE (MBTS)
Rubber World - SA

THIOFLAVIN GREEN TONER
Chem Mktg Rptr - W - NY

THIOGLYCOLIC ACID
Chem Mktg Rptr - W - NY

THIOINDIGOLD: MAROON, REDS
Chem Mktg Rptr - W - NY

THIONEX
Rubber World - SA

THIOSALICYLIC ACID
Chem Mktg Rptr - W - US

THIOTAX (MBT)
Rubber World - SA

THIOVANIC ACID
See THIOGLYCOLIC ACID

THIURAD
Rubber World - SA

THIURAM: E, M, M(TG)
Rubber World - SA

THIXON ADHESIVES: B-SERIES,
N-SERIES, P-SERIES, X-SERIES
Rubber World - SA

THORIUM NITRATE
Chem Mktg Rptr - W - US

THORIUM PELLETS
Iron Age - W

THREAD: INDUSTRIAL
US Labor Stat Bur - Wholesale Prices
& Price Indexes - M

dl-THREONINE
Chem Mktg Rptr - W - US

COMMODITY PRICES

THYME
J of Commerce - W - NY
Natl Provision - W - Chicago

THYME LEAVES
Chem Mktg Rptr - W - NY

THYME OIL
Chem Mktg Rptr - W - NY
J of Commerce - W - NY

THYMOL
Chem Mktg Rptr - W - US
J of Commerce - W - NY

THYMOL IODIDE
Chem Mktg Rptr - W - US

TI-GUM
Rubber World - SA

TILLIA FLOWERS
J of Commerce - W - NY

TIMOTHY
Lancaster Farm - W - Lancaster Pa

TIMOTHY SEED
Seed World - A - US and by states
US Stat Rptg Ser - Agri Prices - M - US, Iowa, Minn, Mo, Ohio
US Stat Rptg Ser - Agri Prices - Annual Summary - A - US and by states

TIN
Am Met Mkt/Met News - D - NY
Barron's - W - NY
Eng Min J - M - NY
Fin Times Can - W - NY
Iron Age - W
Met Wk - W
Min Rec - W - NY
North Miner - W - NY, Toronto
NY Times - D - NY
UN Bul Stat - M - US
Wall Street J - D - NY

TIN: ANODE
Finishers' Mgt - M

TIN: BLOCK PIPE
Comm Bul - W

TIN: PIG, GRADE A
US Labor Stat Bur - Wholesale Prices & Price Indexes - M

TIN: STRAITS
Chem Mktg Rptr - W - NY
Purch World - M - NY

TIN BRONZE INGOT
Foundry - M

TIN BRONZE INGOT: HIGH LEADED
Foundry - M

TINOPAL: BHS, PCR, SFG
Rubber World - SA

TINPLATE
Am Met Mkt/Met News - D - Midwest
Indus Wk - W

TIN POWDER
Am Met Mkt/Met News - D - US

TIN SCRAP
Second Raw Materials - M - Boston, Cleveland, Montreal, NY, Toronto

TINUVIN: 326, 327, 328, P
Rubber World - SA

TIRES: AUTO, TRUCK, TRACTOR
US Stat Rptg Ser - Agri Prices - Annual Summary - A - US and by states

TIRE YARN: VISCOSE FILAMENT
US Labor Stat Bur - Wholesale Prices & Price Indexes - M

2, 4, 5-T ISO-OCTYL ESTER
Chem Mktg Rptr - W - US

TISSUE: CLEANSING
US Stat Rptg Ser - Agri Prices - Annual Summary - A - US and by states

COMMODITY PRICES

TITANIUM
   Eng Min J - M
   Iron Age - W
   Met Wk - W
   Min Rec - W

TITANIUM DIOXIDE
   Chem Mktg Rptr - W - US
   J of Commerce - W - NY
   US Labor Stat Bur - Wholesale Prices
     & Price Indexes - M

TITANIUM DIOXIDE: ANATASE
   Am Paint J - W
   Can Chem Processing - M - East Can
   Purch World - M
   Rubber World - SA

TITANIUM DIOXIDE: RUTILE
   Am Paint J - W
   Rubber World - SA

TITANIUM HYDRIDE
   Chem Mktg Rptr - W - US

TITANIUM ORE
   Eng Min J - M

TITANIUM PIGMENTS
   Am Paint J - W

TITANIUM SHAPES
   US Labor Stat Bur - Wholesale Prices
     & Price Indexes - M

TITANIUM SPONGE
   Eng Min J - M
   Iron Age - W
   J of Commerce - D - NY

TITANIUM TETRACHLORIDE
   Chem Mktg Rptr - W - US

T-MR MINERAL RUBBER
   Rubber World - SA

TOASTERS
   US Stat Rptg Ser - Agri Prices -
     Annual Summary - A - US and
     by states

TOBACCO
   Can Tobacco - 9/yr - Can
   Tobacco/Internatl - BW - Eastern
     district markets
   US Econ Ser - Tobacco Sit - Q
   US Stat Rptg Ser - Agri Prices - M -
     US and by states, areas
   US Stat Rptg Ser - Agri Prices -
     Annual Summary - A - US and
     some states

TOBACCO: CHEWING
   US Labor Stat Bur - Wholesale Prices
     & Price Indexes - M

TOBACCO: FLUE-CURED, FIRE-CURED,
DARK AIR-CURED, LIGHT AIR-CURED
   US Agri Mktg Ser - Tobacco Mkt
     Rev - Q(seasonal coverage)

TOBACCO: SMOKING
   US Econ Ser - Tobacco Sit - Q
   US Labor Stat Bur - Wholesale Prices
     & Price Indexes - M
   US Stat Rptg Ser - Agri Prices -
     Annual Summary - A - US and
     by states

TOBIAS ACID
   Chem Mktg Rptr - W - US
   J of Commerce - W - NY

dl-a-TOCOPHEROL
   Chem Mktg Rptr - W - NY

dl-a-TOCOPHEROL ACETATE
   J of Commerce - W - NY

d-a-TOCOPHEROLS
   Chem Mktg Rptr - W - NY

d-a-TOCOPHERYL ACETATE
   Chem Mktg Rptr - W - NY

dl-a-TOCOPHERYL ACETATE
   Chem Mktg Rptr - W - NY

d-a-TOCOPHERYL ACID SUCCINATE
   Chem Mktg Rptr - W - NY

TODI
   Rubber World - SA

COMMODITY PRICES

TOILETS: CHINA
    US Stat Rptg Ser - Agri Prices -
      Annual Summary - A - US and
      by states

o-TOLIDINE HYDROCHLORIDE
    Chem Mktg Rptr - W - NY

TOLU BALSAM
    Chem Mktg Rptr - W - NY

TOLUENE
    US Labor Stat Bur - Wholesale Prices
      & Price Indexes - M

TOLUENE: COALTAR
    Am Paint J - W
    Chem Mktg Rptr - W - Albany,
      Chicago, Cleveland, Birmingham,
      Houston

TOLUENE: PETROLEUM
    Am Paint J - W
    Chem Mktg Rptr - W - Bayonne,
      Philadelphia, Port Arthur Tex,
      South Bend Ind, Southeast, West
      coast

p-TOLUENESULFONAMIDE
    Chem Mktg Rptr - W - US

TOLUENESULFONIC ACID
    Chem Mktg Rptr - W - US

p-TOLUENESULFONIC ACID
    Chem Mktg Rptr - W - NY

m-TOLUIDINE
    Chem Mktg Rptr - W - US

o-TOLUIDINE
    Chem Mktg Rptr - W - US

p-TOLUIDINE
    Chem Mktg Rptr - W - US
    J of Commerce - W - NY

TOLUIDINE MAROONS
    Chem Mktg Rptr - W - US

TOLUIDINE RED TONER
    Am Paint J - W
    Chem Mktg Rptr - W - US
    J of Commerce - W - NY

o-TOLUIDINE THIONATE
    J of Commerce - W - NY

2, 4-TOLYLENEDIAMINE
    Chem Mktg Rptr - W - NY
    J of Commerce - W - NY

TOLYENE DI-ISOCYANATE
    Chem Mktg Rptr - W - NY

TOMATO CATSUP
    See CATSUP: TOMATO

TOMATOES
    US Agri Mktg Ser - Fruit & Veg
      Prices - A - Calif, Chicago, Fla,
      NY, Ohio
    US Econ Ser - Mktg & Trans Sit -
      Q - US
    US Econ Ser - Veg Sit - Q - Chicago,
      NY
    US Labor Stat Bur - Retail Food
      Prices - M - US and 23 cities
    US Labor Stat Bur - Wholesale Prices
      & Price Indexes - M
    US Stat Rptg Ser - Agri Prices -
      M - US
    US Stat Rptg Ser - Agri Prices -
      Annual Summary - A - US and
      by states

TOMATOES: CANNED
    J of Commerce - W
    US Labor Stat Bur - Retail Food
      Prices - M - US and 23 cities
    US Labor Stat Bur - Wholesale Prices
      & Price Indexes - M

TOMATO JUICE
    Alaska Bev Analyst - M - Alaska

TOMATO JUICE: CANNED
    US Labor Stat Bur - Wholesale Prices
      & Price Indexes - M

COMMODITY PRICES

TOMATO PASTE
 J of Commerce - W

TOMATO SAUCE: CANNED
 US Labor Stat Bur - Wholesale Prices
  & Price Indexes - M

TONKA BEANS
 Chem Mktg Rptr - W - NY
 J of Commerce - W - NY

TONOX
 Rubber World - SA

TOOLS: HAND
 US Labor Stat Bur - Wholesale Prices
  & Price Indexes - M
  See also specific tools

TOTAQUINE
 J of Commerce - W - NY

TOWELS
 US Stat Rptg Ser - Agri Prices -
  Annual Summary - A - US and
  by states

TOXAPHENE
 Chem Mktg Rptr - W
 J of Commerce - W - NY
 US Stat Rptg Ser - Agri Prices -
  Annual Summary - A - US and
  by states

TP PLASTICIZER: -90B, -95, -680
 Rubber World - SA

TRACTORS: USED
 Implement & Tractor - IR - US

TRACTORS: WHEEL TYPE
 US Stat Rptg Ser - Agri Prices -
  Annual Summary - A - US and
  by states

TRAGACANTH GUM
 Chem Mktg Rptr - W - NY
 J of Commerce - W - NY

TRIACETATE: STAPLE & TOW
 Mod Textiles Mag - M

TRIACETATE TRICOT
 Dly News Rec - D
 J of Commerce - W

TRIACETATE YARN
 Mod Textiles Mag - M

TRIACETIN
 Chem Mktg Rptr - W - East
 Rubber World - SA

TRIBUTOXYETHYL PHOSPHATE
 Rubber World - SA

TRIBUTYLAMINE
 Chem Mktg Rptr - W - US

TRIBUTYL CITRATE
 Chem Mktg Rptr - W - East

TRIBUTYL PHOSPHATE
 Am Paint J - W
 Chem Mktg Rptr - W - US
 Rubber World - SA

TRIBUTYRIN
 Chem Mktg Rptr - W - NY

TRICHLOROACETIC ACID
 Chem Mktg Rptr - W - US

1, 2, 4-TRICHLOROBENZENE
 Chem Mktg Rptr - W - US

1, 1, 1-TRICHLOROETHANE
 Chem Mktg Rptr - W - NY

1, 1, 2-TRICHLOROETHANE
 Chem Mktg Rptr - W - US

TRICHLOROETHYLENE
 Chem Mktg Rptr - W - NY
 J of Commerce - W - NY
 Rubber World - SA
 US Labor Stat Bur - Wholesale Prices
  & Prices Indexes - M

TRICHLOROISOCYANURIC ACID
 Chem Mktg Rptr - W - NY

TRICHOLINE CITRATE
 Chem Mktg Rptr - W - NY

COMMODITY PRICES

TRICOT
See ACETATE TRICOT,
NYLON TRICOT

TRICRESYL PHOSPHATE
Am Paint J - W
Chem Mktg Rptr - W - NY
Rubber World - SA

TRIDECYL ALCOHOL
Chem Mktg Rptr - W - NY

TRIETHANOLAMINE
Am Paint J - W
Chem Mktg Rptr - W - East
Rubber World - SA

TRIETHANOLAMINE LAURYL SULFATE
Chem Mktg Rptr - W - US

TRIETHYLAMINE
Am Paint J - W
Chem Mktg Rptr - W - East

TRIETHYL CITRATE
Chem Mktg Rptr - W - East

TRIETHYLENE GLYCOL
Chem Mktg Rptr - W - East
Rubber World - SA

TRIETHYLENE GLYCOL
DIPELARGONATE
Chem Mktg Rptr - W - East

TRIETHYLENETETRAMINE
Chem Mktg Rptr - W - East

TRIETHYL PHOSPHATE
Chem Mktg Rptr - W - NY

TRI-ISOBUTYLENE
Chem Mktg Rptr - W - NY

TRI-ISOPROPANOLAMINE
Chem Mktg Rptr - W - East

TRIMENE & TRIMENE BASE
Rubber World - SA

TRIMETHYLAMINE
Chem Mktg Rptr - W - NY

TRIMETHYLOLETHANE
Am Paint J - W

TRIMETHYLOLPROPANE
Am Paint J - W
Chem Mktg Rptr - W - NY

TRINITROPHENOL
Chem Mktg Rptr - W - Charlotte NC

TRIOXANES
Chem Mktg Rptr - W - US

TRIPENTAERYTHRITOL
Chem Mktg Rptr - W - East

TRIPHENYLGUANIDINE
Chem Mktg Rptr - W - NY

TRIPHENYL PHOSPHATE
Am Paint J - W
Chem Mktg Rptr - W - NY

TRIPOLI
Eng Min J - M - Ark, Ill, Mo

TRIPROPYLENE GLYCOL
Chem Mktg Rptr - W - US

TRIS-(HYDROXYMETHYL)
AMINOMETHANE
Chem Mktg Rptr - W - US

TRITON: A-45, X-100, X-405
Rubber World - SA

TROUSERS: MEN'S
US Labor Stat Bur - Wholesale Prices
  & Price Indexes - M
US Stat Rptg Ser - Agri Prices -
  Annual Summary - A - US and
  by states

TROWELS
US Labor Stat Bur - Wholesale Prices
  & Price Indexes - M

dl-TRYPTOPHAN
Chem Mktg Rptr - W - NY

TUEX
Rubber World - SA

COMMODITY PRICES

TUNA: CANNED
   J of Commerce - W
   US Labor Stat Bur - Retail Food
     Prices - M - US and 23 cities
   US Labor Stat Bur - Wholesale Prices
     & Price Indexes - M

TUNG OIL
   Am Paint J - W - NY
   Chem Mktg Rptr - W - NY
   J of Commerce - D
   US Econ Ser - Fats & Oils Sit -
     5/yr - NY
   US Labor Stat Bur - Wholesale Prices
     & Price Indexes - M

TUNGSTEN
   Chem Mktg Rptr - W - US
   Eng Min J - M
   Met Wk - W

TUNGSTEN: WOLF
   Min Rec - W

TUNGSTEN CARBIDE POWDER
   Am Met Mkt/Met News - D - US

TUNGSTEN ORE
   Eng Min J - M - US
   North Min - W - London
   West Min - M - US

TUNGSTEN POWDER
   Am Met Mkt/Met News - D - US
   J of Commerce - D - NY

TUNGSTIC ACID
   Chem Mktg Rptr - W - US

TURKEY GROWER FEED
   US Stat Rptg Ser - Agri Prices - M-
     US and by states
   US Stat Rptg Ser - Agri Prices -
     Annual Summary - A - US and
     by states

TURKEY POULTS
   US Stat Rptg Ser - Agri Prices -
     Annual Summary - A - US and
     by states

TURKEY RED OIL
   Rubber World - SA

TURKEYS
   US Agri Mktg Ser - Broiler Mktg
     Guide - Q - US
   US Econ Ser - Demand Sit - Q - US
   US Stat Rptg Ser - Agri Prices -
     Annual Summary - A - US and
     by states
   US Stat Rptg Ser Wis - Prices
     Received - M - Wis

TURKEYS: DRESSED
   J of Commerce - D - NY

TURKEYS: HENS
   Calif Farm - S - central Calif
   Man Co-op - W - Winnipeg
   US Agri Mktg Ser - Turkey Mktg
     Guide - A - US
   US Econ Ser - Poultry & Egg Sit -
     5/yr - NY

TURKEYS: LIVE
   Mo Rural - S - Mo
   US Labor Stat Bur - Wholesale Prices
     & Price Indexes - M
   US Stat Rptg Ser - Agri Prices - M -
     US and by states

TURKEYS: READY-TO-COOK,
FROZEN
   US Cons & Mktg Ser - Poultry Mkt
     Stat - A - Ill, Kan, Los Angeles,
     Minn, NY, Seattle

TURKEYS: TOMS
   Calif Farm - S - central Calif
   Man Co-op - W - Winnipeg
   US Agri Mktg Ser - Turkey Mktg
     Guide - A - US
   US Econ Ser - Poultry & Egg Sit -
     5/yr - NY

TURMERIC
   J of Commerce - W - NY

TURPENTINE
   J of Commerce - D - NY
   US Labor Stat Bur - Wholesale Prices
     & Price Indexes - M

COMMODITY PRICES

TURPENTINE: GUM
   Am Paint J - W - NY

TURPENTINE: SULFATE-WOOD
   Am Paint J - W - NY

TURPENTINE: WOOD
   Am Paint J - W - NY

TURPOL NC-1200
   Rubber World - SA

TWEEN 20
   Rubber World - SA

TWILLS
   See COTTON GRAY GOODS,
        RAYON GRAY GOODS

TWINE: BINDER, BALER
   US Stat Rptg Ser - Agri Prices -
      Annual Summary - A - US and
      by states

TYCHEM A-50
   Rubber World - SA

TYPE 50 CLAY
   Rubber World - SA

TYPE METAL (SCRAP)
   Second Raw Materials - M -
      Chicago, Cleveland, Philadelphia,
      Pittsburgh

TY-PLY: 3640, BC, RC, Q, UP, S, T
   Rubber World - SA

U

UC540 CLAY
   Rubber World - SA

ULTRAMARINE BLUE
   Am Paint J - W

ULTRAMARINE BLUE: MEDIUM RED
TO RED, VIOLET
   Chem Mktg Rptr - W - US

ULTRAMARINE VIOLET TONER
   J of Commerce - W - NY

ULTRAWET: DS, KX, 42 K, 45 DS
   Rubber World - SA

UMBER: AMERICAN, BURNT
POWDERED, RAW POWDERED
   Am Paint J - W

UMBER: TURKEY
   J of Commerce - W - NY

UMBER: TURKEY, BURNT POWDERED,
RAW POWDERED
   Am Paint J - W

UMBER PIGMENT
   Chem Mktg Rptr - W - NY

UNADS
   Rubber World - SA

UNDECYLENIC ACID
   Chem Mktg Rptr - W - NY

UNDERWEAR (PANTIES)
   US Stat Rptg Ser - Agri Prices -
      Annual Summary - A - US and
      by states

UNDERWEAR (SHORTS): MEN'S
   US Labor Stat Bur - Wholesale Prices
      & Price Indexes - M
   US Stat Rptg Ser - Agri Prices -
      Annual Summary - A - US and
      by states

UNDERWEAR (SLIPS): WOMEN'S,
MISSES', & JUNIORS
   US Labor Stat Bur - Wholesale Prices
      & Price Indexes - M
   US Stat Rptg Ser - Agri Prices -
      Annual Summary - A - US and
      by states

UNDERWEAR (UNDERSHIRTS):
INFANTS'
   US Labor Stat Bur - Wholesale Prices
      & Price Indexes - M

COMMODITY PRICES

UNDERWEAR (UNDERSHIRTS): MEN'S
  US Labor Stat Bur - Wholesale Prices
    & Price Indexes - M
  US Stat Rptg Ser - Agri Prices -
    Annual Summary - A - US and
    by states

UNICEL: 100, ND, S, SX
  Rubber World - SA

UNICHLOR: SV, 40
  Rubber World - SA

UNIFLEX: 300, 325, 330, 375
  Rubber World - SA

UOP
  Rubber World - SA

UREA
  Chem Mktg Rptr - W - East
  J of Commerce - W - NY
  Mod Pckg-Encyclo & Plan Guide -
    A - US
  US Econ Ser - Feed Sit - Q -
    Fort Worth
  US Labor Stat Bur - Wholesale Prices
    & Price Indexes - M
  US Stat Rptg Ser - Agri Prices -
    Annual Summary - A - US and
    by states

UREA (262)
  Feedstuffs - W - Atlanta, Boston,
    Chicago, Fort Worth, Kansas
    City, Los Angeles

UREX (IMPROVED)
  Rubber World - SA

U.S.P.: DENSE
  Rubber World - SA

UVA-URSI
  J of Commerce - W - NY

UVA-URSI LEAVES
  Chem Mktg Rptr - W - NY

UVITEX OB
  Rubber World - SA

V

VACUUM CLEANERS: CANISTER TYPE
  US Stat Rptg Ser - Agri Prices -
    Annual Summary - A - US and
    by states

VALERIAN ROOT
  Chem Mktg Rptr - W - NY
  J of Commerce - W - NY

dl-VALINE
  Chem Mktg Rptr - W - US

VALONIA
  J of Commerce - W - NY

VANADIUM
  Iron Age - W
  Met Wk - W

VANADIUM OXYTRICHLORIDE
  Chem Mktg Rptr - W - US

VANADIUM PENTOXIDE
  Chem Mktg Rptr - W - US
  Eng Min J - M

VANAX: A, A-7, RODFORM
  Rubber World - SA

VANCIDE 89
  Rubber World - SA

VANDEX
  Rubber World - SA

VAN DYKE BROWN
  Am Paint J - W
  Chem Mktg Rptr - W - NY

VANILLA BEANS
  Chem Mktg Rptr - W - NY
  J of Commerce - W - NY

VANILLA OLEORESIN
  J of Commerce - W - NY

COMMODITY PRICES

VANILLIN
Chem Mktg Rptr - W - NY
Rubber World - SA
US Labor Stat Bur - Wholesale Prices
& Price Indexes - M

VANOX 12
Rubber World - SA

VARNISH: FLOOR
US Labor Stat Bur - Wholesale Prices
& Price Indexes - M

VARNISH: ORANGE, WHITE
Am Paint J - W

VARNISH GUMS
J of Commerce - W

VAROX AND VAROX LIQUID
Rubber World - SA

VEAL
Lancaster Farm - W - NY
US Econ Ser - Livestock Sit - BM - US
US Labor Stat Bur - Wholesale Prices
& Price Indexes - M

VEAL CUTLETS
US Labor Stat Bur - Retail Food
Prices - M - US and 23 cities

VEALERS
US Agri Mktg Ser - Livestock Mkt
News - W - Ga, Louisville,
National stock yards, Portland,
St. Paul
US Econ Ser - Livestock Sit - BM -
St. Paul

VEALERS: LIVESTOCK
Natl Provision - W - Indianapolis,
Louisville, St. Paul

VEGETABLE FAT
Feedstuffs - W - Boston, Buffalo,
Fort Worth, Kansas City

VEGETABLES
See also specific entries

VEGETABLES: FROZEN
J of Commerce - W

VELSICOL: GD 5-28 RESIN, M-144 OIL, XL-30 RESIN
Rubber World - SA

VENETIAN RED
Am Paint J - W
J of Commerce - W - NY

VENTILATORS: UNIT
US Labor Stat Bur - Wholesale Prices
& Price Indexes - M

VERMICULITE
Eng Min J - M - Atlantic ports,
Mont, SC

VERMILLION ENGLISH
Am Paint J - W
J of Commerce - W - NY

VERMOUTH
Alaska Bev Analyst - M - Alaska
Ariz Bev J - M - Ariz
Bev Media - M - NY
Bev News - M
Ill Bev J - M - Ill
Ky Bev J - M - Ky
Md-Wash-Del Bev J - M - DC, Del, Md
Mich Bev News - IR - Mich
Patterson's - M - Calif
RI Bev J - M - RI
Wis Bev J - M - Wis

VERSA-LUBE
Rubber World - SA

VETCH SEED
US Stat Rptg Ser - Agri Prices -
Annual Summary - A - US and
by states

VETIVER ACETATE
Chem Mktg Rptr - W - NY

VETIVER OIL
Chem Mktg Rptr - W - NY
J of Commerce - W - NY

COMMODITY PRICES

VICTORIA BLUE TONER
   Am Paint J - W
   Chem Mktg Rptr - W - NY

VINSOL RESIN
   Rubber World - SA

VINYL
   Mod Pckg-Encyclo & Plan Guide -
   A - US

VINYL ACETATE
   J of Commerce - W - NY

VINYL ACETATE MONOMER
   Chem Mktg Rptr - W - NY
   US Labor Stat Bur - Wholesale Prices
   & Price Indexes - M

VINYL BROMIDE
   J of Commerce - W - NY

VINYL N-BUTYL ETHER
   Chem Mktg Rptr - W - US

VINYL CHLORIDE MONOMER
   Chem Mktg Rptr - W - US
   US Labor Stat Bur - Wholesale Prices
   & Price Indexes - M

VINYL ETHER
   Chem Mktg Rptr - W - NY

VINYL ETHYL ETHER
   Chem Mktg Rptr - W - Calvert City
   Ky

2-VINYLPYRIDINE
   Chem Mktg Rptr - W - US

VINYL SCRAP
   Purch World - M - NY

VINYL STABILIZERS
   Can Chem Processing - M - Ont, Que

VINYLTOLUENE
   Chem Mktg Rptr - W - US

VINYON: STAPLE FIBER
   Mod Textiles Mag - M

VIOLET TONER: PMA, PTA
   Am Paint J - W

VISCOSE: FILAMENT YARN
   US Labor Stat Bur - Wholesale Prices
   & Price Indexes - M

VISCOSE RAYON
   See RAYON

VISE: STANDARD
   US Labor Stat Bur - Wholesale Prices
   & Price Indexes - M

VITAMIN A
   Chem Mktg Rptr - W - NY
   US Labor Stat Bur - Wholesale Prices
   & Price Indexes - M

VITAMIN B1
   Chem Mktg Rptr - W - NY
   US Labor Stat Bur - Wholesale Prices
   & Price Indexes - M

VITAMIN B2
   Chem Mktg Rptr - W - US
   US Labor Stat Bur - Wholesale Prices
   & Price Indexes - M

VITAMIN B6
   US Labor Stat Bur - Wholesale Prices
   & Price Indexes - M

VITAMIN B12
   Chem Mktg Rptr - W - NY
   J of Commerce - W - NY
   US Labor Stat Bur - Wholesale Prices
   & Price Indexes - M

VITAMIN C
   US Labor Stat Bur - Wholesale Prices
   & Price Indexes - M

VITAMIN D
   Chem Mktg Rptr - W - NY

COMMODITY PRICES

VODKA
  Alaska Bev Analyst – M – Alaska
  Ariz Bev J – M – Ariz
  Bev Media – M – NY
  Bev News – M
  Buck Bev J – M – Ohio
  Ill Bev J – M – Ill
  Ky Bev J – M – Ky
  Md-Wash-Del Bev J – M – DC, Del, Md
  Mich Bev News – IR – Mich
  NJ Bev J – M – NJ
  Patterson's – M – Calif
  RI Bev J – M – RI
  Wis Bev J – M – Wis

VODKA: FLAVORED
  Ariz Bev J – M – Ariz
  Bev News – M
  Buck Bev J – M – Ohio
  Ill Bev J – M – Ill
  Ky Bev J – M – Ky
  Md-Wash-Del Bev J – M – DC, Del, Md
  Mich Bev News – IR – Mich
  Patterson's – M – Calif
  Wis Bev J – M – Wis

VOCOL AND VOCOL S
  Rubber World – SA

VOLCLAY
  Rubber World – SA

VULCACIT
  Rubber World – SA

VUL-CUP: 40KE, R
  Rubber World – SA

VULKADUR: A, R, T LIQUID AND POWDER
  Rubber World – SA

VULTAC: 2-6
  Rubber World – SA

W

WAGONS: FARM
  US Stat Rptg Ser – Agri Prices – Annual Summary – A – US and by states

WAHOO ROOT BARK
  J of Commerce – W – NY

WAHOO TREE BARK
  J of Commerce – W – NY

WALLET: MEN'S, MORROCCO
  US Labor Stat Bur – Wholesale Prices & Price Indexes – M

WALNUT OIL
  Chem Mktg Rptr – W – NY

WALNUTS
  J of Commerce – W – NY

WALNUT (WOOD)
  Comm Bul – W

WARECURE: C, T
  Rubber World – SA

WAREFLEX PLASTICIZER
  Rubber World – SA

WARFARIN
  Chem Mktg Rptr – W – Chicago, NY

WASHING MACHINES: ELECTRIC
  US Stat Rptg Ser – Agri Prices – Annual Summary – A – US and by states

WASTE PAPER: BAG CUTTINGS, PRINTED AND UNPRINTED
  Comm Bul – W – Boston, New England

WASTE PAPER: BOXBOARD CLIPPINGS
  Paperbd Pckg – A – Chicago, NY

COMMODITY PRICES

WASTE PAPER: BOXBOARD CUTTINGS
   Comm Bul - W - Boston, New England
   Official Bd Mkts - W - Chicago, Cleveland, Los Angeles, NY, South

WASTE PAPER: COLORED LEDGER
   Comm Bul - W - Boston, Chicago, New England

WASTE PAPER: COLORED TAB CARDS
   Comm Bul - W - Boston, New England
   Paper Trade J - W

WASTE PAPER: CORRUGATED
   Comm Bul - W - Boston, Chicago, New England, NY

WASTE PAPER: CORRUGATED CUTTINGS
   Official Bd Mkts - W - Chicago, Cleveland, Los Angeles, NY, South

WASTE PAPER: DOUBLE LINED KRAFT CORRUGATED CLIPPINGS
   Paperbd Pckg - A - East, Midwest

WASTE PAPER: DOUBLE LINED KRAFT CORRUGATED CUTTINGS
   Comm Bul - W - Boston, Chicago, New England
   Paper Trade J - W

WASTE PAPER: ENVELOPE CUTTINGS
   Comm Bul - W - Boston, New England

WASTE PAPER: FLOUR AND SUGAR BAGS
   Comm Bul - W - Boston, New England

WASTE PAPER: FOLDED NEWS
   J of Commerce - W - NY

WASTE PAPER: HARD WHITE ENVELOPE CUTTINGS
   Comm Bul - W - Boston, New England
   Official Bd Mkts - W - US
   Paper Trade J - W

WASTE PAPER: HARD WHITE SHAVINGS
   Official Bd Mkts - W - US
   Paperbd Pckg - A - East, Midwest
   Paper Trade J - W

WASTE PAPER: MANILA TAB CARDS
   Comm Bul - W - Boston, New England
   J of Commerce - W - NY
   Official Bd Mkts - W - US
   Paperbd Pckg - A - East, Midwest
   Paper Trade J - W

WASTE PAPER: MILL WRAPPERS
   Paper Trade J - W

WASTE PAPER: MIXED
   Comm Bul - W - Chicago, NY

WASTE PAPER: MIXED COLORED SHAVINGS
   Comm Bul - W - Boston, New England

WASTE PAPER: .009 MIXED KRAFT CLIPPINGS
   US Bur Dom Comm - Pulp Q - Q

WASTE PAPER: NEW BROWN KRAFT BAG WASTE, PRINTED
   Paper Trade J - W

WASTE PAPER: NEW BROWN KRAFT BAG WASTE, UNPRINTED
   Paper Trade J - W

WASTE PAPER: NEW BROWN KRAFT ENVELOPE CUTS
   Paper Trade J - W

WASTE PAPER: NEW DOUBLE KRAFT LINED CORRUGATED CUTS
   Official Bd Mkts - W - US

COMMODITY PRICES

WASTE PAPER: NEWS
  Comm Bul - W - Chicago, NY

WASTE PAPER: NO.1 BALED NEWS
  Comm Bul - W - Boston, New England
  Paperbd Pckg - A - Chicago, NY

WASTE PAPER: NO. 1 BOOKS
  Comm Bul - W - Boston, New England

WASTE PAPER: NO. 1 COLORED LEDGER
  Paper Trade J - W

WASTE PAPER: NO. 1 FREE OF GROUNDWOOD SHAVINGS
  Comm Bul - W - Boston, New England

WASTE PAPER: NO. 1 GROUNDWOOD SHAVINGS
  Comm Bul - W - Boston, New England
  Paper Trade J - W

WASTE PAPER: NO. 1 HARD COLORED CUTTINGS
  J of Commerce - W - NY

WASTE PAPER: NO. 1 HARD WHITE ENVELOPES
  J of Commerce - W - NY

WASTE PAPER: NO. 1 HARD WHITE SHAVINGS
  Comm Bul - W - Boston, New England
  J of Commerce - W - NY

WASTE PAPER: NO. 1 MIXED
  Comm Bul - W - Boston, New England
  J of Commerce - W - NY
  Official Bd Mkts - W - Chicago, Cleveland, NY, South
  Paperbd Pckg - A - Chicago, NY
  Paper Trade J - W
  Purch World - M - NY
  US Bur Dom Comm - Pulp Q - Q

WASTE PAPER: NO. 1 NEWS
  Official Bd Mkts - W - Chicago Cleveland, Los Angeles, NY, South
  Paper Trade J - W
  US Bur Dom Comm - Pulp Q - Q

WASTE PAPER: NO. 1 SOFT WHITE SHAVINGS
  J of Commerce - W - NY
  Official Bd Mkts - W - US
  Paper Trade J - W

WASTE PAPER: NO. 1 WHITE NEWS BLANKS
  Comm Bul - W - Boston, New England

WASTE PAPER: OLD CORRUGATED
  J of Commerce - W - NY

WASTE PAPER: OLD CORRUGATED BOXES
  Paperbd Pckg - A - Chicago, NY
  Purch World - M - Chicago, NY
  US Bus Dom Comm - Pulp Q - Q

WASTE PAPER: OLD CORRUGATED CONTAINERS
  Paper Trade J - W

WASTE PAPER: ONE CUT SOFT WHITE SHAVINGS
  Comm Bul - W - Boston, New England

WASTE PAPER: OVERISSUE NEWS
  Comm Bul - W - Boston, New England
  Paper Trade J - W

WASTE PAPER: .009 SEMICHEM KRAFT CLIPPINGS
  US Bur Dom Comm - Pulp Q - Q

WASTE PAPER: SOFT WHITE COATED SHAVINGS
  Comm Bul - W - Boston, New England

COMMODITY PRICES

WASTE PAPER: SORTED WHITE LEDGER
  Official Bd Mkts - W - Chicago, Cleveland, Los Angeles, NY, South

WASTE PAPER: SULPHITE NEWS (WRAPS)
  Comm Bul - W - Boston, New England

WASTE PAPER: SUPER BOOKS
  Comm Bul - W - Boston, New England

WASTE PAPER: SUPER MIXED
  Comm Bul - W - Chicago

WASTE PAPER: SUPER SOFT WHITE SHAVINGS
  Paper Trade J - W

WASTE PAPER: TRIPLE SORTED BROWN KRAFT
  J of Commerce - W - NY

WASTE PAPER: TRIPLE SORTED KRAFT
  Comm Bul - W - Boston, New England

WASTE PAPER: WHITE LEDGER
  Comm Bul - W - Boston, Chicago, New England
  Paperbd Pckg - A - Chicago, NY
  Paper Trade J - W

WASTE PAPER: WHITE NEWS BLANKS
  Official Bd Mkts - W - US
  Paperbd Pckg - A - East, Midwest
  Paper Trade J - W
  US Bur Dom Comm - Pulp Q - Q

WATERMELONS
  US Agri Mktg Ser - Fruit & Veg Prices - A - Calif, Chicago, Fla, NY, Tex
  US Econ Ser - Veg Sit - Q - US
  US Labor Stat Bur - Retail Food Prices - M - US and 23 cities
  US Stat Rptg Ser - Agri Prices - M - US

WATER-SOLUBLE FILM
  Mod Pckg-Encyclo & Plan Guide - A - US

WATER SUCTION HOSE: RUBBER
  US Labor Stat Bur - Wholesale Prices & Price Indexes - M

WATTLE BARK
  J of Commerce - W - NY

WAX: FLOOR
  US Stat Rptg Ser - Agri Prices - Annual Summary - A - US and by states

WAX: ROSS SUNPROFFING
  Rubber World - SA

WAX 118
  Rubber World - SA

WAXES
  J of Commerce - W

WEBNIX
  Rubber World - SA

WESTERN SPRUCE: FRAMING LUMBER
  Comm Bul - W

WESTERN WHITE SPRUCE BOARDS
  Comm Bul - W - east of Chicago

WHEAT
  Agri Let - W - US
  Barron's - W - Chicago
  Comm Rev - W - US
  Dly Mkt Rec - D - Chicago, Kansas City, Minneapolis
  Fin Post - W - Chicago
  Fin Times Can - W - Chicago
  Free Press Farm - W - Chicago
  J of Commerce - D - Baltimore, Chicago, Kansas City, NY
  Lancaster Farm - W - Lancaster Pa
  NY Times - D - Chicago, Kansas City
  UN Bul Stat - M - Can, US
  US Econ Ser - Demand Sit - Q - US

COMMODITY PRICES

US Econ Ser - Wheat Sit - Q - US markets
US Stat Rptg Ser - Agri Prices - M - US and by states
US Stat Rptg Ser - Agri Prices - Annual Summary - A - US and by states
Wall Street J - D - Chicago, Kansas City, Minneapolis
West Producer - W - Chicago, Sask

WHEAT: AMBER DURUM
Dly Mkt Rec - D - Minneapolis

WHEAT: DARK NORTHERN SPRING
Mont Farm - S - Portland

WHEAT: FEED
Feedstuffs - W - Kansas City, Los Angeles

WHEAT: HARD RED WINTER
Ida Farm - S
Mont Farm - S - Portland
Ore Farm - S - Portland
Utah Farm - S - Ogden Utah
Wash Farm - S - Portland

WHEAT: HARD WINTER
Dly Mkt Rec - D - Minneapolis
US Labor Stat Bur - Wholesale Prices & Price Indexes - M

WHEAT: NORTHERN SPRING
Dly Mkt Rec - D - Minneapolis

WHEAT: NO. 1 DARK NORTHERN SPRING
US Agri Mktg Ser - Grain Mkt News - W - Minneapolis

WHEAT: NO. 1 HARD AMBER DURUM
US Agri Mktg Ser - Grain Mkt News - W - Minneapolis

WHEAT: NO. 1 HARD WINTER
Neb Farm - S - Omaha
US Agri Mktg Ser - Grain Mkt News - W - Houston, Kansas City, Omaha, Portland

WHEAT: NO. 2
Calif Farm - S - Los Angeles, Stockton

WHEAT: NO. 2 HARD
Barron's - W - Kansas City

WHEAT: NO. 2 HARD WINTER
US Agri Mktg Ser - Grain Mkt News - W - St. Louis

WHEAT: NO. 2 RED
NY Times - D - Chicago

WHEAT: NO. 2 SOFT RED WINTER
US Agri Mktg Ser - Grain Mkt News - W - Baltimore, Chicago, St. Louis, Toledo

WHEAT: NO. 2 SOFT WHITE
US Agri Mktg Ser - Grain Mkt News - W - Portland, Toledo

WHEAT: NO. 2 YELLOW HARD WINTER
US Agri Mktg Ser - Grain Mkt News - W - Chicago

WHEAT: RED WINTER
US Labor Stat Bur - Wholesale Prices & Price Indexes - M - St. Louis

WHEAT: SEED
US Stat Rptg Ser - Agri Prices - Annual Summary - A - US and by states

WHEAT: SOFT RED WINTER
Mich Farm - S - central Mich

WHEAT: SOFT WHITE
Ida Farm - S - Portland
Ore Farm - S - Portland
US Labor Stat Bur - Wholesale Prices & Price Indexes - M - Portland
Utah Farm - S - Ogden Utah
Wash Farm - S - Portland

WHEAT: SPRING
US Labor Stat Bur - Wholesale Prices & Price Indexes - M - Minneapolis
US Stat Rptg Ser - Agri Prices - M - Colo, Ida, Minn, Mont

COMMODITY PRICES

WHEAT: WHITE
　Mich Farm - S - central Mich

WHEAT: WINTER
　US Stat Rptg Ser - Agri Prices - M - Colo, Ida, Minn, Mont

WHEAT BRAN
　Dly Mkt Rec - D - Minneapolis
　US Agri Mktg Ser - Feed Mkt News - W

WHEAT BRAN: STANDARD
　Dairynews - S - Boston, Buffalo, NY, Philadelphia

WHEAT GERM OIL
　Chem Mktg Rptr - W - NY

WHEAT MIDDLINGS
　Dly Mkt Rec - D - Minneapolis
　US Agri Mktg Ser - Feed Mkt News - W

WHEAT MIDDLINGS: STANDARD
　Dairynews - S - Boston, Buffalo, NY, Philadelphia

WHEAT MILLFEEDS
　Feedstuffs - W

WHEAT MILLRUN
　Calif Farm - S - Los Angeles, San Francisco
　US Agri Mktg Ser - Feed Mkt News - W - Denver, Los Angeles, Portland, San Francisco

WHEAT SHORTS
　Mo Rural - S - Kansas City Mo

WHEY: DRIED
　Feedstuffs - W - Baltimore, Buffalo, Chicago, Kansas City, San Francisco
　US Cons & Mktg Ser - Dairy Mkt Stat - A - East, Midwest

WHEY: SPRAY
　Dairy Rec - M - East

WHEY POWDER
　Dairy Rec - M - East, Midwest

WHISKEY: BLENDED, CANADIAN, IRISH, LIGHT
　Alaska Bev Analyst - M - Alaska
　Ariz Bev J - M - Ariz
　Bev Media - M - NY
　Bev News - M
　Buck Bev J - M - Ohio
　Ill Bev J - M - Ill
　Ky Bev J - M - Ky
　Md-Wash-Del Bev J - M - DC, Del, Md
　Mich Bev News - IR - Mich
　NJ Bev J - M - NJ
　Patterson's - M - Calif
　RI Bev J - M - RI
　Wis Bev J - M - Wis

WHISKEY: BONDED
　Alaska Bev Analyst - M - Alaska
　Ariz Bev J - M - Ariz
　Bev News - M
　Ill Bev J - M - Ill
　Ky Bev J - M - Ky

WHISKEY: BOTTLED-IN-BOND
　Ariz Bev J - M - Ariz
　Bev Media - M - NY
　Ky Bev J - M - Ky
　Md-Wash-Del Bev J - M - DC, Del, Md
　NJ Bev J - M - NJ
　Patterson's - M - Calif
　RI Bev J - M - RI
　Wis Bev J - M - Wis

WHISKEY: CORN
　Alaska Bev Analyst - M - Alaska
　Ariz Bev J - M - Ariz
　Bev Media - M - NY
　Bev News - M
　Buck Bev J - M - Ohio
　Ky Bev J - M - Ky
　Md-Wash-Del Bev J - M - DC, Del, Md
　Mich Bev News - IR - Mich
　NJ Bev J - M - NJ
　Patterson's - M - Calif

WHISKEY: GERMAN
　Ill Bev J - M - Ill

COMMODITY PRICES

WHISKEY: JAPANESE
   Ariz Bev J – M – Ariz
   Ill Bev J – M – Ill
   Ky Bev J – M – Ky
   Mich Bev News – IR – Mich
   RI Bev J – M – RI
   Wis Bev J – M – Wis

WHISKEY: RYE
   Alaska Bev Analyst – M – Alaska
   Ariz Bev J – M – Ariz
   Bev News – M
   Buck Bev J – M – Ohio
   Ky Bev J – M – Ky
   Md-Wash-Del Bev J – M – DC, Del, Md
   Patterson's – M – Calif
   RI Bev J – M – RI
   Wis Bev J – M – Wis

WHISKEY: SCOTCH
   Alaska Bev Analyst – M – Alaska
   Ariz Bev J – M – Ariz
   Bev Media – M – NY
   Bev News – M
   Buck Bev J – M – Ohio
   Ill Bev J – M – Ill
   Ky Bev J – M – Ky
   Md-Wash-Del Bev J – M – DC, Del, Md
   Mich Bev News – IR – Mich
   NJ Bev J – M – NJ
   Patterson's – M – Calif
   RI Bev J – M – RI
   Wis Bev J – M – Wis

WHISKEY: STRAIGHT
   Alaska Bev Analyst – M – Alaska
   Ariz Bev J – M – Ariz
   Bev Media – M – NY
   Bev News – M
   Ill Bev J – M – Ill
   Ky Bev J – M – Ky
   Md-Wash-Del Bev J – M – DC, Del, Md
   NJ Bev J – M – NJ
   Patterson's – M – Calif
   RI Bev J – M – RI
   Wis Bev J – M – Wis

WHISKEY: TENNESSEE
   Ariz Bev J – M – Ariz
   Bev Media – M – NY
   Bev News – M
   Buck Bev J – M – Ohio
   Md-Wash-Del Bev J – M – DC, Del, Md
   Mich Bev News – IR – Mich
   Patterson's – M – Calif
   Wis Bev J – M – Wis

WHISKEY: WHITE
   Md-Wash-Del Bev J – M – DC, Del, Md
   Wis Bev J – M – Wis

WHITE: NOS. 1 & 3, 10, WINGDALE, YORK, SNOWFLAKE
   Rubber World – SA

WHITE FACTICE: 56, 56-S, 57-S, E SPECIAL, LAC SPECIAL
   Rubber World – SA

WHITE FIR: SELECTS AND SHOP
   Comm Bul – W

WHITE FIR BOARDS
   Comm Bul – W

WHITEFISH: UNPROCESSED
   US Labor Stat Bur – Wholesale Prices & Price Indexes – M

WHITE OIL
   J of Commerce – D

WHITE PINE BARK
   J of Commerce – W – NY

WHITE PRECIPITATE
   Chem Mktg Rptr – W – US

WHITETEX
   Rubber World – SA

WHITING
   US Labor Stat Bur – Wholesale Prices & Price Indexes – M

WHITING: ALLIED
   Rubber World – SA

COMMODITY PRICES

WHITING: DOMESTIC, PRECIPITATED; IMPORTED, COMMERCIAL
   Am Paint J - W

WILD CHERRY BARK
   J of Commerce - W - NY

WILLOW
   Comm Bul - W

WILTROL: N, P
   Rubber World - SA

WINDOWS: HOUSE
   US Stat Rptg Ser - Agri Prices - Annual Summary - A - US and by states

WINDSOR CLAY
   Rubber World - SA

WINES
   Alaska Bev Analyst - M - Alaska
   Ariz Bev J - M - Ariz
   Bev Media - M - NY
   Bev News - M
   Calif Farm - S - Calif
   Calif Wine - S - Calif
   Ill Bev J - M - Ill
   Ky Bev J - M - Ky
   Md-Wash-Del Bev J - M - DC, Del, Md
   Mich Bev News - IR - Mich
   Patterson's - M - Calif
   RI Bev J - M - RI
   Wis Bev J - M - Wis

WINES: KOSHER
   Bev Media - M - NY

WINGDALE WHITE
   Rubber World - SA

WINGSTAY
   Rubber World - SA

WINGSTROK 10
   Rubber World - SA

WINGTACK: 95, 115
   Rubber World - SA

WINTERGREEN OIL
   J of Commerce - W - NY

WINTER PEA SEED
   US Stat Rptg Ser - Agri Prices - Annual Summary - A - US and by states

WIRE SCREEN: GALVANIZED
   US Stat Rptg Ser - Agri Prices - Annual Summary - A - US and by states

WITCH HAZEL BARK
   Chem Mktg Rptr - W - NY

WITCH HAZEL LEAVES
   Chem Mktg Rptr - W - NY
   J of Commerce - W - NY

WITROL: N, P
   Rubber World - SA

WOLLASTONITE
   Am Paint J - W
   Chem Mktg Rptr - W - US

WOOD FLOUR
   Rubber World - SA

WOOD PULP
   UN Bul Stat - M - US

WOOD PULP: BLEACHED HARDWOOD SULFATE DOMESTIC, CANADIAN, EUOPEAN
   Official Bd Mkts - W

WOOD PULP: BLEACHED SOFTWOOD KRAFT
   Paperbd Pckg - A

WOOD PULP: CHEMICAL, SULFATE, BLEACHED
   US Labor Stat Bur - Wholesale Prices & Price Indexes - M

WOOD PULP: CHEMICAL, SULFATE, SEMI-BLEACHED
   US Labor Stat Bur - Wholesale Prices & Price Indexes - M

COMMODITY PRICES

WOOD PULP: CHEMICAL, SULFATE, UNBLEACHED
    US Labor Stat Bur - Wholesale Prices & Price Indexes - M

WOOD PULP: CHEMICAL, SULFITE, BLEACHED
    US Labor Stat Bur - Wholesale Prices & Price Indexes - M

WOOD PULP: CHEMICAL, SULFITE, UNBLEACHED
    US Labor Stat Bur - Wholesale Prices & Price Indexes - M

WOOD PULP: GROUNDWOOD
    Paperbd Pckg - A
    Paper Trade J - W
    US Bur Dom Comm - Pulp Q - Q
    US Labor Stat Bur - Wholesale Prices & Price Indexes - M

WOOD PULP: GROUNDWOOD, BLEACHED
    Paper Trade J - W

WOOD PULP: GROUNDWOOD, DOMESTIC, CANADIAN, EUROPEAN
    Official Bd Mkts - W

WOOD PULP: KRAFT, BLEACHED HARDWOOD
    Paper Trade J - W

WOOD PULP: KRAFT, BLEACHED SOFTWOOD
    Paper Trade J - W

WOOD PULP: KRAFT, SEMI-BLEACHED
    Paper Trade J - W

WOOD PULP: KRAFT, UNBLEACHED
    Paperbd Pckg - A
    Paper Trade J - W

WOOD PULP: SULFATE, BLEACHED
    US Bur Dom Comm - Pulp Q - Q

WOOD PULP: SULFATE, BLEACHED, CANADIAN, DOMESTIC, & EUROPEAN
    Official Bd Mkts - W

WOOD PULP: SULFATE, SEMI-BLEACHED
    US Bur Dom Comm - Pulp Q - Q

WOOD PULP: SULFATE, SEMI-BLEACHED, CANADIAN, DOMESTIC, & EUROPEAN
    Official Bd Mkts - W

WOOD PULP: SULFATE, UNBLEACHED
    US Bur Dom Comm - Pulp Q - Q

WOOD PULP: SULFATE, UNBLEACHED, CANADIAN, DOMESTIC, & EUROPEAN
    Official Bd Mkts - W

WOOD PULP: SULFITE, BLEACHED
    Paperbd Pckg - A
    Paper Trade J - W
    US Bur Dom Comm - Pulp Q - Q

WOOD PULP: SULFITE, BLEACHED, CANADIAN, DOMESTIC, & EUROPEAN
    Official Bd Mkts - W

WOOD PULP: SULFITE, UNBLEACHED
    Paperbd Pckg - A
    Paper Trade J - W
    US Bur Dom Comm - Pulp Q - Q

WOOD PULP: SULFITE, UNBLEACHED, CANADIAN, DOMESTIC, & EUROPEAN
    Official Bd Mkts - W

WOOD ROSIN
    Am Paint J - W - NY
    J of Commerce - D - NY

WOOL
    Fin Post - W
    Ida Farm - S - Northwest
    Mont Farm - S - Northwest
    Natl Wool - M - US states (varies)
    NY Times - D - NY
    UN Bul Stat - M - US
    US Stat Rptg Ser - Agri Prices - M - US and by states

COMMODITY PRICES

US Stat Rptg Ser - Agri Prices -
   Annual Summary - A - US and
   by states
Wall Street J - D - NY

WOOL: CARPET
   Comm Bul - W - Boston
   US Labor Stat Bur - Wholesale Prices
     & Price Indexes - M

WOOL: CROSS BRED
   J of Commerce - D - NY

WOOL: DOMESTIC
   Comm Bul - W - Boston
   World Wool Dig - M - Boston

WOOL: DOMESTIC APPAREL
   US Labor Stat Bur - Wholesale Prices
     & Price Indexes - M

WOOL: FINE STAPLE
   Barron's - W - Boston
   Wall Street J - D - Boston

WOOLS: FLEECE
   J of Commerce - W

WOOL: FOREIGN GROWTHS, ARGENTINA
   J of Commerce - W

WOOL: FOREIGN GROWTHS, AUSTRALIA
   Comm Bul - W - Boston
   J of Commerce - W
   US Labor Stat Bur - Wholesale Prices
     & Price Indexes - M
   World Wool Dig - M - Boston

WOOL: FOREIGN GROWTHS, BUENOS AIRES
   World Wool Dig - M - Boston

WOOL: FOREIGN GROWTHS, MONTEVIDEO
   J of Commerce - W
   US Labor Stat Bur - Wholesale Prices
     & Price Indexes - M

WOOL: FOREIGN GROWTHS, NEW ZEALAND
   Comm Bul - W - Boston
   J of Commerce - W
   US Labor Stat Bur - Wholesale Prices
     & Price Indexes - M
   World Wool Dig - M - Boston

WOOL: FOREIGN GROWTHS, SOUTH AFRICA
   Comm Bul - W - Boston
   J of Commerce - W
   US Labor Stat Bur - Wholesale Prices
     & Price Indexes - M
   World Wool Dig - M - Boston

WOOL: PULLED
   J of Commerce - W

WOOL: RAW
   J of Commerce - W

WOOL: SHORN
   US Econ Ser - Wool Sit - 4/yr

WOOL FABRICS
   US Labor Stat Bur - Wholesale Prices
     & Price Indexes - M

WOOL FABRICS: SUITING BLEND, POLYESTER/WOOL
   US Labor Stat Bur - Wholesale Prices
     & Price Indexes - M

WOOL FABRICS: SUITING, MEN'S
   US Labor Stat Bur - Wholesale Prices
     & Price Indexes - M

WOOL GREASE
   Comm Bul - W - NY
   Dly News Rec - D
   Free Press Farm - W - NY
   J of Commerce - D - NY

WOOL NOILS
   Comm Bul - W - Boston
   J of Commerce - W

COMMODITY PRICES

WOOL TOPS
  Comm Bul - W - Boston
  J of Commerce - W
  Purch World - M - NY
  US Labor Stat Bur - Wholesale Prices
    & Price Indexes - M

WOOL YARN
  UN Bul Stat - M - US
  US Labor Stat Bur - Wholesale Prices
    & Price Indexes - M

WORMSEED
  J of Commerce - W - NY

WORMWOOD HERB
  J of Commerce - W - NY

WORMWOOD OIL
  Chem Mktg Rptr - W - NY
  J of Commerce - W - NY

WRENCHES
  US Labor Stat Bur - Wholesale Prices
    & Price Indexes - M

WRENCHES: END, ADJUSTABLE
  US Stat Rptg Ser - Agri Prices -
    Annual Summary - A - US and
    by states

WT GUM
  Rubber World - SA

WYTOX: 312, 345, XL-PAP, ADP-X, 438, 540
  Rubber World - SA

X

XYLENE
  J of Commerce - W - NY
  Purch World - M
  US Labor Stat Bur - Wholesale Prices
    & Price Indexes - M

XYLENE: COALTAR, PETROLEUM
  Am Paint J - W
  Chem Mktg Rptr - W - US

m-XYLENE
  Chem Mktg Rptr - W - NY

p-XYLENE
  Chem Mktg Rptr - W - US
  US Labor Stat Bur - Wholesale Prices
    & Price Indexes - M

XYLENOL
  Chem Mktg Rptr - W - NY

2, 4-XYLIDINE
  Chem Mktg Rptr - W - NY

XYLIDINES: MIXED
  Chem Mktg Rptr - W - NY

Y

YACCA GUM
  Am Paint J - W

YARA YARA
  Chem Mktg Rptr - W - NY

YARN
  See also specific types

YARN: CARDED
  Dly News Record - D - NY

YARN: CARDED, KNITTING
  US Labor Stat Bur - Wholesale Prices
    & Price Indexes - M

YARN: CARDED, WEAVING
  US Labor Stat Bur - Wholesale Prices
    & Price Indexes - M

YARN: COMBED
  Dly News Rec - D - NY
  Purch World - M

COMMODITY PRICES

YARN: COMBED, KNITTING
US Labor Stat Bur - Wholesale Prices & Price Indexes - M

YARN: COMBED, WEAVING
US Labor Stat Bur - Wholesale Prices & Price Indexes - M

YEAST
Chem Mktg Rptr - W - US

YELLOW OXIDE
J of Commerce - W - NY

YERBA SANTA LEAVES
Chem Mktg Rptr - W - NY

YLANG-YLANG OIL
Chem Mktg Rptr - W - NY
J of Commerce - W - NY

YORK WHITE
Rubber World - SA

Z

ZALBA SPECIAL
Rubber World - SA

Z-B-X
Rubber World - SA

ZEIN
Chem Mktg Rptr - W - NY

ZENITE AND ZENITE SPECIAL
Rubber World - SA

ZEOLEX 23
Rubber World - SA

ZEOSYL 100
Rubber World - SA

ZETAX: DP
Rubber World - SA

ZINAR
Rubber World - SA

ZINC
Am Met Mkt/Met News - D - Can, US
Barron's - W
Chem Mktg Rptr - W - NY
Comm Bul - W
Eng Min J - M
Fin Post - W
Fin Times Can - W - NY
Indus Wk - W
Iron Age - W
Met Wk - W
Min Rec - W - St. Louis
UN Bul Stat - M - Can, US
UN Lead & Zinc Stat - M - Can, US
Wall Street J - D
West Miner - M - Can, US

ZINC: ANODE
Finishers' Mgt - M

ZINC: DIECASTING ALLOY
Comm Bul - W
Purch World - M
US Labor Stat Bur - Wholesale Prices & Price Indexes - M

ZINC: DIECASTING ALLOY, INGOT
Foundry - M

ZINC: HIGH GRADE, INGOT
Foundry - M

ZINC: PRIME WESTERN
Am Met Mkt/Met News - D - Can, US
J of Commerce - D
North Miner - W - Can, US
Purch World - M - St. Louis

ZINC: PRIME WESTERN, CONTINUOUS GALVANIZING GRADE, HIGH GRADE, SPECIAL HIGH GRADE
Am Met Mkt/Met News - D - Can, US

ZINC: SLAB
US Labor Stat Bur - Wholesale Prices & Price Indexes - M

COMMODITY PRICES

ZINC: SMELTERS' SCRAP
Am Met Mkt/Met News - D - US

ZINC: WET, 40, A, CW, P
Rubber World - SA

ZINC ACETATE
Chem Mktg Rptr - W - US

ZINC-AMMONIUM CHLORIDE
Chem Mktg Rptr - W - US

ZINC BORATE
Chem Mktg Rptr - W - NY

ZINC CARBONATE
Rubber World - SA

ZINC CHLORIDE
Chem Mktg Rptr - W - NY
J of Commerce - W - NY

ZINC CHROMATE
Am Paint J - W
Chem Mktg Rptr - W - NY
J of Commerce - W - NY

ZINC CHROMATE: BASIC
Am Paint J - W

ZINC CYANIDE
Chem Mktg Rptr - W - NY
Finishers' Mgt - M
J of Commerce - W - NY

ZINC DUST
Am Met Mkt/Met News - D - US
Am Paint J - W
Chem Mktg Rptr - W - US
J of Commerce - W - NY

ZINC FLUOBORATE
Chem Mktg Rptr - W - US

ZINC-FORMALDEHYDE SULFOXYLATE
Chem Mktg Rptr - W - NY

ZINC HYDROSULFITE
Chem Mktg Rptr - W - NY

ZINC LAURATE
Rubber World - SA

ZINC NAPHTHENATE
Chem Mktg Rptr - W - NY

ZINC NITRATE
Chem Mktg Rptr - W - NY
J of Commerce - W - NY
Rubber World - SA

ZINC NAPHTHENATE: LIQUID
Am Paint J - W

ZINC OCTOATE
Am Paint J - W

ZINC OXIDE
Can Chem Processing - M - Ont & Que
Chem Mktg Rptr - W - NY
J of Commerce - W - NY
US Labor Stat Bur - Wholesale Prices
& Price Indexes - M

ZINC OXIDE: AMERICAN PROCESS,
FRENCH PROCESS
Am Paint J - W

AINC OXIDE: AMERICAN PROCESS,
FRENCH PROCESS, DISPERSED
Rubber World - SA

ZINC PHENOLSULFONATE
Chem Mktg Rptr - W - NY

ZINC POWDER
Am Met Mkt/Met News - D - US

ZINC RESINATE
Chem Mktg Rptr - W - NY

ZINC SCRAP
Iron Age - W
J of Commerce - W - NY
Purch World - M - East
Second Raw Materials - M - Chicago,
    Houston, Los Angeles, Montreal,
    NY, Toronto

ZINC SILICOFLUORIDE
Chem Mktg Rptr - W - US

ZINC STEARATE
Am Paint J - W
Chem Mktg Rptr - W - NY
Rubber World - SA

COMMODITY PRICES

ZINC STEARATE: PLYMOUTH
   Rubber World - SA

ZINC SULFATE
   Chem Mktg Rptr - W - East
   Finishers' Mgt - M

ZINC UNDECYLENATE
   Chem Mktg Rptr - W - US

ZINEB
   US Stat Rptg Ser - Agri Prices -
      Annual Summary - A - US and
      by states

ZIRCON (G)
   Chem Mktg Rptr - W - US

ZIRCONIUM
   Eng Min J - M
   Met Wk - W

ZIRCONIUM ACETATE
   Chem Mktg Rptr - W - US

ZIRCONIUM HYDRIDE
   Chem Mktg Rptr - W - US

ZIRCONIUM OCTOATE
   Am Paint J - W

ZIRCONIUM OXIDE
   Chem Mktg Rptr - W - US

ZIRCONIUM OXYCHLORIDE
   Chem Mktg Rptr - W - US

ZIRCONIUM POWDER
   Am Met Mkt/Met News - D - US

ZIRCONIUM SPONGE
   Iron Age - W

ZIRCON ORE
   Eng Min J - M

ZIREX
   Rubber World - SA

ZMBT
   Rubber World - SA

ZMBT: WAXED, WETTABLE
   Rubber World - SA

ZO-9
   Rubber World - SA

ZONAREZ: 3115, 7115
   Rubber World - SA

LIST OF PUBLISHERS OF PERIODICALS INDEXED

Aberdeen-Angus Journal
Aberdeen-Angus Journal Publishing Co.
808 Des Moines Street
Webster City, Iowa 50595
Monthly

Agricultural Letter
Federal Reserve Bank of Chicago
230 South La Salle Street
Chicago, Illinois 60690
Weekly

Alaska Beverage Analyst
Golden Bell Press
2403 Champa Street
Denver, Colorado 80205
Monthly

American Metal Market/Metalworking News
Fairchild Publications, Inc.
7 East 12th Street
New York, New York 10003
Weekly

American Paint Journal
American Paint Journal Co.
2911 Washington Avenue
St. Louis, Missouri 63103
Weekly

American Shoemaking
Shoe Trades Publishing Co.
15 East Street
Boston, Massachusetts 02111
Weekly

America's Textile Reporter/Bulletin
Bennett Enterprises, Inc.
Daniel Building
Greenville, South Carolina 29602
Biweekly

Arizona Beverage Journal
Diamond Publications, Inc.
3302 North 3rd Street
Phoenix, Arizona 85012
Monthly

Automotive Market Report
Automotive Publishing, Inc.
1101 Fulton Building
Pittsburgh, Pennsylvania 15222
Biweekly

Automotive News
Slocum Publishing Co., Inc.
965 East Jefferson
Detroit, Michigan 48207
Weekly

Barron's National Business and Financial Weekly
Dow Jones and Co., Inc.
22 Cortlandt Street
New York, New York 10007
Weekly

Beverage Media
Beverage Media, Ltd.
251 Park Avenue, South
New York, New York 10010
Monthly

Beverage News
Beverage News, Inc.
150 North Rock Island
Wichita, Kansas 67201
Monthly

Buckeye Beverage Journal
Midwest Beverage Publications
2511 East 46th Street, Suite G-1
Indianapolis, Indiana 46205
Monthly

California Farmer
83 Stevenson Street
San Francisco, California 94105
Semimonthly

California Wineletter
Box 70
Mill Valley, California 94941
Semimonthly

Canadian Chemical Processing
Southam Business Publications, Ltd.
1450 Don Mills Road
Don Mills, Ontario, Canada
Monthly

Canadian Mining Journal
National Business Publications, Ltd.
Gardenvale, Quebec, Canada
Monthly

LIST OF PUBLISHERS OF PERIODICALS INDEXED

Canadian Tobacco Grower
Cash Crop Farming Publications, Ltd.
222 Argyle Avenue
Delhi, Ontario, Canada
Nine Times Yearly

Chemical Marketing Reporter
Schnell Publishing Co.
100 Church Street
New York, New York 10007
Weekly

Chemical Purchasing
Myers Publishing Co., Inc.
381 Park Avenue, South
New York, New York 10016
Thirteen Times Yearly

Chicago Daily Hide and Tallow Bulletin
Jacobsen Publishing Co.
300 West Adams Street
Chicago, Illinois 60606
Daily

Commercial Bulletin
Curtis Guild and Co. Publishers, Inc.
88 Broad Street
Boston, Massachusetts 02110
Weekly

Commercial Review
Commercial Review, Inc.
1812 Northwest Kearney Street
Portland, Oregon 97209
Weekly

Cotton Digest
Cotton Digest Co., Inc.
708 Cotton Exchange Building
Houston, Texas 77002
Weekly

Cotton-Monthly Review of the World
   Situation
International Cotton Advisory Committee
Washington, D.C. 20250
Monthly

Daily Market Record
Minneapolis Grain Exchange
150 Grain Exchange Building
Minneapolis, Minnesota 55415
Daily

Daily News Record
Fairchild Publications, Inc.
7 East 12th Street
New York, New York 10003
Daily

The Dairyman
Box 819
Corona, California 91720
Monthly

Dairynews
Dairylea Cooperative, Inc.
One Blue Hill Plaza
Pearl River, New York 10965
Semimonthly

Dairy Record
141 East 4th Street
St. Paul, Minnesota 55101
Monthly

Dakota Farmer
1216 South Main Street
Aberdeen, South Dakota 57401
Semimonthly

Earnshaw's Infants, Girls and Boyswear
   Review
Earnshaw Publications, Inc.
393 7th Avenue
New York, New York 10001
Monthly

E/MJ Engineering and Mining Journal
McGraw-Hill Mining Publications
1221 Avenue of the Americas
New York, New York 10020
Monthly

Farm and Dairy
Lyle Printing and Publishing Co.
185-189 East State Street
Salem, Ohio 44460
Weekly

Fats and Oils Bulletin
Jacobsen Publishing Co.
300 West Adams Street
Chicago, Illinois 60606
Daily

LIST OF PUBLISHERS OF PERIODICALS INDEXED

The Feed Bulletin
Jacobsen Publishing Co.
300 West Adams Street
Chicago, Illinois 60606
Daily

Feedstuffs
Miller Publishing Co.
2501 Wayzata Boulevard
Minneapolis, Minnesota 55405
Weekly

Financial Post
Maclean-Hunter Ltd.
481 University Avenue
Toronto 2, Ontario, Canada
Weekly

Financial Times of Canada.
10 Arundel Street
Place Bonaventure
Montreal 114, Quebec, Canada
Weekly

Finishers' Management
National Association of Metal Finishers
248 Lorraine Avenue
Upper Montclair, New Jersey 07043
Monthly

Florida Field Report
Deitenbeck Publishing Co., Inc.
320 North Magnolia Avenue
Orlando, Florida 32801
Weekly

Foundry
Penton Publishing Co.
Penton Building
Cleveland, Ohio 44113
Monthly

Free Press Weekly Report on Farming
Free Press Co., Ltd.
300 Carlton Street
Winnipeg 2, Manitoba, Canada
Weekly

Fueloil and Oil Heat
200 Commerce Road
Cedar Grove, New Jersey 07009
Monthly

Handbags and Accessories
Business Journals, Inc.
Box 1257
Stamford, Connecticut 06904
Monthly

Hide & Leather Bulletin
Jacobsen Publishing Co.
300 West Adams Street
Chicago, Illinois 60606
Daily

High Plains Journal
High Plains Publishers, Inc.
1500 East Wyatt Earp Boulevard
Dodge City, Kansas 67801
Weekly

Hog Farm Management
Miller Publishing Co.
2501 Wayzata Boulevard
Minneapolis, Minnesota 55440
Monthly

Idaho Farmer-Stockman
Northwest Farm Paper Unit
Cowles Publishing Company
212 Review Building
Spokane, Washington 99210
Semimonthly

Illinois Beverage Journal
Illinois Beverage Media, Inc.
One North La Salle Street
Chicago, Illinois 60602
Monthly

Implement and Tractor
Intertec Publishing Corp.
1014 Wyandotte Street
Kansas City, Missouri 64105
Semimonthly

Industry Week
Penton Publishing Co.
Penton Building
Cleveland, Ohio 44113
Weekly

Iron Age
Chilton Co.
Chilton Way
Radnor, Pennsylvania 19089
Weekly

LIST OF PUBLISHERS OF PERIODICALS INDEXED

Journal of Commerce
Twin Coast Newspapers, Inc.
99 Wall Street
New York, New York 10005
Daily

Kansas Farmer
Harvest Publishing Co.
109 West 9th Street
Topeka, Kansas 66612
Semimonthly

The Kentucky Beverage Journal
Feature Publications, Inc.
100 East Main Street
Frankfort, Kentucky 40601
Monthly

Lancaster Farming
22 East Main Street
Lititz, Pennsylvania 17543
Weekly

Leather and Shoes
Rumpf Publishing Co.
300 West Adams Street
Chicago, Illinois 60606
Weekly

Livestock Breeder Journal
1506 Hardeman Avenue
Macon, Georgia 31201
Monthly

Manitoba Co-operator
Manitoba Pool Elevators
220 Portage Avenue
Winnipeg 1, Manitoba, Canada
Weekly

Maryland-Washington-Delaware
    Beverage Journal
Beverage Journal, Inc.
3110 Elm Avenue
Baltimore, Maryland 21211
Monthly

Metals Week
McGraw-Hill, Inc.
1221 Avenue of the Americas
New York, New York 10020
Weekly

Michigan Beverage News
Michigan Beverage News, Inc.
7425 East Jefferson Avenue
Detroit, Michigan 48214
Semimonthly

Michigan Farmer
4415 North Grand River Avenue
Lansing, Michigan 48906
Semimonthly

Mining Record
2829 East 2nd Avenue, Suite 212
Denver, Colorado 80206
Weekly

Missouri Ruralist
Harvest Publishing Co.
9800 Detroit Avenue
Cleveland, Ohio 44102
Semimonthly

Modern Packaging – Encyclopedia and
    Planning Guide
McGraw-Hill, Inc.
330 West 42nd Street
New York, New York 10036
Annually

Modern Textiles Magazine
Rayon Publishing Corp.
303 Fifth Avenue
New York, New York 10016
Monthly

Montana Farmer – Stockman
Northwest Farm Paper Unit
Cowles Publishing Co.
212 Review Building
Spokane, Washington 99210
Semimonthly

National Live Stock Producer
National Live Stock Publishing
    Association
155 North Wacker Drive
Chicago, Illinois 60606
Monthly

National Petroleum News
McGraw-Hill, Inc.
1221 Avenue of the Americas
New York, New York 10020
Thirteen Times Yearly

LIST OF PUBLISHERS OF PERIODICALS INDEXED

National Provisioner
National Provisioner, Inc.
15 West Huron Street
Chicago, Illinois 60610
Weekly

National Wool Grower
National Wool Growers Association
600 Crandall Building
Salt Lake City, Utah 84101
Monthly

Nation's Restaurant News
Lebhar-Friedman, Inc.
2 Park Avenue
New York, New York 10016
Semimonthly

Nebraska Farmer
Nebraska Farmer Co.
5601 O Street
Lincoln, Nebraska 68501
Semimonthly

New Jersey Beverage Journal
Gem Publishers, Inc.
1180 Raymond Boulevard
Newark, New Jersey 07102
Monthly

New York Times
New York Times Co.
229 West 43rd Street
New York, New York 10036
Daily

Northern Miner
Northern Miner Press, Ltd.
77 River Street
Toronto 247, Ontario, Canada
Weekly

Official Board Markets
Magazines for Industry, Inc.
20 North Wacker Drive
Chicago, Illinois 60606
Weekly

Oil and Gas Journal
Petroleum Publishing Co.
211 South Cheyenne Avenue
Tulsa, Oklahoma 74101
Weekly

The Oil Daily
Oil Daily, Inc.
59 East Van Buren Street
Chicago, Illinois 60605
Daily

Ontario Milk Producer
The Ontario Milk Marketing Board
P.O. Box 4027, Postal Station "A"
Toronto, Ontario, Canada
Monthly

Oregon Farmer - Stockman
Northwest Farm Paper Unit
Cowles Publishing Co.
212 Review Building
Spokane, Washington 99210
Semimonthly

The Packer
Vance Publishing Co.
One Gateway Center
Kansas City, Kansas 66107
Weekly

Paperboard Packaging
Magazines for Industry, Inc.
777 Third Avenue
New York, New York 10017
Monthly

Paper Trade Journal
Lockwood Trade Journal Co.
551 Fifth Avenue
New York, New York 10017
Weekly

Patterson's California Beverage
    Gazetteer
Wolfer Printing Co., Inc.
422 Wall Street
Los Angeles, California 90013
Monthly

Pennmarva
Pennmarva Dairymen's Cooperative
    Federation, Inc.
1717 Gwynn Oak Avenue
Baltimore, Maryland 21207
Monthly

LIST OF PUBLISHERS OF PERIODICALS INDEXED

Pennsylvania Farmer
Harvest Publishing Co.
Harcourt, Brace and World
9800 Detroit Avenue
Cleveland, Ohio 44102
Semimonthly

Platt's Oilgram Price Service
McGraw-Hill Publications Co.
1221 Avenue of the Americas
New York, New York 10020
Daily

Poultry and Egg Marketing
Poultry and Egg News, Inc.
345 Green Street, Northwest
Gainesville, Georgia 30501
Biweekly

The Poultry Times
Poultry and Egg News, Inc.
345 Green Street, Northwest
Gainesville, Georgia 30501
Weekly

Poultry Tribune
Watt Publishing Co.
Mount Morris, Illinois 61054
Monthly

Producers' Guide
Northeast Dairy Cooperative Federation
Box 1344
Syracuse, New York 13201
Monthly

Purchasing World
Technical Publishing Co.
1301 South Grove Avenue
Barrington, Illinois 60010
Monthly

Red Poll News
Red Poll Cattle Club of America
3275 Holdrege Street
Lincoln, Nebraska 68503
Semiannually

Rhode Island Beverage Journal
Beverage Publishing Co. of Rhode
   Island, Inc.
603 Hope Street
Providence, Rhode Island 02906
Monthly

Rubber World
Box 5417
77 North Miller Road
Akron, Ohio 44313
Monthly

Secondary Raw Materials
Market News Publishing Corp.
156 Fifth Avenue
New York, New York 10010
Monthly

Seed World - Seed Trade Buyers' Guide
   and Directory
434 South Wabash Avenue
Chicago, Illinois 60605
Annually

Shorthorn World
16 South Locust Street
Aurora, Illinois 60506
Sixteen Times Yearly

Soybean Digest
American Soybean Association
Hudson, Iowa 50643
Thirteen Times Yearly

Statistical Sugar Trade Journal
Willet and Gray, Inc.
P.O. Box N
Bright Waters, New York 11718
Weekly

Super Service Station
Irving-Cloud Publishing Co.
7300 North Cicero Avenue
Chicago, Illinois 60646
Monthly

Tea and Coffee Trade Journal
Tea and Coffee Trade Journal Co.
79 Wall Street
New York, New York 10005
Monthly

Tobacco/International
Lockwood Trade Journal Co.
551 Fifth Avenue
New York, New York 10017
Biweekly

LIST OF PUBLISHERS OF PERIODICALS INDEXED

United Nations Lead and Zinc Study Group - Lead and Zinc Statistics
United Nations Building, Room 903
New York, New York 10017
Monthly

United Nations - Monthly Bulletin of Statistics
United Nations Statistical Office
New York, New York 10017
Monthly

U.S. Agricultural Marketing Service - Bean Market News
U.S. Department of Agriculture
712 19th Street, Room 373
Denver, Colorado 80202
Weekly

U.S. Agricultural Marketing Service - Broiler Marketing Guide
U.S. Department of Agriculture
Washington, D.C. 20250
Quarterly

U.S. Agricultural Marketing Service - Egg Marketing Guide
U.S. Department of Agriculture
Washington, D.C. 20250
Semiannually

U.S. Agricultural Marketing Service - Feed Market News
U.S. Department of Agriculture
Independence, Missouri 64050
Weekly

U.S. Agricultural Marketing Service - Fresh Fruit and Vegetable Prices
U.S. Department of Agriculture
Washington, D.C. 20250
Annually

U.S. Agricultural Marketing Service - Grain Market News
U.S. Department of Agriculture
Independence, Missouri 64050
Weekly

U.S. Agricultural Marketing Service - Honey Market News
U.S. Department of Agriculture
Washington, D.C. 20250
Monthly

U.S. Agricultural Marketing Service - Livestock, Meat and Wool - Market News
U.S. Department of Agriculture
Washington, D.C. 20250
Weekly

U.S. Agricultural Marketing Service - Peanut Market News
U.S. Department of Agriculture
Washington, D.C. 20250
Weekly

U.S. Agricultural Marketing Service - Tobacco Market Reviews
U.S. Department of Agriculture
Washington, D.C. 20250
Quarterly

U.S. Agricultural Marketing Service - Turkey Marketing Guide
U.S. Department of Agriculture
Washington, D.C. 20250
Annually

U.S. Agricultural Stabilization and Conservation Service - Sugar Reports
U.S. Department of Agriculture
Washington, D.C. 20250
Monthly

U.S. Bureau of Domestic Commerce - Pulp, Paper and Board Quarterly Industry Report
U.S. Department of Commerce
Washington, D.C. 20230
Quarterly

U.S. Consumer and Marketing Service - Cotton Price Statistics
U.S. Department of Agriculture
Box 17723
Memphis, Tennessee 38117
Monthly

LIST OF PUBLISHERS OF PERIODICALS INDEXED

U.S. Consumer and Marketing Service -
  Dairy Market Statistics
U.S. Department of Agriculture
Washington, D.C. 20250
Annually

U.S. Consumer and Marketing Service -
  Poultry Market Statistics
U.S. Department of Agriculture
Washington, D.C. 20250
Annually

U.S. Economic Research Service - Cotton
  Situation
U.S. Department of Agriculture
Washington, D.C. 20250
Five Times Yearly

U.S. Economic Research Service - Dairy
  Situation
U.S. Department of Agriculture
Washington, D.C. 20250
Five Times Yearly

U.S. Economic Research Service -
  Demand and Price Situation
U.S. Department of Agriculture
Washington, D.C. 20250
Quarterly

U.S. Economic Research Service - Fats
  and Oils Situation
U.S. Department of Agriculture
Washington, D.C. 20250
Five Times Yearly

U.S. Economic Research Service -
  Feed Situation
U.S. Department of Agriculture
Washington, D.C. 20250
Five Times Yearly

U.S. Economic Research Service -
  Livestock and Meat Situation
U.S. Department of Agriculture
Washington, D.C. 20515
Bimonthly

U.S. Economic Research Service -
  Marketing and Transportation
  Situation
U.S. Department of Agriculture
Washington, D.C. 20250
Quarterly

U.S. Economic Research Service -
  Poultry and Egg Situation
U.S. Department of Agriculture
Washington, D.C. 20250
Five Times Yearly

U.S. Economic Research Service -
  Statistics on Cotton and Related Data
  1930-1967, Annual Supplement
U.S. Department of Agriculture
Washington, D.C. 20250
Annually

U.S. Economic Research Service -
  Tobacco Situation
U.S. Department of Agriculture
Washington, D.C. 20250
Quarterly

U.S. Economic Research Service -
  Vegetable Situation
U.S. Department of Agriculture
Washington, D.C. 20250
Quarterly

U.S. Economic Research Service -
  Wheat Situation
U.S. Department of Agriculture
Washington, D.C. 20250
Quarterly

U.S. Economic Research Service -
  Wool Situation
U.S. Department of Agriculture
Washington, D.C. 20250
Quarterly

U.S. Labor Statistics Bureau -
  Estimated Retail Food Prices by
  Cities
U.S. Department of Labor
Washington, D.C. 20250
Monthly

U.S. Labor Statistics Bureau -
  Retail Prices and Indexes of Fuels
  and Electricity
U.S. Department of Labor
Washington, D.C. 20250
Monthly

LIST OF PUBLISHERS OF PERIODICALS INDEXED

U.S. Labor Statistics Bureau -
  Wholesale Prices and Price Indexes
U.S. Department of Labor
Washington, D.C. 20250
Monthly

U.S. Market News Section - Monthly
  Cotton Linters Review
U.S. Department of Agriculture
Box 17723
Memphis, Tennessee 38117
Monthly

U.S. Market News Section - Weekly
  Cotton Market Review
U.S. Department of Agriculture
Box 17723
Memphis, Tennessee 38117
Weekly

U.S. Statistical Reporting Service -
  Agricultural Prices
U.S. Department of Agriculture
Washington, D.C. 20250
Monthly

U.S. Statistical Reporting Service -
  Agricultural Prices - Annual Summary
U.S. Department of Agriculture
Washington, D.C. 20230
Annually

U.S. Statistical Reporting Service -
  Dairy Products
U.S. Department of Agriculture
Washington, D.C. 20250
Monthly

U.S. Statistical Reporting Service
  (Wisconsin) - Average Price Received
  by Farmers for Milk of Manufacturing
  Grade in the Minnesota-Wisconsin
  Area
U.S. Department of Agriculture
Box 5160
Madison, Wisconsin 53705
Monthly

U.S. Statistical Reporting Service
  (Wisconsin) - Prices Received
U.S. Department of Agriculture
Box 5160
Madison, Wisconsin 53705
Monthly

Utah Farmer-Stockman
Northwestern Farm Paper Unit
Cowles Publishing Co.
212 Review Building
Spokane, Washington 99210
Semimonthly

Wall Street Journal
Dow Jones and Co., Inc.
30 Broad Street
New York, New York 10004
Daily

Washington Farmer-Stockman
Northwest Farm Paper Unit
Cowles Publishing Co.
212 Review Building
Spokane, Washington 99210
Semimonthly

Weekly Bulletin of Leather and Shoe News
77 Summer Street
Boston, Massachusetts 02110
Weekly

Western Livestock Journal
Nelson R. Crow Publications
1730 South Clemente Street
Anaheim, California 92802
Weekly

Western Miner
Gordon Black Publications, Ltd.
1200 West Pender Street
Vancouver, British Columbia, Canada
Monthly

Western Producer
Modern Press
446 Second Avenue, North
Saskatoon, Saskatchewan, Canada
Weekly

LIST OF PUBLISHERS OF PERIODICALS INDEXED

Wisconsin Beverage Journal
Zien Enterprises, Inc.
606 West Wisconsin Avenue
Milwaukee, Wisconsin 53203
Monthly

Wool Sack
South Dakota, Minnesota, Iowa and
 Nebraska Wool Growers Association
306 Fourth Street
Brookings, South Dakota 57006
Monthly

World Wool Digest
International Wool Secretariat
Wool House
6-7 Carlton Gardens
London S.W.1, England
Monthly